T0326307

BOOK OF FOOLS

BOOK OF FOOLS

An Intelligent Person's Guide to

Fops, Jackasses,

Morons, Dolts, Dunces, Halfwits and Blockheads

TERRY REED

Algora Publishing
New York

Library of Congress Cataloging-in-Publication Data —

Reed, Terry, 1937-
    The book of fools: an intelligent person's guide to fops, jackasses, morons, dolts,
dunces, halfwits and blockheads / Terry Reed.
        pages cm
    Includes bibliographical references.
    ISBN 978-1-62894-033-6 (soft cover: alk. paper) — ISBN 978-1-62894-034-3 (hard
cover: alk. paper) — ISBN 978-1-62894-035-0 (ebook) 1. Stupidity—Humor. 2. American
wit and humor. I. Title.
    PN6231.S77R44 2013
    818'.602—dc23
                            2013027409

Printed in the United States

The author extends his appreciation to the American Council
on Inanity, in corrupt Washington, D.C., without which this
Icarian volume would never have hiked its wheels

TABLE OF CONTENTS

Chapter I. Leaving No Fool Behind

As our title forecasts, this provocatively assertive book addresses the disarmingly fertile subject of fools in their broad cultural contexts and in their not infrequently bizarre manifestations. Our objective, certain to fall quite short, is to *leave no fool behind*. This is not to infer (by which we mean to *surmise*, *imply* or even *hint*) that either the author or his readership is in any demonstrable sense of the word *foolish*, now or at any other time. After all (and let's be plain on this point), no fool would write a book like this, and no fool would read it. Precisely who does read it is a discretely personal decision we leave to those gifted with more than ordinarily inquiring minds.

Foolishness, we hasten to add, can be deceptive. Let us begin by cautioning that whereas certain specimens of the world's great literature that over the centuries are read, nay, scrutinized, with the straightest of faces, and in the pristine light of utmost seriousness, are not always recognized for the madcap material that they assuredly are. An amusing instance of this literary misunderstanding turns up in the work of unpredictable cleric and *littérateur* Thomas More (1478–1535), universally toasted these days as a Roman Catholic martyr who was not so amusingly imprisoned and beheaded, which is one of those things that happen to people purveying decidedly not foolish opinions. His celebrated narrative *Utopia* (composed in Latin 1515–1516) has by some been rightly called *a fool's paradise*. The word *utopia*, as any schoolboy knows, derives from the Greek *outopia* that means *nowhere*, which it usually is. It purports to be an ideal, if authentically communistic (yes, *communistic*) template of an impeccably ordered society, except that it's rendered as a social catastrophe of the highest (or shall we say *lowest*) order. In the first of its two parts, More coyly directs our attention to a certain "hanger on...who played the fool so well that he seemed to be one." He may indirectly have been pointing an umbrella tip at himself. After all, as the old saw goes, "it's a cunning part to play the fool well." *Utopia* evades a goodly proportion of our more (excuse the pun) or less literate fools of greater than ordinary naiveté who have taken *Utopia* seriously as a revolutionary blueprint for visionary societies, except the whole thing is manifestly a joke.

The meaning of *fool* and its approximate synonyms, if such exist in any language, cries out for definition such as might be uncovered in *The Oxford English Dictionary*, second edition, popularly and henceforth referred to as the *OED*, that cites its linguistic mutations as *folle, fole, foyl, foule, foolle* and *fule*, all of which denote an *insane person*, a *madman*. In its feminine form it appears as *folle*. Its Latin derivation is *follem* or *follies*, meaning *bellows*, or to put it another way, *windbag*, or *chatterbox*. Languages and their meanings evolve constantly, however; and *fool* comes eventually to denote "one deficient in judgment or sense, one who acts or behaves stupidly, a silly person, a simpleton." The Bible, as we shall amply discover, uses the terms *fool* and its derivations with cloying frequency, often (but not always) to expose stupidly impious persons. The OED further notes that "the word has [in modern English] a much stronger sense than it had in any earlier period," continuing, "it now has an implication of insulting contempt which does not in the same degree belong to any of its synonyms, or to the derivative *foolish*."

Fools have been mercilessly derided in celebrated remarks attributed to people who deemed themselves graced with superior wisdom. As a phrase, *to be a fool to*, for instance, we take to mean to be *in every way inferior to*, but not always. The German theologian Martin Luther said that a fool "remains a fool his whole life long," with apparently no prospect of escaping from the shackles of intellectual vacuity. Francis Beaumont, the English dramatist, identified by bookish types with his collaborator John Fletcher, felt the same way, referring to a certain fool who "had resolved to live a fool for the rest/ Of his dull life." The poet Edward Young, today identified with the so-called *Graveyard School* of British versifiers, said (and we've heard this before), "at thirty man suspects himself a fool," and later, "a fool at forty is a fool indeed." Everyone is familiar with the Lincolnesque-attributed remark that "you can fool some of the people all of the time and all of the people some of the time; but you can't fool all of the people all of the time." Less known are the lines of English poet laureate John Dryden (1631–1700) that read, "For I am young, a Novice in the Trade, / The Fool of Love, unpractic'd to persuade."

The ostensible object in all these cerebral observations is to eschew commonplace stupidity. In its place we are encouraged to live intelligently and stay well clear of the flawed mental, procedural, philosophic, moral and theological habits that some fools embrace. Even so, some of the more intelligent of our number dread coming to terms with the fool who dwells within. The Scotch-born actor Alastair Sim commented candidly and bravely in the year of his death that, "it was revealed to me many years ago with conclusive certainty that I was a fool and that I had always been a fool," adding ironically that "since then I have been as happy as any man has a right to be." This surprising disclosure is more common than one might first imagine. It was Theodore Rubin, the celebrated and well-published New York psychiatrist who wrote, "I must learn to love the fool in me—the one who feels too much, takes too many chances, wins sometimes and loses often." His conciliatory comments put us in mind of Lewis Mumford, another New Yorker, who established his international reputation as a social philosopher and brilliant student of urban social structural and architectural modalities, as recorded for example in *The Sticks and Stones: A Study of American Architecture and Civilization* (1924), *American Taste* (1929), *The Culture of Cities* (1938), *The Story of Utopias* (1941), *The Condition of Man* (1944) and *The City in History* (1961). Mumford, with characteristic self-effacement, bravely conceded that, "I wanted to die happily if I knew that on my tombstone could there be written the words, 'This man was an absolute fool. None of the disasters that he reluctantly predicted ever came to pass!'" Such ingratiating outbursts of public modesty invite knowing amusement, an endearing aspect of character that genuine fools, whether born into foolishness or having acquired it own their own, have traditionally overlooked.

Aristotle, who had a great deal to say and *infer* (allege, adduce) about tragedy, had damnably little to pronounce on comedy, but what he does say moves directly to the essence of what constitutes humor. He calls it (in the Wheelwright translation) "a representation of men who are morally inferior, but only in the sense of being ludicrous. For the ludicrous is a subdivision of the morally ugly, consisting of some defect or ugliness which does not produce actual harm, and hence causes no pain to the beholder as a comic mask is ugly and distorted without causing pain...." In other words, humor derives from our willingness to recognize our superiority (in any sense of it we can justify) over someone else, such as a fool who, in appearance, is as foolish as his behavior—so long as the object of our humor does not produce injury to its subject. The objects of Aristotle's tragic theory are elevated specimens, persons of high or even highest station possibly best illustrated by royalty. His remarks on humor apply to people of lower station. So it is that Aristotle's distinction between what's been called *superior action* (in tragedy) and *inferior action* (in comedy) among our lessers, is all too clear. Should some high-toned old Christian woman expertly execute a pratfall (such as a humiliating tumble on her fanny) by slipping on a wet banana, it may be construed as low comedy. If she breaks her back in the process, all comedy vanishes. It's not funny anymore.

People find children and dogs amusing because they feel superior to them. So-called *base* characters (if one regards dogs and children as base) behave in a predictably ridiculous manner and may, on occasion, seem to execute it surprisingly well. All the same, one of them may, and probably does, represent what we regard as the earmarks of a simpleton (a figure to be scrutinized more closely later) or a fool, whether that foolish disposition is innate or whether it is merely affected as in a circus clown or a late night television wise guy. He may affect a certain naïve ignorance toward which we are made to feel securely and smugly superior, partly because we are not threatened, and (to the contrary) feel reassuringly encouraged at how cleverly, even cunningly, above everyone we assuredly are. Hence, comedy arises out of our insecurities and the need to be reassured that ordinary fops, jackasses, morons, dolts, halfwits and blockheads somehow fall well short of our cerebral cleverness, to an extent quite over and above what one finds in such carnivals of malicious stupidity as governments composed of flunkies doing little more than attending political apes who in turn have been elected there by a predominantly moronic nation of ill-informed and uneducated voters. Fools that politicians be, their potential for uproarious comedy has been undermined by the inestimable damage that they inflicted upon a trusting nation that foolishly directed them supposedly to govern.

Observing fools is a self-congratulatory gesture that makes even a fool believe that he is worthy and valuable, whereas he's likely to be little more than a blockhead who, over a lifetime, in all probability has done little or nothing productive in any sense whatsoever. Accordingly, his derisive laughter derives from viewing television programs that cue their slack-jawed viewers when to laugh, how robustly and for how long. Just as we may need someone toward whom we *look up*, so too we require someone whom we may *look down upon*. Consequently, most people find themselves situated half way on a scale between heroes and Neros, conquerors and comics, inglorious *role models* (as some dunces call them) and goons. Yet the closer one identifies with greatness and character, the more fulfilled his life may be and the greater his capacity for sophisticated nuances of humor. You are, to view it another way, what you find humorous, just (as some used to say), you are what you eat, or perhaps what eats you.

Comedy comes in various packages. In Dante Alighieri's day (1265–1321) a comedy was a busy narrative with a happy (or otherwise satisfactory) conclusion, as in his *Divine Comedy* (the *comedy* part having been appended to the title after Dante's passing) that ushers us through the horrific depths of hell (some regions of which are, yes, frozen over), providing a tourist's perfunctory familiarity with purgatorial humiliation. We finally advance to the eternal bliss that attends our privileged glimpse at paradise, culminating with cameo appearances by Mary, John the Baptist, the archangel Gabriel and St. Bernard, before whom shines the radiant light of God's all-knowing. If that's not a happy ending, it's darned close. One may be inclined to say that there are no fools in Heaven, but then again, because of their simple and perhaps inoffensive ways (if such there be), some fools may be heaven-eligible after all. The fool, one of whose manifestations is as a born simpleton similar to a *village idiot* was, in the good old days, physically beaten. Makes sense, does it not? If you happen to encounter a dodo, you flog him. There are, of course, a number of idiots in Dante's hell, where one identifies evil with darkness, that being the absence of light, and therefore stygian blackness, that aptly represents evil, which is in turn a manifestation of ignorance. In the Middle Ages, fools became identified with Satan, an embodiment of evil and stupidity.

That said, did not the Franciscans think of themselves as *fools for Christ*? Did not St. Francis call himself God's Jester? Is there not an old Jewish one-liner that says, "a whole fool is half a prophet"? It was St. Paul who wrote (*Oxford New English Bible* translation), "Let no one deceive himself. If any among you thinks that he is wise in this age, let him become a fool that he may become wise, for the wisdom of this world is folly with God" (*I Corinthians* 3:18–19). In Paul's second letter to the Corinthians comes familiar advice: "how gladly you bear with fools, being yourself so wise! (elsewhere rendered as "you suffer fools gladly, seeing yourselves are wise"). Paul himself said that he spoke as a fool, and averred that it was out of God's own foolishness that He saved the world, possibly in the sense provided in *Galatians* that "divine folly is wiser than the wisdom of man."

Condemnation of fools turns up with monotonously redundant frequency in biblical contexts other than Paul's. *Job* 2:10 warns us that "you talk as any wicked fool of a woman might talk," and *Proverbs* 5:23 tells us that "he will perish for want of discipline wrapped in the shroud of his boundless folly," then in 12:15 it advises that "a fool thinks that he is always right; wise is the man who listens to advice." Such counsel we find amply supported by other choice moralistic and rhetorically balanced admonitions, among them: "a fool shows his ill humor at once; a clever man slighted conceals his feelings." We also learn that "a clever man has the wit to find the right way [whereas] the folly of stupid men misleads them." Similarly, "a fool is too arrogant to make amends; upright men know what reconciliation means." In 15:2 we read, "a wise man's tongue spreads knowledge; stupid men talk nonsense." Presuming, like the Greeks, that with age comes wisdom, 15:5 posits "a fool spurns his father's correction, but to take reproof to heart shows good respect." Turning to animal imagery, 17:12 counsels that it's better to confront a she-bear robbed of her cubs "than a stupid man in his folly," in the knowledge that, in 17:21 "a stupid man is the bane of his parent, and his father has no joy in a boorish son." Likewise, we are earnestly advised, "do not answer a stupid man in the language of his folly" (26:4-5) "or you will grow like him," and moreover, "answer a stupid man as his folly deserves, or he will think himself a wise man," a point jolly well taken. More graphically, we are apprised that "he who sends a fool on an errand cuts his own leg off and displays the stump" (26:6); and speaking of limbs (26:7), we are apprised again by way of simile, "a proverb in the mouth of a stupid man dangles help-less as a lame man's legs."

Over in *Isaiah* (19:11–13) the same arguments prevail. "Fools that you are, you princes of Zoan/ Wisest of Pharaoh's counselors, you may be, but stupid counselors you are," and shortly after, "Zoan's princes are fools; the princes of Noph are dupes." We are notified in 35:8 that "there shall be a causeway there which shall be called the Way of Holiness...it shall become a pilgrim's way, [and] no fool shall trespass on it."

Biblical onslaughts aimed at fools carry a certain accusatory malicious-ness, ever asserting that fools and foolishness constitute a menace to com-mon decency and godliness. The biblical narrator, to the contrary, represents himself (whoever he may be) as faultlessly upright, and therefore generously qualified to recommend codes of behavior to all who have ears. Observe, for example, *Jeremiah* 4:22, where we're assured that "my people are fools, with no understanding. They are clever only in wrongdoing, and of doing right they know nothing." In 5:21-22 the narrator seizes his audience by the collar, admonishing them to "listen, you foolish and senseless people, Who have eyes and see nothing, ears and hear nothing, Have you no fear of me? Says the Lord; will you not shiver before me.... In *Solomon*, the biblical voice again threatens its listener (11:23-24), asserting that "this is why the wicked who have lived their lives in heedless folly were tormented [it served them right] by thee with their own abominations," continuing, "they had strayed far down the paths of error taking for gods the most contemptible and hid-den creatures, deluded like thoughtless children," and moreover (13:2) "what born fools are men who, having lived in ignorance of God [as we shall see, one of the primary prerequisites for foolhood is a failure to endorse the Christian mysteries] from the good things before their eyes could not learn who really is, and failed to recognize though they observed his works." Then in 13:19 we confront a threat "to make men stumble and to catch the fret of fools." In 15:4 the narrator inveighs against "the perverted invention of human skill [and] the barren labor of printers...the sight of which arouses in fools the passion-ate desire for a mere image without life or breath."

Finally, in *Ecclesiastes* 19:23-24 fools again occupy the lowest rung on God's theological ladder, since "there is a cleverness that is loathsome and [there are] some fools [who] are merely ignorant." What to do? It is clearly "better to be Godfearing and lack brains [at risk of becoming another fool, perhaps?] than have intelligence and break the law." But if you're a fool, even a fool for God, maybe, there's no defending your foolhardiness, as is empha-sized in 20:16 where "the fool says in desperation, 'I have no friends; I get no thanks from my own kindness; though they eat my bread, they speak ill of me,'" after which we are warned "how everyone will laugh at him," followed by a caveat concerning a fool's ill sense of timing: "a proverb will fall flat when uttered by a fool, for he will produce it at the wrong time." So it goes.

Matthew 7:26 points our attention to someone who "was foolish enough to build his home on sand," exclaiming shortly after, "You fools!" *Romans* 1:23 addresses those who, God help us, "made fools of themselves," be it for better or worse.

We are gradually bludgeoned into accepting one inescapable conclusion, namely that a fool, or someone perceived as a fool, is not much more than a moral and social nuisance which one finds a convenient target for moralistic sermonizing. The message becomes all the clearer when the accusatory voices of biblical admonition spend all their wind upon fools without proposing much more than empty moralistic rhetoric as an alternative. To say it another way, we know what the words on the page say, but we are uncertain about what they recommend as an alternative, since they have endlessly represented the dogmatic convictions of what might be someone else's theology.

Our investigation of fools and their cultural history inexorably confronts the question of how, and even if, they are fools at all. As Gershwin's *Porgy and Bess* reminds us, it ain't necessarily so. There have been occasions in human history when anyone who speculated that the world was round was taken for a fool. There were other regrettable times in human history when anyone who believed the world to be flat was also taken to be a fool. Consequently, anyone who is of a speculative cast of mind is at risk for being foolishly assumed as foolish. Meanwhile, looming in the shadows of biblical sententiousness is the *wise fool*, whom we shall consider in subsequent pages. He is an irony (certainly) as well as an intellectual anomaly, ever intellectually threatening. To be sure, fools, real ones, are out there and in dangerously, even perilously overwhelming numbers. It remains always a question whether they are as they appear or whether they are, in spite of their costumes, wise men in caps, bells, ass's ears, prancing and carrying on as fools customarily do.

As we shall see, certain words used in our inquiry deserve, nay demand, closer definition, among them *impious*, which means, in the words of the OED, "not pious, without piety or reverence for God and his ordinances; presumptively irreligious, wicked or profane," and later, "wanting in natural reverence and dutifulness." The term *ordinance* refers to "the action of ordaining, ordering, or arranging," denoting "arrangement in regular sequences of things or matters according to rule" and moreover "the action of ordering or regulating, authoritative appointment or dispensation, control, disposal." Still later, the definition expands to embrace "that which is ordained or decreed by the Deity or by Fate; a dispensation, decree, appointment of Providence or of Destiny."

Threatening admonitions abound, but they ultimately revert to someone else's notion of how things are and prescribe precisely how *they ought to be*. Ergo, to behave any differently is to be a fool, but not necessarily a fop (by which we do not mean a mystical member of the Fraternal Order of Police), but to be passed off as a mere *flapdoodle* (so to speak), the food of fools. If one flies in the face of conventionality, he may better be described as a *simpleton*, something that means what it says. The OED defines it as simply "one who is deficient in sense or intelligence; a silly person; a fool," derivations of which include rather bizarre terms such as *simpletonian* (that may put us in mind of *Smithsonian*), *simpletonic*, *simpletonish* or the more elegant *simpletonianism* (suggesting a learnedly asinine persuasion), or the statesman-like *simpleton-ism*, that would present well if engraved in granite. That form is not quite so genteel, since it suggests childliness in its more pejorative sense, meaning not so much a school of thought but something easily confused with *simplic-ity*. All considered, it's one more synonym (albeit in the narrowest sense of that word, synonyms don't exist) for a fool, except this time it leans toward the *puerile*, which denotes the childish, silly, juvenile, after the Latin *puer* (boy), boyish, that also directly puts us in mind of what some sociologists call *puericulture* which addresses the rearing of children.

It is demeaning in most cases to refer to an adult as a child; and to call a man a boy or a woman a girl, unless it's playfully intended, is an egregious insult just as it would be to call a military man a mere *soldier boy*, or an air-plane pilot a *fly boy*—nothing more than an airborne simpleton (although some of them do exist, such as in the ridiculous case of the October 2009 Northwest Airlines flight that missed its Minneapolis airport destination by a mere one hundred miles while its moonstruck crew were foolishly lost in metaphysical contemplation over their laptop computers). George Bernard Shaw concocted a play entitled *The Simpleton of the Unexpected Isles* in 1934. It is an hour-long comedy concerning a British clergyman, an alleged simple-ton, who comes upon what Shaw called "a single little household with four children." He happens to be an *impotent simpleton*, although in reality he is no simpleton at all. Shaw refers to his drama as "the fantasy that the race will be brought to judgment by a supernatural being, coming literally out of the blue."

The French feminine singular *la niaise* translates loosely into the English *simpleton* and further suggests a tendency toward naiveté or the *sotte* (fool) that derives from *sottise* that means, among other things, *folly* and *foolish-ness*. There is a French drama called *La Niaise*, remotely similar to Shaw's, but concerning a woman of obvious, but still suspect, intelligence who is assumed by those around her to be a blatant simpleton. The somewhat over-looked British novelist and playwright Charles Reade published *A Simpleton: A Story of the Day* (posthumously, 1896) illustrating that a person who would hardly be taken for a fool may turn out to be entirely the opposite of what he seems. Aside from having been passed off as a common simpleton, the fool has occasionally been guilty of *impudence*, a failure of what otherwise would be in the minds of most *sound judgment*. Instead, he may present certain errors of received opinion, as for example in matters surrounding shamelessness, immodesty, indelicacy, indecency, effrontery, disrespect, insolence, and unabashed presumptuousness. These minor imperfections may be included beneath the disrespectable title of *impudicity*, not to be confused with *impotency*, which is an irksome shortcoming of an entirely different sort.

Shamelessness is neither more nor less than what's been quite frankly called destitution *of shame*, i.e., without an apprehension of shame. It is sometimes applied to person with an appalling shortage of modesty such as those who belong to the exalted order of *ecdysiasts* who have little to no hesitation presenting themselves nude in public places, particularly when the price for admission is propitious. It may be applied to those around us who have no sense of shame at all and who therefore are quite willing to engage in acts that a few of us can only salaciously imagine. Oh, to be unfettered! Like unto it is immodesty which is fundamentally another form of *shamelessness*, but more inclined toward repulsive things like *assertiveness*, something that certain people feel quite free to express but who condemn its practice in others. Its odiousness rests heavily upon who one is and precisely what he is asserting, not to say how currently in vogue it may be to flagrantly endorse certain outrageous opinions. To assert what is currently presumed to be unassailably sound opinion, we'd say without hesitation, is altogether acceptable.

This, alas, raises the matter of pretense or pretension, call it what you will. It assumes the form of posturing, pretending, *acting out*, forcing one's unpalatable opinions on defenseless guests at morbid dinner parties from which easy and ready escape is ordinarily difficult to arrange without being socially obvious. Worse, it involves an unhealthy dollop of arrogance, which is little more than overwhelming others with one's delusions of innate superiority, itself not the product of what one has achieved but of what one has assumed to be superior birth that carries with it a preposterous estimate of elevated rank and station. We have no problem with any of that. Such fools may give the impression, but only that, of an overwhelmingly generous familiarity with the world's treasure chest of knowledge available in the repositories of the world's most generously endowed libraries. One can accomplish this if one is equipped with the requisite law-enforcement grade arrogance and a far greater than usual penchant for common effrontery, a cunning weapon for initiating a combative assault on a cocktail party prisoner who, because of his excessive alcoholic quotient, is ill prepared to defend himself, partly because he is trapped, and partly because alcohol has appreciably compromised his capability for protecting himself. An affront, let us all agree, is usually in the form of a protractedly unpleasant exchange leading to nothing very worth the trouble. It trades upon the endless possibilities of conveying disrespect spiced with indignation that usually ends in horridly assertive expressions of outrage.

An affront is a frontal attack on one's fragile sense of dignity. Wrote John Dryden, "to one well-born, the affront is worse and more," to which we might add, to one low-born affront comes as no surprise, since a person of lower station may well command a lesser sense of both dignity (because he has so little of it at risk) and modesty. That too, not to say that he's far more inclined to accept what life hurls his way. As to modesty, the average bloke does not necessarily have any to guard, if by modesty we mean an arsenal of allied virtues such as an overweening abundance of moderation, a virtue that one observes ever often less these turbulent days. A modest individual, on the considerable other hand, seems to carry in his quiver a refined instinct for self-control born of self-discipline along with a gift for *clemency*, by which we're saying a tendency toward certain gentleness and mercy that guides him toward civil leniency.

So it is that fools are under siege from a fertile variety of insults aimed at destroying their fragile and uncertain sense of self-worth, substantially undermined by the merciless bludgeoning they receive in the blessed pages of the Holy Bible. But fools, to say it quite directly, are everywhere unpopular and unwelcome. Thomas Carlyle in his *Latter-Day Pamphlets* (1850) estimated that in his time and place there were "Twenty-seven million, mostly fools." A politician with the unlikely name of Champ Clark, U.S. Speaker of the House between 1911 and 1919, responded, "the percentage of fools is not so great as Carlyle states it, but nevertheless it is quite large." You bet it was. Anyone ceaselessly assailed by fools carries a tendency to retreat into a cage he has constructed for himself. Where else, then, is he to repair? The obvious first response is to take cover in a foolocracy, a foolish fortress of security surrounded by a more than generous moat, an ideal setting to maintain or fortify foolification. A foolocracy, allow us to reiterate, is nothing in the world but a government under hopeless mismanagement of fools, a form of governance not totally unfamiliar to Americans in the recent past. It has the advantage of recognizing fools as not only a social class, but as an absurd and hopeless governing body. If mem'ry serves, Sydney Smith may have been the first to render comment upon this, drawing liberally upon what's been appropriately called his *Swiftian wit*. Smith lent what support he had at his command to certain liberation movements, one of them directed at Catholics and others whom he viewed as oppressed, not excluding unmarried women facing as their eternal penalty the unenviable task of guiding apes through hell. Nor was he unmindful of the plight of fools, wherever they may be discovered. Allow us, for example, to cite the old fellow's attitude toward Tories who, he tells us, "will do everything by slow degrees which the Whigs propose to do at once. Whether the delay be wise or mischievous is a separate question, but such I believe to be the man in whom fools of the earth put their trust."

These days, persons belonging to the foolocracy, like other fools, have opened a cyber website; the one in question pays homage to certain individuals designated as *fool of the week*. Mindful that a foolish hypocrisy is the mark of a foolish mind, one such designee was (not surprisingly) a politician; he had allegedly attempted to entice a woman into a sadomasochistic interlude, in which the woman was choked and beaten from head to heel. All went comparatively well until, awakened from having blacked out, she discovered herself bound by a leather belt. The politician, it appears, was on record as opposing homosexual activities on grounds that they were horridly inconsistent with *family values*. According to police, said politician had plied the woman with alcoholic beverages as a means of promoting a certain ease of consensuality.

Meanwhile, the UK's North Kent Police Station contracted a private company to maintain every aspect of its building for a span of 30 years. This meant, among other absurd things, that when a roll of bathroom tissue expired, it was necessary to pass the problem through certain bureaucratic channels to be addressed along with other such urgent *issues*, as jackasses now call such things. The first step in rectifying the problem was to make a call on a certain *hot line*, and at the same time present certain paper documents, both of which were to be evaluated and, if the deemed necessary, would in due time be evaluated and, quite possibly, addressed officially. Moreover, if the police had a mind to move a table or attach a document to a wall, they were obliged to observe the same prescribed fool's customary ritual. Elsewhere, Iran's less than universally popular elected president–dictator Mahmoud Ahmadinejad had been telling his followers that Americans were interfering with the anticipated arrival of *mankind's savior*. "We have documented proof," said the Iranian leader, claiming that Americans envision a "descendant of the prophet of Islam [who] will rise in these parts and [then] will dry the roots of injustice in the world." Continuing, "they have devised all these plans to prevent the coming of the Hidden Imam because they know that the Iranian nation is the one that will prepare the grounds for his coming, and will be the supporter of his rule."

A source appropriately calling itself *Foolocracy* reported that in Asheville, N.C., a chap known to prance the streets wearing a Confederate soldier's uniform while brandishing a Confederate flag, took umbrage with another chap who had publicly declared himself an *atheist* but who nonetheless wished to be seated on Asheville's city council. The neo-Confederate objected on grounds that the North Carolina constitution prohibits political office for "any person who shall deny the being of Almighty God," in spite of the North Carolina supreme court's having unambiguously declared in 1961 that no religious test would enjoin a citizen from holding public office. Meanwhile, the fellow in the Confederate uniform (who, it developed, was a once president of the local NAACP chapter and an avowed promoter of something called *Southern Heritage*) continued to hold his ground. *Foolocracy*, by the way, disclosed that Indiana University had won $221,000 of taxpayers' money for the laudable purpose of discovering why young gentlemen (who may prefer blondes) do not prefer condoms. *Foolocracy* also disclosed that the widely-held view that Saddam Hussein could not wage war on the West originated with information secured from a taxi driver; and that the governor-elect of New Jersey had attended 122 Bruce Springsteen concerts.

Such disclosures of idiocy lend support to the notion that a foolocracy will always be with us, and that it is one aspect of what we might call the absurdist persuasion (to be mercilessly examined later), that something is ever lurking in cultural shadows the world over. There is little else we can do but look longingly toward antiquity for cultural guidance in the face of outright foolishness that threatens to destroy us all. Consider *uno absurdo dato, mille sequuntur* that, to trust our imperfect recollection of Latin, we render as "a man may build a thousand absurdities upon one." We are reminded too of the wonderfully Latin *credo quia absurdum est*: "I believe it because it is absurd." The word comes to us more directly from the Latin *absurde*. The *ab* part of the word means *off*, and the *surd* or Latin *surdus* means something *like silent, mute, dumb, dull, indistinct, deaf, inaudible, and offensive to the ear*. In music it means inharmonious, perhaps out of tune. In our time, it has come to mean something out of step with what might suspiciously be called *good sense* (if we can agree upon what that may be) or with propriety. The OED defines *absurd* as incongruous, unreasonable, illogical, something "plainly opposed to reason, and hence ridiculous, silly." Absurdity, being innately foolish and foolhardy, has been a rich and ongoing source of feverish comment.

Consider, for example, that the man known to some of us as *Marcus Tullius*, or more playfully as *Tully*, remarked over his chop, "*Nihil tam absurde dici potest, quod non dicatur, ab aliquo philosophorum*," in other words, "there is nothing so absurd but some philosopher has said it," suggesting that out of the mouths of purportedly wise men of philosophic predisposition come the most foolish of abject stupidities. Oliver Goldsmith, conversant in both jurisprudence and medicine, and possibly best remembered for *The Vicar of Wakefield* (1766), was thus a bookish gentleman who, amply acquainted with libraries, remarked on that subject, "a book may be amusing with numerous errors, or it may be very dull without a single absurdity," suggesting that to introduce absurdity is also to entertain through what is upon closer scrutiny unabashed *foolishness*. One is mindful of Gilbert and Sullivan's *Patience* (1881), directed at absurd aestheticism, where we listen attentively while a chorus of dragoons belt out, "now is not this ridiculous—and is not this preposterous? /A thorough-paced absurdity—explain it if you can." But you can't. As an unidentified chap opined, "Even absurdity has a champion to defend it, for error is always talkative," as for ludicrous example some nonsense lines from the pen of near-forgotten William Cosmo Monkhouse who drew breath between 1840 and 1901. Twice married, he jotted the following thoughts, posthumously collected in his *Nonsense Rhymes* (1902): "There was an old man of Lyme/ Who married three wives at a time, / When asked 'why a third?' / He replied, 'One's absurd!/ And bigamy, Sir, is a crime!" Similarly,

Max Beerbohm, writing for the once influential *Yellow Book*, a miscellany of poetry, fiction and commentary, observed in 1895 that "there is always something rather absurd about the past," if only because one has the benefit of hindsight's wisdom. Others have come to grip with reality as it strikes them in the present. George Duhamel was a medical doctor who turned to humane commentaries, mostly before World War II, defending individuals against what he viewed as the menace of catechism. "Je respecte trop l'idée de Dieu," he wrote, "pour la rendre responsable d'un monde aussi absurd. ("I have too much respect for the idea of God to make it responsible for such an absurd world.")

Absurdity, of course, has long infiltrated, if not enhanced, the arts. Literary chaps as far back as Aristophanes, Plautus, Terence, Dante, Boccaccio, Chaucer, Shakespeare and Rabelais have, all by way of satire, introduced the absurdity of fools into their work. In 1980 a then associate professor, Dick Penner, at the University of Tennessee, brought out a soft-bound anthology of absurdist fiction gleaned from Nikolai Gogol, Daniil Kharms, Franz Kafka, Vladimir Nabokov, Flann O'Brien, Samuel Beckett, Eugene Ionesco, Tommaso Landolfi, Juan Carlos Onetti, Voltaire, Joseph Heller, Ingeborg Bachman and Albert Camus. He called it, not absurdly, *Fiction of the Absurd*, redefining *absurd* as "away from all reason or right sense; laughably foolish and [significantly enough] true." Penner cited the Hungarian theater critic and scholar Martin Esslin, able author of *The Theatre of the Absurd* (1962), who argued the "plausible theory that the spirit of Absurd Theatre evolved from the early Greek *mimus*, a spectacle of dancing, singing, juggling, and clowning" that we find today in absurdist writers who trade in "the same kind of invented logical reasoning, false syllogism [and] free association" that carried forth in the film comedians Charlie Chaplin, the Keystone Cops and Buster Keaton, Laurel and Hardy, W.C. Fields and the Marx Brothers — all of whom superbly donned the fool's absurd mask.

As Penner noted, the absurd in literature owes something to surrealism and Dadaism. The former is also known as the *absurdist movement* and generally likened to *super realism*, an artistic attempt to siphon off the subconscious through a series of dreams, arcane symbols and an unbridled spectacle of irrationality. The term *surrealism* apparently originated with Guillaume Apollinaire in about 1917. You can call him *Guillaume*, or you can call him *Apollinaire*, but his real name was (begging your pardon) *Wilhelm Albert Wlodzimierz Apolinary Kostrowicki*. An Italian chap born of a Polish mother who knew him by that absurd name, he was, we regret to say, carried off by the influenza at age 38 in 1918, by which time he had gamely tried his hand at acting, poetry, essays, one erotic novel called *The Gas Heart* (1921) and another titled (sadomasochically) *Les Onze Mille Verges* (The Eleven Thousand Rods).

Viewed from another side, the absurdist movement is generally recognized as an outbranch of something called *Dada*, as absurd as its infantile name, believed to have sprung to life from a fine old French expression, *être sur son dada* (to ride one's hobby horse). Dada is most often identified with its premier crackpot proponent, that being Tristan Tzara, an obscure Romanian versifier and earnest-looking little fellow (real name Sammy Rosenstein) who devoted his life to Marxism and (in the words of one thumbnail biographer) attempted to *disintegrate the structures of language* while methodically sipping Pernod in Parisian cafes. Among Dada's lofty principles was its raising "inconsequential bayonets and the Sumatral head of German babies." Dada is occasionally remembered as something expressing "life with neither bedroom slippers [nor] flabby cushions." Let us here proclaim that there's nothing better than being an intellectual, or better still a bogus intellectual. As Gilbert and Sullivan remind us,

> I am an intellectual chap,
> And I think things that would astonish you.

Tzara, as avant-garde as anyone you could dredge from Parisian gutters, argued that reason doesn't get in the way of thought, and that everything means exactly nothing, as we had long suspected. Tzara had, to be quite honest about it, destructive tendencies that encouraged him to destroy art, so far as that may have been possible. To be fair about it, Tzara was influenced (in a negative sort of way) by the madness of armies, war and death. Of course, he was correct. We can without reservation at least credit him for that much.

Every age reinvents what doesn't need reinventing. The Theater of the Absurd appeared to have invented irrationality, as if the world had never imagined such preposterous a thing. But it was the same old stuff in a postmodern package, although one wonders how anything could be quite so self-contradictory as *postmodern*. Because of theater's practical limitations, the absurd theater has substantially narrower limitations than fiction, inasmuch as there are things that can be accomplished in fiction that are impossible on any kind of stage. The theater, after all, is itself somewhat absurd because it is rather aesthetically archaic. Be all that as it may, playwrights most identified with the absurdist movement are the Franco-Romanian Eugene Ionesco (1909 [not 1912, as often reported]–1994), remembered today for *The Lesson* (1951), *The Chairs* (1952), *Jack, or the Submission* (1955), *The Rhinoceros* (1959, and *The Bald Soprano* (1965). Ionesco is long on absurdity in the form of non-sequiturs, contradictions, irrelevancies, impossibilities, incoherencies and inarticulations—all of which we encounter daily and have no desire to see presented in theaters as some remarkably brilliant discovery.

His theatrical *message* is perilously close to that of the Anglo-American poet, playwright and essayist T(homas) S(tearns) Eliot, namely what's been called the dehumanizing influence of contemporary life and the apparent meaninglessness of existence in a world characterized by despair and stupefying hopelessness. Such sprightly notions are also to be found in the work of Irish-born Samuel Beckett, for a time a secretary to the great James Joyce. Beckett wrote prolifically and is best identified with *En Attendant Godot* (*Waiting For Godot*) written in 1949, presented in 1952 and published in English in 1954. Godot is, in all probability, a cynical representation of God, the center of all meaning, *destiny* and fulfillment, except that he never shows up. The play introduces two tramps, Gogo and Didi, whom we encounter beneath a dead tree, probably an oblique allusion to Calvary. Beckett is also fondly remembered among old timers for his *End Game* (1958), a cheerful little drama with four characters, three of whom appear to be paralyzed. It is a nihilistic classic, if ever there was one, that deservedly crowned Beckett the *Archangel of Absurdity*. Much to his credit, he turned down a Nobel Prize, something that in our time has become as absurd as anything that ever crossed Beckett's perverse mind, since it also has been awarded to a disquieting succession of *imbéciles*. Not long ago, we must add by way of an aside, a nihilistic American auto repair garage generously offered a gratuitous Nobel Prize with every oil change. We should explain here that nihilism is a powerfully loaded term derived from the Latin *nihil*, meaning *nothing*, or something of no value, no worth. One is put immediately in mind of Hemingway's "A Clean, Well-Lighted Place" that toward its end reads, "Our *nada* who art in *nada*, *nada* be thy name thy kingdom *nada* thy will be *nada* in *nada* as it is in *nada*. Give us this *nada* our daily *nada* and *nada* us our *nada* as we *nada* our *nada*...Hail nothing full of nothing, nothing is with thee." Nothing delights a nihilist more than denying any objective basis for truth, and therefore allowing him to believe in nothing. Nihilism, by the way, borrows its name from a 19th and 20th century Russian movement that, having advanced various schemes for supposed reform, eventually devoted its creative energies to terrorist projects.

Of course, there are a number of other notable playwrights identified with the absurdist movement, among them Harold Pinter, son of a Jewish tailor, who concocted *The Room* and *The Dumb Waiter* (1957), followed by *The Caretaker* (1960) and *The Homecoming* (1965); Edward Albee (1928, the adopted son of theater magnate Reed Albee), who gave us *The Zoo Story* (1959), *The Death of Bessie Smith*, *The American Dream* (1961), and *Who's Afraid of Virginia Woolf?* (1962); and Jean Cocteau (1889–1963) the clever man of letters who left us with *The Human Voice* (1930), *The Infernal Machine* (1936), and *The Typewriter* (1947); Jean Genet, the *succès-de-scandale* who lived a criminal life but who nonetheless expected us to explain, as best we know how, *The Maids* (1947), *The Balcony* (1957), *The Blacks* (1959) and *The Screens* (1964); and of course Albert Camus who, in an existential error, accepted a Nobel Prize in 1957 when, to be quite honest about it, he could not have known better. He (whose name is usually pronounced *camoo*, but sometimes articulated as *camoose* to avoid association with certain foolish slang terms) became far better known for his novels such as *The Stranger* (1942) and *The Plague* (1948), but he was nonetheless identified with the absurd theater through his *Caligula* and *Cross Purpose* (1947) and through his forward-looking theatrical friends with whom he opened what they called their *Theatre du Travail* in 1935 that morphed into the *Theatre de L'Equipe* two seasons later. Their intention (and we've heard this many times) was to deliver theater to working class blokes as well as to the intellectually advantaged. French literature, perhaps more than any other, tends toward the philosophic, and it led Camus to absurdist, even nihilist views, such as the notion that Christ was entirely divine and in no sense human. *Nihilism* is a doctrine of denial, often rejecting outright such doctrinal matters as morality and religion. It is, as the American Calvinist Timothy Dwight called it, "a total disregard for all moral obligation." It is also an extreme form of skepticism that leads even to the denial of existence, ending in nothingness, sometimes driving its proponents into depression and madness. Some later psychologists have described the movement as *delusionary*.

During World War II Camus, for all his negativism, became actively involved with the French Resistance, something that may later have turned him away from nihilism and toward constructive rebellion. He somewhat ironically embraced moral responsibility while at the same time developing an anti-Christian position, although scholars have on occasion claimed him as a Christian in spite of himself. Remaining always the skeptic and metaphysical quester, Camus in his *Myth of Sisyphus* (1942), a philosophic essay, emphasized the hopelessness and the absurdity of life as represented in that mythic figure whom Hades sentenced eternally to roll a boulder up to the apex of a hill only to have it roll back down. It was an astutely selected, apt symbol, Camus recognized, capturing the essence of life's abject futility. He is, as much as any writer, identified with existentialism that has as one of its philosophic ends to resolve the problem of despair born of utter futility and frantic desperation among those who could make no sense of *existence*, which includes darned near everyone. Existentialism, over the years, has meant widely different things to different minds. It pertains, obviously, to dilemmas associated with existence. The OED characterizes existentialism as "a doctrine that concentrates [upon] the existence of the individual, who, being free and responsible, is held to be what he makes himself by the self development of his essence through acts of the will." In simpler terms, one sorts out for himself his reason for existing, and then follows his own philosophic path.

Existentialism ostensibly reaches back to the Danish philosopher Søren Kierkegaard and then to such 20th century figures as Karl Jaspers, who advanced certain points of existentialism in his *Man in the Modern Age* (1931) and his three-volume *Philosophy* (1932); his fellow German thinker Friedrich

Nietzsche, wistfully remembered for his *Thus Spake Zarathustra* (1883–1891) and his *Beyond Good and Evil* (1886); and Jean-Paul Sartre who, as much as any French cognoscente, recommended the cause of existentialism through the publication of his *Being and Nothingness* (1943) that represented man as a desperate creature hopelessly adrift in a senseless universe. Sartre's phrase "existence precedes essence" summarizes the *existential problem*, acknowledging that one first exists, and second, is left to make sense of that existence, which is to say explain his motives and ends for existing. He may then be equipped to identify his personal plight and his life mission. It is as easy, and as difficult, as that. One may, for example, devote himself to building, to healing, to finding God or to launching any number of other quests that one might presumably construe as productive and wholesome. One's reason for existing pivots upon what he makes of himself. To view it from another side, we are, as they say, *condemned to be free*, to discover who, what and where we are, and to what purpose. Hence, existentialism became both a philosophic movement and a literary passion, although by the 1970s it had as a movement degenerated into something of a sophomoric catnip.

Granted, for all their real or feigned absurdities, fools seldom investigate existential solutions, one of which is to seek wisdom in any of the world's civilized religions, if such exist. They are far more likely, like most people, to float aimlessly from day to day without objectives, goals or even fantasies. One choice can be merely to float serenely through life as a flaming fool, that being an option for those gifted with absurdly comedic and absurdist inclinations. Of course not everyone possesses these carefree characteristics, and may lapse into profound mental and emotional distress to exacerbate their madness. The popular Scottish experimental psychiatrist R. D. (Ronald David) "Ronnie" Laing addressed exactly this dilemma when he wrote in his *Politics of Experience* (1967) that "madness need not be all breakdown," and that "it may also be break-through. It is a mental liberation as well as an enslavement and existential death." Let us hope not, but if indeed that's where it leads, we don't want to go there. Granted, Laing was something of a crackpot and therefore as absurd as certain of his patients. For all his obvious faults, Laing was, in the 1970s, the most read, if not the most endorsed, psychiatrist of his day, although, to be sure, his readers were not themselves students of the mind. Laing was mired in the existential and speculated about what he called *psychiatric existentialism* without ever having worked out its implications. As near as we know, existential psychotherapy seems to have been predicated upon everyone's being alone, the solution to which is familiarly existential: that everyone discover, however foolish it may appear, his own reason for drawing breath. Women, we are told, rest their very existence upon love, whatever that may mean; possibly that one should become warmly affectionate, and let it go at that. Byron, who knew a thing or two about love and women, or let on that he did, wrote in his protracted ottava rima *Don Juan* (1823–1824) that "Man's love is of man's life a thing apart, [but that] 'Tis woman's whole existence," something that we might construe as the center of a woman's existential constitution.

This may or may not sound patently ridiculous, depending upon how one regards *les choses du coeur*, as they're called. Playing at being the fool trades heavily upon the ridiculous, to present oneself deliberately as preposterous. Ridiculousness involves a number of preposterously awful manifestations in such disparate roles as dolts, halfwits, jack-asses dunces, morons and all such rubbish. *Ridiculous* mostly means being subject to ridicule (something that someone, we don't know who, called a *weak weapon*) which in turn means to be approached in mockery, as a fool might be if he's a real fool worth the name, leading inexorably toward derision. Woodrow Wilson said in 1916 that "the best way to silence a friend of yours whom you know to be a fool is to induce him to hire a hall. Nothing chills pretense like exposure." It is all pretty terrible, any way you approach it. It means that if you're ridiculous, people laugh (as they say) *at* you, rather than *with* you, simply because they have reason to believe that you're stupid, which may or may not be justified, whereas they are under the fallacious impression that they are, by their stupidity, somehow superior, although it is seldom clear how or why.

Maybe they are. The awful word *ridiculous* refers to something or someone who (or that) invites derisive laughter (derisive meaning derision, which means deride, meaning jeer, gibe, flout). *Ridiculous* entails such familiar terms as absurdity and preposterousness. Shakespeare, for example, writes in *The Tempest* of "a most ridiculous Monster, to make a wonder of a poor drunkard." The ridiculous and the sublime are friends. Wit that he was, our own Tom Paine cleverly observed, "the sublime and the ridiculous are often so clearly related that it is difficult to class them separately. One step above the sublime makes the ridiculous, and one step above the ridiculous makes the sublime again." So also the Irish poet Derek Mahon (1941) felt moved to say, "I am just going outside and may be some time/ The others nod, pretending not to know./ At the heart of the ridiculous, the sublime," illustrating that, as we have suggested, the sage and the fool are not so distant, and may in fact be the same person. So too the American outsider Ambrose Bierce, who left us wondering what to do with his *Cobwebs from an Empty Skull* (1874) and *The Devil's Dictionary* (1911), wryly called *ambition* "an overmastering desire to be vilified by enemies while living and made ridiculous by friends when dead."

A fool's life consists primarily of a long and arduous journey during which he blatantly invites derision, common ridicule, alienation, humiliation, disgust, avoidance, exclusion, and vilification. He is even designated as a fool in the Tarot deck that numbers its cards and attaches sometimes *mystic* significance to them. Tarot is both an allegorical playing card and an arcane means of fortune telling, alleged to have originated in 14th century Italy. There are 22 Tarot cards to a deck, 12 of which are numbered and regarded as trumps, then added to 56 more cards to total 78. T. S. Eliot cites Tarot in Part I of *The Waste Land* (1922), entitled "The Burial of the Dead," where he introduces a certain Madame Sosostris, the not so *famous clairvoyant* lifted from the pages of Aldous Huxley in his novel entitled *Chrome Yellow* (1921) and referred to by Eliot as the "wisest woman in Europe, / With a wicked pack of [Tarot] cards." According to the unimaginably mystic *Hermetic Order of the Golden Dawn*, the deck is "one of the most powerful sources of information in the world," since it promises to transport one mystically "in contact with one's higher self." We have no problem with any of that, because it may lead us to discover happiness without really trying, and may show us how to prevent our pants from falling down.

The zero Tarot card, which is numbered 22, the last of the trump cards, belongs to the Fool, who carries the synonymous identification of *Le Mat, Il Matto, Matello, Il Pazzo* or plain old *Le Fol*. Tarot authority Robert Hudson, whose *Mystical Origins of Tarot: From, Ancient Roots to Modern Usage* tells us more than we want to know, not omitting that the fool "stands outside the social order of medieval life" which explains why he is depicted as a "homeless, placeless, frequently mentally ill person," whose theatrical role was to invent an entertainment of his own devising, since there may or may not have been any dialogue furnished for his use by any playwright. In Germany, he became identified as a *Narr* (fool). Suffice it to say that the Narr, or any other equivalently pejorative name, became little more than a strolling biped, a walking joke, whose estate, as we shall also see in later pages, evolved over the ages and is, regrettably, still in our midst. Hudson explains that the Tarot Fool is sometimes identified as the *skys* that he renders as *the excuse* which in turn is an *expendable card*. He also explains that in Tarot decks, the Fool arrives variously dressed in *penitential white* and other times in the rags of a wandering beggar under siege by a dog and by children who taunt him. He surfaces from time to time in what was to become the fool's customary uniform of cap (with feathers), bells and a jackass's ears. Customary too was his donning fools' customary colors of green and yellow.

June Kaminski, a contributor to "The Voice of Women," further informs us that the fool represents what we have long known as *Everyman*, an archetype, representing us all, great and small. The Fool in Tarot, she again reminds us, "is known as the most worthless," although she hastens by way of contradiction to add that it's "also the most valuable one," which settles the matter with unambiguous precision. So too, he is both first and last, a remark that comes from a woman in a state of metaphysical overdrive. Kaminski continues by notifying us that the fool somehow "represents the negative space above the Tree of Life," as we had long suspected but were hesitant to say except in the strictness of privacy. But why is the fool assigned the zero ranking? Simple. It is, she informs us, merely the Qabalistic Zero. By Jove, we've got it. Continuing, Ms. Kaminski gently stresses that our fool "is intricately linked with all 21 cards of the Major Arcana." Major Arcana! We had somehow suspected as much: a fool in charge of the Eternal Arcana: a delicious thought, and yet a provocative one. Give us words of eternal comfort, O Fool, if you can unearth them. "The Fool coaxes us to walk our own path, not the path of the herd," something that, quite frankly, we had not resolved until this moment.

Elevating us to ever higher Platonic spiritual regions, Ms Kaminski then draws a distinction so perplexing that we frankly had not the courage to wrestle with it. We refer (obviously) to the differences that separate the *Upright Fool* from what is known among Tarot travelers as a *Reversed Fool*. Let's grope our way to the bottom of the matter by way of our own Madame Sosostris. Let's also come directly to the point: an Upright Fool represents what we might familiarly know as a *fresh start*, a *new beginning*, a sort of *clean sweep of life and destiny*. It reaches us through foolish delusion and recommends that we react to life with a certain forthright resolve, a limitless optimism and, above all, a faith that we can prevail anywhere we may elect. The Reverse Fool, to proceed directly to the point of our investigation, "gives us a clear warning that we must resist the template to race recklessly or immaturely in any new situation." Impeccably articulated, we dare say; we could not have expressed it with more gravity and basic down-on-the-farm, straight-talking good sense. Is there more? More or less, yes. Try this on: the Reverse Fool will forever be peering over your shoulder, begging you to accept your real or imagined responsibilities as well as your commitment. Don't forget them, for heaven's sake. Any further advice? Yes, but it's metaphysically murky, and generally inappropriate for learned minds. We thank Ms. Kaminski for her concise and yet painfully enlightening words that seem to have come from some mystically divine origin. She leaves us now, bullwhip in hand, striding circumspectly out of the room.

Tarot! By Jove, it offers a variety of spiritual purposes behind its deceptively coy appearance as a silly card game suitable for a Sunday afternoon after church. But is it time to call for a fresh deck? Not quite. Our subject, lest we forget, is *foolishness*, something that we have not yet beheld in all his brilliant colors. Had we but world enough and time, we might have strolled pleasantly, a few respectful paces behind Ms. Kaminski, and beheld more of Tarot's unfathomable mysteries, thereby throwing wide the gate to perfect knowledge by gazing thoughtfully into things like *Feng Shui* astro locations, *Kui Energy Reports*, *Rider West Tarot*, *Aquatic Tarot*, Tarot's 78 levels of enlightenment, with Kung Foo sauce and so like. But we have other obligations that oblige us to leave our Tarot friends by the wayside, extending them a hearty *Heigh Ho* and good luck in their greater than metaphysical glances into Ultimate Destiny. Onward, we say, our hands outstretched in lasting friendship and earnest good wishes. Don't neglect to write in lucid

English, that you may share your mysteries the world over, as well as to our friends on other planets.

We know fools by their foolspeak, by their predictably foolish discourse. "Silence," Sir Francis Bacon is alleged to have said in a grave interlude of introspection, "is the virtue of the fool," meaning, we presume, that fools are far better off with their lips sealed. As conventional wisdom (if indeed such exists) tells us, "it is better to remain silent and be thought a fool than to speak and remove all doubt." Such linguistic gaffes are usually the fault of wretched grammar, hideous reliance upon clichés and recklessly illogical substance—any of which can serve deservedly as an occasion for uncontrollably derisive laughter. As someone said, "Where ignorance is bliss, 'tis folly to be wiser." Consider, for instance, the popularity of so-called *Pig Latin* in the 1940s, the infamous implementation of a code language for use among children. It was as elemental as placing the first letter of a word at the end of it, and then adding a sound similar to an *ay* or *ei* also at the end. The big idea was to evade enemies' ears by befuddling them, thereby enabling one to speak with impunity by uttering things like *ropday* in place of *drop*. Foolish or not, both speaker and listener must have been more than routinely keen at distorting English in such a way as to baffle almost anybody by use of a contrived language. The mystery scrivener Raymond Chandler made famous through his novels *The Big Sleep* (1939), *The Lady in the Lake* (1943) and *Double Indemnity* (1944) recorded *in passim* through the divine pages of *Dime Detective Magazine*, "big white father say come now...don't give me any more of your pig Latin." Nor was it unfamiliar to F. Scott Fitzgerald, who remarked, also *in passim*, "when anything Latin or Pig Latin was ever put up to me, I could always rise to meet that." We also seem to recall that Flower Children of those glorious 1960s revived it so as to communicate in a loopy manner with their fuzzed up fellows while in police custody. Criminals in England, we are reminded, relied upon it as a code language devised by rearranging letters within a word. Lusty Samuel Pepys, who married a 15-year-old, concealed his multifarious secrets in an arcane shorthand of his own devising. Even Benjamin Franklin, the ever-resourceful inventor and rational American man for all seasons, developed such a coded system for his messages. Franklin, heaven help us, was anything in the world except a fool (although in later times fools did rely upon Pig Latin to make a mockery of language by distorting it). There was also a brief fad called Dog Latin (*Canis Latinicus*), a mongrelization of Virgil's mighty language. With Dog Latin, fools attached things like *us* or *ics* to words, thereby investing them with bogus Latinate sounds best appreciated by fools of all stripes, especially the most sententious of them who might employ such lofty language appropriate to the grand opening of a budget-priced brothel or a visit to the White House. It was rightly referred to by some of our betters as *Bad Latin*, which is to say no Latin at all, but something bred and barked in a filthy kennel.

While we are on the sensitive subject of universal languages, we must not omit of what in fools' parlance was, if not is, *Bebop* that, as Henry Mencken said in his *History of the American Language* (1919, 1921) acquired its unique sound (since it carried no sense) in a *flattened fifth*, best illustrated in Miles Davis's *Weird-O*, and variously called *bebop, rebop* and so forth to accommodate various emergent occasions which, even in spelling, consisted of nonsense words such as *doowop*, identified with other musicians like Dizzy Gillespie and Charlie Parker, who seized language for its onomatopoetic *effect* rather than its significance and devoted it to other versatile applications in books, clothing, hotrods and underground unwritten significances known only to persons of a certain covert condition. There was a 1949 article that appeared in the "Desert News" that raised the sensitive question of whether the District of Columbia street car company could oblige its riders to suffer bebop while in transit, saying, "readers, dreamers, philosophers and other people on the ragged edge of being driven nuts by modern civilization call it a dark plot against sanity." Bebop, we are obliged to record, mutated into a fool's language, used for utterances by fools like Teddy Boys and other *avant-garde* scoundrels, and ever still foolish cliques. Eventually, signs reading *Bebop Spoken Here* appeared in the filthy windows of Village bistros and accorded it a certain modicum of acceptance among persons of a certain cultural edge, even though bebop didn't mean anything, becoming as it was the *non-language of nowhere and nothing*, notwithstanding that you could write it, play it, sing it, smoke it, dance it, eat it for breakfast even if it had no taste.

Bismarck is reputed to have said that God looks out for fools, drunks, little children and travelers. Bebop survived, probably on grounds that it was harmless enough. Some fools are by their nature harmless enough, although they are often irritating; and in the end they usually do not present a vexatious problem to the rest of us. We nevertheless continue not to suffer them gladly, with or without their historic attraction to bebop and other evidences of nonsense that persons of breeding, education and civility are more than likely to eschew. One can suffer fools, yes; but only so long as they remain resolutely invisible, inaudible, inarticulate, out of hearing, out of one's front yard and out of sight. Only thus can they coexist without gravely endangering other peoples' sense of emotional equilibrium, encouraged by the conviction that fools present themselves in various subspecies and can therefore be handled with little more than adroit social leverage.

Steward, kindly bring forth the sort of chap upon whom we apply the degenerate term *fop*, by which (we repeat) we do not mean to denigrate (let us be clear) the Fraternal Order of Police, a perfectly respectable assemblage of constables and public safety and enforcement public service officers upon whom the sovereign safety of our streets and our honor depend. Most of us have little other dealing with the FOP except to receive telephone solicitations and other humanely warm and brotherly gestures calculated to elevate police to the station to which they rightfully belong. Nay, the fop to whom we refer is a permutation of *fool*, a subject to which we have devoted our unswerving attention lo, these many erudite pages. Simply put, a fop is merely another foolish person, identified in other times and places as a *foppie*, which is to say a *coxcomb*, which is nothing but a silly cap warn by a professional fool, which is also to say a person who earns his keep doing silly things for the uproarious regalement of other fools. In the immortal words of little Tommy, "a fool and his money are soon parted." Tusser, the farmer, poet, all around good neighbor and Sunday morning philosopher, "he shall strive for a coxcomb and thrive as a daw," meaning *jackdaw*: a contemptuous name for a loquacious *idiot*. *Fop*, in more enlightened times, has come to signify a conceited, superficial ass, a fake and an insufferable pretender. *Coxcomb* has also been applied to a whimsical sort of husband, an effeminate man, a fashion plate and traveling head idiot.

As to *fop*, medical authorities have judiciously selected it as an appropriate name for a disease, known to those learned in medical science a *Fibrodysplasia Ossificanus Progressiva*, a somewhat arcane muscular complaint that unaccountably transmutes muscle and other tissue into bone. Laugh if you must, but it's no laughing matter. FOP is sufficiently troubling to occasion formation of a *support group* numbering (at last count) 200 perfectly earnest persons, worldwide. Fops have traditionally found their way into our drama, to name but three: George Etherege's *The Man of Mode, or Sir Fopling Flutter* (1676); Aphra Behn's *The Town Fopp* (so spelled, 1676) *Sir Timothy Tawdrey* (also so spelled, 1676); and Colley Cibber's *Love's Last Shift, or Virtue Rewarded* (1696).

Exactly three centuries later *The Onion*, a British publication, took careful note of a local dandy who caused a stir among the constables who had been summoned to assist his removal from public view. The headline read, "Foppish Dandy Disregards Local Constabulary," explaining that the subject "who is a well-known socialite and composer of light verse, is said to have behaved most rudely to the constables, responding in their attempts to subdue him" with what one witness called "an air of casual dismissal," adding too that such regrettable behavior "was most irregular and boorish, and by no means appropriate to a gentleman of his standing." It all began when the offender consumed "a great amount of port," after which he "seemed lost in reverie," singing mightily, tossing his curls to and fro, gesturing madly about the rooms and laughing gaily all the while." Responded the "wife of a prominent captain of industry, 'what a hearty person.'"

Back on our majestic shores a regrettably foppish incident occurred in the Hamptons when, according to a source identifying himself as the *Gawker*, "a social gay [name withheld] was below average." We regret to hear it. "On Saturday he was hanging out at Georgica being fabulous, when someone 'assaulted' him by calling him a 'Jew' and a 'fag.' Worse, the 'douche' wasn't kicked out, because he was a big spender." The subject himself was reported "last seen engaged in the most retarded social feuds, spoke to a Guest of the Guest about the incident [and] said something about the gay's socks or something. However, he didn't hold back on painting himself as the gay Rosa Parks for having the courage to speak out against gay slur words." We feel secure in assuming that the incident itself resolved in a satisfactory conclusion. Elsewhere in the great *beau monde*, in a source calling himself *Foppish Dandy* we encountered a certain animated chap who was, according to reports, "a very sophisticated psyche...well-spoken...[with] advanced vocabulary...an English accent and a huge sexual orientation" and was "frequently depicted wearing women's clothes and sometimes makeup." We conclude our glimpses of foppish life from a source calling itself *MechaMonkey* that observes, "you may have taken notice that fops such as ourselves sport only the finest of attires, and our impeccably styled hair surely needs no introduction." Continuing, "in watching my manservant Manservante, play my games for me that I don't strain my hands...I begin to suspect that they have given nary even a glance into their pocket mirrors...I do love a man in a fine uniform. I chanced upon some Greek fellow as well the other day. I won't go into the travesty of his outfit, but I will say that body paint has never ever been fashionable. Manservante was fortunately close enough to catch me and carry me home when I swooned upon witnessing the tragedy of his accoutrements."

Such is the magnificently gorgeous world of foppery through which certain personalities project themselves to stunning advantage, by which they seem best to navigate life, never an easy task. The fop assumes a certain blithe nonchalance, a rather flippant way of confronting his obstacles. In a site called "Lowposts" we meet bewildering Pistol Brandisher and his mate Tex Mecks Brandner who introduces himself as a "foppish British Dandy turned wild west cowboy," adding that "we scour through the western conference of this sport you call basketball, and the mysteries it entails." He continues, "I have met a few Mormons on the wagon train out here to the plains of Utah. They're good people, but they seem to be hogging all the bloody women. How much buggering can one man possibly do?" Brandner begins to sound reminiscent of that British dandy to end them all, Oscar Fingal O'Flaherty Wills Wilde, himself a refined fop and an elegantly flamboyant, self-parodying social disgrace who was at Magdalene College, Oxford, when he recorded the following lines:

> Adieu! Adieu! You silver lamp the moon,
> Which turns our midnight into perfect noon,
> Doth surely light thy towers, guarding well
> Where Dante sleeps, where Byron loved to dwell.

In his outrageously foppish way, Wilde was nonetheless nothing if not quotable. Wrote he, "One should never trust a woman who tells her real age. A woman who would tell one that, would tell one anything," or perhaps, "it takes a thoroughly good woman to do a thoroughly stupid thing," or maybe "I prefer women with a past. They're always damned interesting to talk to," or "the book of life begins with a man and a woman in a garden. It ends in Revelations."

Like unto fops are jackasses who, like fools in general, have traditionally discovered a home in Washington, D.C., which is not only our *nation's* capital, and the (once) capital of the "free" world, but currently, at the very least, the world center of abject stupidity and rampant corruption. But what of the jackass and his unique characteristics? The term *jack*, in one of its etymologic senses, directs us to what one might call a *common bloke*, a *good fellow* such as one might encounter on the street or in a commodious pub enjoying a pint with his mates. The phrase *to play the jack* means, as one might well surmise, to spring some kind of unpleasant stunt. At other times, it has denoted some sort of constabulary person one might encounter at a convention of the aforementioned Fraternal Order of Police. In still another context one might use *jack* to refer to a common sailor, or to say it another way, a *sea-going chap*, one who is at his best form contentedly riding the waves and eddies that Fate places before him. In games of chance, the *jack* applies to the knave of trumps in games of all forms, especially one we know on these shores as *California Jack*. It may also refer to *Monterrey Jack* (a form of cheese) or the kind of jack that one relies upon to lift an automobile. It may oft times refer to lending someone a *jack*, something that in the old days denoted a *farthing*. There are those, yes, who use the term to describe a soap-making machine or a sailing vessel, or even the male gender of animals. One might also become, as idiots say, a *jack of all-trades and master of none.*

Or it can refer to a *jackass*, commonly taken to be nothing more nor less than a male ass, of whom are we acquainted with not a few, since they are used to breed mules. We must not omit to say that jackasses have deservedly found their way into song and legend. We've all heard the good one about how a jackass makes no progress when he's kicking, something that he does most of the time. We are also amply acquainted with a beloved maxim advising that "any jackass can make money; it takes a wise man to keep it." On a learnedly philosophic level, we've been told more times than we care to remember that the braying of a jackass never reaches heaven. Mark Twain introduced us all to his Jackass Gulch, a California mining camp where he shared a cabin on Jackass Hill with Tom Quartz, the cat. A jackass can also be an African penguin and a so-called *Kookaburra* bird, but it is not in these senses of the word that most people comprehend the term, for to them a jackass is (to be quite unequivocal about it) a stupid person or, in common vulgar parlance, a *dumb ass*, referred to among our German friends and enemies as a *dummkopf*, although others have identified it as a *pied-à-terre* in Nevada's Jackass Flats that had once been employed as a nuclear blasting ground. Still others have discovered Nirvana in the Jackass outpost situated near Dewey, Arizona, or the Jackass Ridge in Coulterville, California, while yet others have acquired a taste for Jackass Meadow in the High Sierra. This, like all things, is a function of taste. Marc Cooper published an enlightening treatise on that subject called "Thinking of Jackasses" in the April 2005 *Atlantic Monthly*. We are all uncomfortably aware that the jackass is the mascot of the Democratic Party. This unfortunate circumstance began, legend has it, after populist Andrew Jackson had been undiplomatically identified by a less than adulatory cognomen in or about 1828, nine years after which it was deployed as an unkind (to say it mildly) cartoon by one Thomas Nash in *Harper's Weekly* calling Democrats *asses*.

Down in North Carolina citizens amused themselves by electing some sorry bloke as the state's Jackass of the Year, as for example a person named Tony Rand, whom these scoundrels described as *ethically challenged*, or another chap named Hugh Holimen whom they affectionately call the *smartest man in the world* and who reportedly is, by North Carolina standards, "smarter than you are, so shut up and do what he says." Another of their favorites was Kay Hagan, remembered as the "U.S. Senator [who] voted for the porkulus bill that will indebt the grand kids you don't even have yet"; Beth Perdue, "NC's first year governor [who] has one of the lowest approval ratings in the country," as well as Mike Easly, described as an "Ex-Gov [and] clown-ass...making more news out of office than he did in it"; and of course Cal Cunningham, described as possibly "another John Edwards," once celebrated as a *Jackass of the Year*.

The Chicago Tribune's Washington Bureau presented an article on September 10, 2009, titled "Traficant: Still 'Jackass' After All these Years," disclosing that "the former Ohio congressman [was] released from prison last week after serving seven years for racketeering, bribery, obstruction of justice and tax evasion," referring warmly to his fellow felons as *almost like a family*, concluding, 'I'm still, I guess, the same jackass that I was." A source calling itself "A Tangled Web: A dissenting review of contemporary British and American politics" published an item on August 24, 2008, entitled "Joe Biden: Career Hack and Natural Born Ass," directing attention to his being "a career politician [who] other than a short stint in a law firm in Wilmington for a couple of months...has never held a job other than public office," mentioning too that "through his longevity of living off the public dole, he had never acquired immense knowledge on all matters of our lives, and considers himself an expert on all of them...especially Foreign Relations, the Military, Health Care," and to hold in mind that "this genius has had no education other than law school [from] which he graduated at the bottom of his class." It continues by recording the Vice President's remarks on East Indians in America, to wit: "I've had a great relationship with [them]. In Delaware, the greatest growth population is Indian Americans—moving from India. You cannot go to a 7-11 or a Dunkin Donuts unless you have a slight Indian accent. I'm not joking." The preceding remarks were addressed to a less than appreciative audience of Indian Americans. In September of 2010 Vice President Biden, affectionately known as *Slow Joe*, explained to a reporter that, should the less than esteemed *president* go to his eternal reward, he (Biden) would not, under Constitutional rules of succession, become the next Commander in Chief.

Biden, curiously enough, has been called a *moron*, but in precisely what sense of the word we have yet to learn. Let us be quite clear that when we here deploy that term it is never in reference to a mentally handicapped person. Truman Capote was once himself believed to be mentally disadvantaged or, as we say these days, *mentally challenged*, but he rather overcame that suspicion. On a related subject, he commented once that whereas some people are born bastards, others earn that distinction on their own. So too is it with morons, inasmuch as some are born with that *distinction*, while others develop it through hard work, sustained application and extraordinary determination. Such designations have neither escaped the attention of etymologists nor the attention of more or less ordinary chaps on the street. Let's begin by observing that the word *morology* refers, plain and simple, to the meaningless chattering one encounters at cocktail parties and other such convivial exercises in utter meaninglessness that one may discover in the company of dunces who prefer chattering over cogitation. The OED calls it variously *corrupt communication*, something that fools propagate for the scrutiny of other fools, just as *gizmology* serves the same purpose for those absorbed in the crypto science of *gizmos*.

The word *moron* traces its illustrious history to the Latin *moras*, and to a Greek expression meaning *stupid*. *Morone*, by the way, refers to a certain species of a salamander reported in 1774 as *venomous to the last degree*, something as true today as it was in those stimulating times. A true moron is an adult with a mental age of someone between eight and twelve, so described by the American Association for the Study of Feeble Minded in 1910, the year when the Boy Scouts was founded. Calmer heads have since prevailed, enforcing the belief that a person with an IQ of between 50 and 69 is closer to the mark. Social workers, at least in America, often substituted the word *imbecile*, which they took to mean a slow-witted person, or common fool, to which we have all enjoyed greater than cursory introduction. In more enlightened times, the moron became more gently referred to as a person with a "mild degree of mental sub normality."

Today the term has little or nothing to do with all that, since it now applies to anyone whom we even suspect of perpetrating stupid acts, which applies to damned nearly everyone we can name, excluding, of course, the author of this volume and his infinitely patient readers. We are mindful of David Ogilvy in his *Confessions of an Advertising Man* (1963) that tells us, "the consumer isn't a moron; she's your wife." One might do well to thumb the pages of the *Eugenics Review* for July of 1929, where we encounter a chap's light but still didactic verse:

> See the happy moron,
> He doesn't give a damn;
> I wish I were a moron,
> By God! Perhaps I am!

One has always the uneasy, possibly paranoid sensation that he is surrounded and threatened by morons, and thereby perpetually at the mercy of their moronic atrocities. Accordingly to *National Geographic* magazine, 80% of Americans have not read a book since high school (where there is an odds-on probability that they, along with their teachers, hadn't read one either); and half of Americans cannot locate any given state on a national map. Nearly all Americans cannot find most foreign countries; half of American teenagers have no idea what World War II (also known as *World War Eleven*) was all about, nor who won it, nor over whom, nor when it was fought; nearly half of Americans believe that the sun revolves around the earth; almost half believe that one can beneficially swill antifreeze; and over half think that the earth is 6,000 years old. Recent statistics purport that between 1992 and 2003 only 13% were deemed *proficient* enough in literacy to "perform complex and challenging literary activities." Only 22% of them possess even basic literacy. By *literacy* moronic government bureaucrats had in mind "using printed and written information" to function in society, to achieve one's goals and "to develop one's knowledge and potential." By March of 2007, 85% had completed high school, such as it has become, and 28% qualified for a bachelor's degree, albeit some of those degrees are awarded in *education* that are intended for teachers, and are therefore all but intellectually vacant.

Consequently, it's a fool's nation, as evidenced by its mindless voting. American anti-intellectualism has undermined the possibilities for anything approaching a cultured society with a recognized, encouraged and adequately nourished *intelligentsia*, by which we mean a social class devoted to the beleaguered life of the mind, the cultivation of theory and idea, a university-educated class circumspectly equipped to reflect critically and to serve as cultural standard bearers. In America this is a near impossibility. Intellectuals are widely misunderstood and marginalized partly as a result of their growing tendency to commandeer university lecterns to proselytize petty politics instead of teaching physics. The Anglo-American poet W. H. Auden (1907–1973) wrote,

> To the man on the street, who I am sorry to say
> Is a keen observer of life,
> The word Intellectual suggests straightaway
> A man who's untrue to his wife.

What is an intellectual, after all, but a chap who cannot read a book without a pencil in hand? The definition is not as absurd as it sounds, in that a) he has a book, b) he has a pencil, c) he reads the book, and d) he can actually write, and e) that he feels an overwhelming compunction to supplement his remarks to what's on the page before him. There is a rapidly declining segment of the population that some call the *reading class*, that begs the question of what this *reading class* is reading. If *best seller* lists were to be taken seriously, it would appear that the reading class is reading mere pap. Publishers, understandably, publish what they believe will sell, which is reasonable enough. A best seller, after all, is a best seller, something that sells relatively well because a) other people seem to be reading it, and b) someone is spending lots of promotional money that may encourage retail sales but at the same time exact a ruinous bite out of net profits.

"Books," Ralph Waldo Emerson with characteristic irony wrote in *The American Scholar* (1837), "are for the scholar's idle times," meaning that there's nothing quite as beneficial as confronting life directly rather than thumbing through someone else's leaves. One must at least become bibliographically selective, exercising prudence, caution, taste, and civilized discrimination in the selection of his books. Fools read nothing, and therefore become nothing except what they are. In recent years, small, independent presses have been subsumed by publishing behemoths who in turn are ever more interested in which titles have been well received by largely less than qualified reviewers and by those who make acquisition choices in libraries, since it is impossible to shelve a copy of everything published. It has been reported that more than three million books were published in America in 2010. The number of new-print titles produced by stateside publishers ranged from an estimated 215,777 in 2002 to a reported 316,480 in 2010, not including 2.7 million self-published titles, reprints of previously books out of copyright, and various print-on-demand titles and cascades of English language books printed outside U.S. borders. Some of these books compete for shelf space in book stores, where publishers pay booksellers premiums for preferred sales space and other conspicuous displays. Store managers are aware of their inventory, and when books fail to sell, they return them to the publisher—at the publisher's expense. In the meantime, larger book publishers are ever more inclined, unlike decades past, toward items that will return a profit for shareholders. Only recently, however, have books been presented not only in hard and soft cover, but also in electronic formats that reportedly present an entire volume on an electronic screen.

Bibliophiles may find fault with electric books, since they love their tomes, enjoy handling them, inhaling the aroma of their musty pages, jotting comments in their margins, taking them to bed and perusing them at meals and on public conveyances. To them, a book is a personal companion, a refuge, a source of renewable information and entertainment. Milton, who considered books his best friend, said that "as good almost to kill a Man as kill a good Book," remarking also that men's lives are "preserved and stored up in books" or other such mortuaries of information. Johnson, in his lexicon, declared that the term *bookish* "is generally used contemptuously." Those on the foolish side of our national culture cannot begin to comprehend loving books the way they love their shabby television entertainments and their popular music. All this is a question of taste, and taste is what divides the social classes—far more than financial condition, as most idiots seem to believe. Books (or *bucks*, as some dolts call them) are on the surface little more than printed documents containing information on everything from here to the moon, so that one may seek, and possibly even find, what he longs for in counsel and even ammunition, as for example throwing a book at someone, literally or figuratively, as in persecuting him in some setting that imagines itself a court of law. One also may *keep books*, in the form of financial records, or learn how to use other people's methods of culinary concocting. One can occasionally bring someone *to book*, which apparently means showing him the error of his ways. Some people *go by the book*, i.e., proceed in orthodox ways. One can also *book* someone else, which means send him into incarceration, something that law enforcement people dearly love to do as a way of demonstrating their limitless authority over everyone except themselves. One can at times *close the book*, meaning to bring some matter to its conclusion. There is such a thing as a *handbook*, a tome that one not necessarily holds in one's hand, but has *at hand*, as may be needed, should one forget how to uncork a bottle or flush a latrine. There are those who burn books, but that has a pejorative side to it, since it seems to suggest destroying books so that no one else can read them, although computer manuals and other product user books ought at first sight be consigned to bonfires as being of no use except to enrage people. A 1942 message on censorship by the American Booksellers Association, during World War II's darkest days when America's existence was at stake, opined, "We all know that books burn—yet we have the greater knowledge that books cannot be killed by fire. People die, but books never die. No man and no force can abolish memory...in this war, we know, books are weapons."

Books have, over the centuries, invented slogans, possibly contrived by people, including a few morons, who spent more time inventing morals and maxims than opening and devouring books. They've stumbled upon witless comments such as "a book is like a garden carried in the pocket." Pleasant thought, say what? This reminds us too that certain bibliophiles tote their bibliographic treasures everywhere they roam. Here's a more serious one: "a book may be as great a thing as a battle." By Jove, yes. It might. Try this: "a book that remains shut is a block." Precisely. For learned generations, university students have besieged their libraries for the purpose of identifying and borrowing the largest tomes that collection has stuffed in its stacks. The purpose is not to open them, but use them to support planks that become temporary bookshelves. It's always been a damned fine idea, notwithstanding that "a closed book does not produce a learned man," something that we all might have assumed. Today's anti-intellectuals, corrupted by institutions of lower learning, feel that any good book is a closed book. Consider this for its inspirational properties: "a few good books well chosen are of more use [if we view libraries for their utilitarian purposes] than a great library."

Then there are more less the same slogans expressed differently, for example, "a good book (as Milton suggested) is the best of friends" or, if you please, "a good book is a great friend," or possibly "a great book is a good friend" that we find elsewhere as "a good book is the best companion." Idiots, as a rule, don't endorse any of these litt'ry maxims, nor do they subscribe to the notion that "a man without books is like a king without money," or if you may, "a wicked book is the wickeder because it cannot repent." We do know that many a book has been reprinted, but what book has ever been *repented*? Another cautionary message holds that one should "beware of the man of one book," that one might construe to mean that the man is a menace who has read a single book, or possibly written one, as well. We can all enthusiastically agree that such a person is quite likely a menace to us all because of his intellectual limitations. We've seen this point of view expressed as "God protect us from him who has read but one book," a cautionary notice well worth forgetting. Books, after all, can inflict harm, such as transmitting venereal diseases and precipitating mental irregularities that occasion urgent professional attention. In the vernacular: "buck larnin spiles a man ef he's got mother wit [we could hardly agree more]; and ef he han't got that, it don't do him no good." Well expressed, as is the bond that exists between "men who have read the same book," unlikely though that may be. Another wag advises us that "the two most useful books in married life are the cookbook and the checkbook." By George, if only we had conceived that great notion. There are also the old saws about books and their covers, that advise (hold your breath) "you can't tell a book by its cover," except that you most certainly can. If not, you can size it up quite handily by glancing surreptitiously at its table of contents (if any) or by turning to any paragraph on any page. There are other silly variations on cover-judging, such as "don't judge a book by its cover," or "never judge a book by its cover," or with a bit more originality, "you can't tell a book by its binding," and all such foolishness.

Other dubious bibliographic advice: "read much, but not too many books," the meaning of which we leave to persons better prepared to interpret. Here's another: "some books leave us free and some books make us free," which sounds like darned good counsel, provided that we can discover what it is. Tuck this one in your girdle: "something is learned [we love the passive voice] every time a book is opened." Try this for a puzzler: "The best part of a book is not the thought it contains, but the thought it suggests," meaning possibly that we *read between the lines* (as idiots call it), and cause the book to say anything we want it to say. Here's an old anti-intellectual favorite: "too many books spoil the student," that places us immediately in mind of "too many cooks spoil the broth." Such pronouncements about books and reading appeal to folks who haven't opened many covers, except perhaps those on beds and manholes. Other comments appear, at least, to have been developed by those who have opened a few books and learned a few things. This one is of Spanish origin: "books and friends should be few and good." Bravo! Shakespeare's *As You Like It* gloriously declaims that "our life, exempt from public haunt, finds tongues in trees, books in running brooks, sermons in stones, and good in everything." In a lonely bit of prose, Charles Lamb (1775–1834) recorded inside his splendid *Last Essays of Elia: Detached Thoughts on Books and Reading* (1833), that "I love to lose myself in other men's minds. When I am not walking, I am reading; I cannot sit and think. Books think for me," which, when you reflect on it, is a rather suspicious comment, suggesting that he turned his mind off and turned the book's on. Lamb, by the way, also complained about "borrowers of books, those mutilators of collections, spoilers of the symmetry of shelves, and creators of odd volumes." His friend Willie Wordsworth commented, somewhat disparagingly, "Books! 'tis a dull and endless strife:/ Come, hear the woodland linnet, /How sweet his music! On my life, / There's of wisdom in it," remarks consistent with a romanticist's innate anti-intellectualism and his preference for nature's sublimity. Milton, in his *Paradise Regained* (1671) complained (Milton spent his entire life complaining) about one who is "deep-versed in books and shallow in himself." My word! Hilaire Belloc! Remember Hilaire Belloc (1870–1953)? Nobody's nitwit, Pierre (as his mates called him, although his real name was Joseph) we remember today as a versatile Catholic man of letters who collaborated with G. K. Chesterton (1874–1936) on novels, was a Member of Parliament, composed some children's books (*Bad Child's Book of Beasts, Cautionary Tales*) and biographies of Robespierre, Napoleon and Cromwell. Said he, "when I am dead, I hope it may be said:/ His sins were scarlet, but his books were read"—a comment which most authors with a talent for whimsy enthusiastically endorse. One of the anonymous contributors to the British periodical *Punch* said that "I never read books—I write them," apparently so as not to encounter any surprises. No less a sovereign authority than *Ecclesiastes* dourly warns us (as any author would) "of making many books there is no end; and much study is a weariness of the flesh." No less weary is the 17th century cleric Thomas Fuller who (probably from the pulpit) warned us that "learning has gained most by those books by which printers have lost," the message of which we defer to the reader, except to say that the cause of learning has been irreparably damaged by books that are no longer on our shelves. Granted, this is a bizarre comment, and yet one deserving of additional investigation. A silly character in Goldsmith's *She Stoops to Conquer or, The Mistakes of a Night* (1773) proclaims that he's fond of anything with age on it. "I love everything that's old," says the idiot, adding, "old friends, old times, old manners, old books," but he's not entirely facetious, since odds are that if a book has survived, it's a favorable signal. Other books have come to an ignominious end in landfills, in shredders, or on remainder tables. Books have been known to cause damage, of course, by spreading vile and repugnant ideas that have caused revolutions and uprisings and even precipitated health problems. An old maxim carries the caveat, "Up! Up! my Friend, and quit your books;/or surely you'll grow double" from having too long slouched over a reading table and morphing into a hunchbacked dwarf.

Such, such is the lore of books. Dimwits occasionally ask (as a way of *breaking the ice*) *have you read any good books lately?* To which one responds, yes: one written by the partially crippled Richard Harris Barham (1788–1845), aka Thomas Ingoldsby, the curate, poet, novelist and roving wit, who wrote, "The jack daw sat on the Cardinal's chair,/ Bishop and abbot, and all were there. /Never, I ween,/ Was a prouder seen,/ Read of in books, or dreamt of in dreams,/Than the Cardinal Archbishop of Rheims!" To be read of in books! The very thought of it endears us to the printed folio, quarto and octavo! Life hardly gets better. As Thomson so bountifully captured it in our language, "An elegant sufficiency content, / Retirement, rural quiet, friendship, books, / Ease an alternate labor, useful life, / Progressive virtue and approving Heaven," Who but Shakespeare might with greater grandeur place books in their most elegant presentments? Consider *Love's Labor's Lost* where we encounter, "From women's eyes this doctrine I derive. / They sparkle still the right Promethean fire. / They are the books, the arts, the academies,/ That show, contain, and nourish, all the world," so says the character Rosaline. Books are the most elegant of things, fine architecture, splendid illustrations, the world's best and most distinguished discourse captured on parchment, hemmed with buckram, held in the hand of a prince or princess, a scholar or student. A prospect of elegance.

There is, among fools, at least, a certain paranoid distrust of books and their dubious, ambiguous contents, although to be sure, one must evaluate what he reads as much as he evaluates what he eats. There is certain distrust too, of persons who have a decent education, pursuant to which they read a great many books, so long as they did not take up *teacher education*, something that does not reward or expect that anyone knows anything in preparation for teaching children. Then too, better books have some reputation for belonging to the better social classes, and are all the more the object of skepticism among fools, although it does not only involve them. Joseph Trapp (1679–1747), who translated Virgil and who became Oxford's first professor of poetry, took a decidedly dim view of England's primary universities, complaining that Oxford wanted *loyalty*, while Cambridge, despite its treasury of books, "wanted learning." So too did Thomas Carlyle (1795–1881), the mighty author of *Sartor Resartus* (1833–1834), grumble that "the true university of these days is a collection of books," as if libraries kept learning afloat without discerning readers, besides which (as Mark Twain wryly remarked), a classic is "a book people praise and don't read."

As to banning books, something that in decades past was a certain guarantee of substantial sales, novelist Rebecca West (1892–1983), like most of the rest of us, condemned the practice, saying that it was as "indefensible as infanticide." Nonetheless, fools may burn books, although most books are rubbish, but banning them is equally damaging because it too disallows a book to be in common circulation. Of course, forbidding also begs the question of what precisely is objectionable, to whom, and why. If anything deserves banning, it is 98% of the rubbish that clutters television screens and therefore sullies the public mind with programming and is to no purpose (even as entertainment) whatsoever. The choice of books that have been banned by certain bureaucrats for certain purposes in certain places is nothing if not astonishing, more often than not outright horrific. Morons, being as they are moronic, have historically sought and sometimes succeeded to incinerate items among the best and brightest titles, the selection of which depends upon which of us exercised his divine judgment.

For the nonce, let us review certain titles banished by government bureaucrats who are themselves a palpable public menace. We cite such dangerous titles alphabetically, beginning with Carroll's *Alice's Adventures in Wonderland*, Remarque's *All Quiet on the Western Front*, Orwell's *Animal Farm* and *Nineteen Eighty-Four*, Milton's *Areopagitica*, Huxley's *Brave New World*, Voltaire's *Candide*, Frank's *The Diary of Anne Frank*, Gray's *Dick and Jane*, Balzac's *Droll Stories*, Cleland's *Fanny Hill*, Steinbeck's *The Grapes of Wrath*, Solzhenitsyn's *The Gulag Archipelago*, Ginsberg's *Howl*, Lawrence's *Lady Chatterley's Lover*, Bannerman's *Little Black Sambo*, Jackson's *The Lottery*, Flaubert's *Madame Bovary*, Kafka's *The Metamorphosis*, Burroughs's *Naked Lunch*, Paine's *The Rights of Man*, Rushdie's *The Satanic Verses*, Miller's *Tropic of Cancer*, Joyce's *Ulysses*, Stowe's *Uncle Tom's Cabin*, McNamara's *United States–Vietnam Relations: 1945–1967*, Russell's *Unarmed Victory* and Hall's *The Well of Loneliness*.

So much for tax dollars in action. Among the more recognizable titles that other (non-governmental) parties have conspired to burn and bury, try Twain's *The Adventures of Huckleberry Finn*, Warren's *All the King's Men*,

Faulkner's *As I Lay Dying*, Wright's *Black Boy*, London's *Call of the Wild*, Pilkey's *Captain Underpants*, Salinger's the *Catcher in the Rye*, Burgess's *A Clockwork Orange*, Walker's *The Color Purple*, Hemingway's *A Farewell to Arms* and *For Whom the Bell Tolls*, Baldwin's *Go Tell It On the Mountain*, Fitzgerald's *The Great Gatsby*, Conrad's *Heart of Darkness*, Capote's *In Cold Blood*, Ellison's *Invisible Man*, Nabokov's *Lolita*, Golding's *Lord of the Flies*, Mailer's *The Naked and the Dead*, Wright's *Native Son*, Steinbeck's *Of Mice and Men*, Updike's *Rabbit Run*, Knowles' *A Separate Peace*, Vonnegut's *Slaughterhouse Five*, Morrison's *Song Solomon*, Lee's *To Kill A Mockingbird*, Miller's *Tropic of Cancer* (again) and Lawrence's *Women in Love*.

To have read and well digested these titles would for most people constitute a fairly satisfactory cultural matrix upon which to continue reading. To be quite sure, not all books are worth preserving, but that is a matter of taste and judgment. Failed books constitute a mountain of dead and deadening weight waiting to be transmigrated into another literary life. As Auden said, "some books are undeservedly forgotten; none are undeservedly remembered." Shakespeare in his sonnets advanced the notion of immortality in literature, and other writers' earnest desire was to see themselves live eternally on bookshelves stuffed within the yellowed leaves of their own books. Some bookshelves, however, are little more than literary graveyards intended to make some oblique cultural statement by way of books that are possessed but never opened. Someone, we cannot recall who, said that possession of a book becomes a substitute for reading it. Anthony Burgess two years before *The Clockwork Orange* had written *The Doctor is Sick*, although it is more probable that the reader is sick, and that the nature of that sickness is common stupidity that in our time is far more the rule than the exception.

An unlettered public is a moronic one that virtually guarantees the continuance of a foolish underclass to be reckoned with in one means or another. One can presume to rescue fools from their foolishness, but this too is foolish. One can submit to foolishness and become a moron without trying awfully hard. More likely, one may be more obliged to recognize a nation of fools, itself more than enough capitulation to life's stupidity, a subject upon which we have posited a few observations. But that too is an unsatisfactory position to assume, because it makes fools of us all. Books may or may not lead us further into despair, because they are nearly always negatively inclined, as great literature amply illustrates. Optimistic assessments of life arouse suspicion, since there is something about them that the human animal knows better, and that causes him to envision life as little more than (as we used to hear) a *veil of tears*, something to no positive end unless perhaps he can possibly can turn to theology for rescue. Johnson, in his *Life of Savage* (1744), wrote that "the general lot of mankind is misery." Books, the good ones, at least, can enlighten, and occasionally offer (if only by implication) a modicum of hope amid the stygian darkness of foolery.

Morons cannot understand, nor can they be made to understand even if they want to, that *fiction is fact*. That's not merely an irony; an irony means a whole bag of things, but mainly it's saying one thing but meaning quite the opposite. It's also having a result that is contrary to what we anticipated. The expression *fiction is fact* is instead a paradox, a term that means, contrary to what we call *received opinion* (which is those opinions that most morons accept as the truth), contrary to the way things are and, in their minds, the way they're *supposed to be*. Paradox strikes ordinary people, therefore, as preposterous, simply because it contradicts what they've always been told, what is commonly held to be valid, something beyond contradiction, *ipso facto* (something that means *absolutely, beyond any doubt*), altogether beyond contradiction. Therefore it is fair game for contradiction and challenge, perhaps an occasion for acrimonious contention. It's a conclusion contrary to what he has any reason to expect, or thinks he does. Possibly the most oft-cited paradox is the one conceived, or at least propagated, by Wordsworth in "My Heart Leaps Up When I Behold" where he wrote, "The child is the father of the man," a notion that strikes the average chronologically challenged fools as back-asswards, inasmuch as the man, obviously and clearly without question, *ipso facto*, is the father of the child. That, as the song tells us, is the way we were told it should be, but that's not how way it actually is. This begs the question of precisely how a child can father a man and also raises the possibility that anyone who believes this ought to be sent into exile, placed in chains, and summarily be relieved of his Velveeta. What the poetical line says (if not *means*) is that the child shapes what the man will be. Out of the boy comes the man. As the twig is bent, so inclines the tree. As Pope tweaked it, "Tis education forms the common mind,/Just as the twig is bent so grows the tree." It's quite as simple as that: a person's past influences, maybe even dictates, his present and future.

But when we suggest that fiction is fact, it has folks of limited comprehension stumped and sometimes altogether befuddled. After all, fiction is falsehood; fact is truth. Pressed on it, the best that a fool can respond is to suggest that certain fiction seems (but probably is not) so real that we might be fooled into thinking that it's a fact. But no; that's not what we mean, either. There is only one way of saying one thing, albeit that one thing may be reliably interpreted in several ways. Fools have the devil's own time with this, but the worst is yet to surface. When we suggest that fiction (let's say the very best of it) is fact, then what sort of fact is it? Is it true that the fictional Aunt Fanny fell out of a plum tree? No. But the best of imaginative writing presents certain circumstances that we are obliged to recognize as being transcendently (which is to say, surpassing, rising above, surmounting) self-evidently true. The Bible is stuffed liberally with such passages that strike us as fiction on one hand and profound truth on the other, and not merely because we're *supposed* to believe whatever we think it says, but because it is mysteriously, self-evidently so. Consider, for example, Adam and Eve in their prelapsarian Edenic garden where at the beginning they live in innocence and blissful happiness until a devil shows up and spoils everything. Is this fiction? Yes. Is it fact? Yes. Is it true? Yes. Does it represent the truth as it is usually defined as a virtuous word inviting other words such as faithfulness, fidelity, loyalty, veracity, sincerity, and integrity? It often denotes things such as a *covenant*, a pledge, a promise, a sense of genuineness, an honor, as well as conformity to rule, fact, and reality. What constitutes reality, on the other hand, is sophisticated and, to be sure, potentially contentious. We are not suggesting that the Bible is fiction, although it may be read as such if one elects to do so. One can read a narrative document (the Bible is but one example) in various ways, providing that we agree that the text neither *means* one thing nor does it mean anything we want it to mean.

This obliges us to consider the nature and identification of *myth*, another word that demands clarification. In the popular mind, myth signifies a falsehood. When we say *that's a myth*, we mean that it is unreliable, nothing more than a cock-and-bull story, something that's bogus, untrue, misleading, false, and so forth. To fools, it involves some silly narrative such as one might find on television, intended to amuse morons, but which is so profoundly irrelevant and pointless that it will be passed over by any thinking person. However, the word *myth* also means quite the opposite, in that educated people apply it to that same transcendent truth as earlier described, in the sense of ancient Greek *myths*, or the Christian *myths* or the *myth of America* and such like. Not all such things are falsehoods; to the contrary, they also refer to profound truths, transcendent realities, and all but magical veracity. The term *mythologem* essentially means the isolation of a fundamental, recognizable, familiar truth, usually something with which we are all familiar such as revenge, honor, betrayal, bravery sacrifice and endlessly on. Consider a homely example of a myth in two senses of the term. Might we consider that Santa Claus is a foolish myth invented for the entertainment of children? Or would we argue, to the contrary, that Santa is a more *mythic figure*, as some call it, pointing toward a profound probity and reality self-evidently representing generosity, kindness, benevolence and love? Ought one therefore to *believe* in Santa Claus? Chances are that a fool would unhesitatingly answer in the negative. Chances are also that a sophisticated person would unhesitatingly respond with an affirmative. Might he be delusional? Possibly, but probably not. Why not? Because he sees the prevailing myth inside Santa's *child friendly* presentment. Meaning what? Meaning that yes: there is a spirit of Christmas (or whatever one wishes to call a mid-winter celebration), a spirit of joy, a spirit of giving, a spirit of laughter—all of which the old figure in a false white beard and a red snowsuit precisely represents. Moreover, in a still more sophisticated sense, he is more than a fat man in red; he is an allegorical representation.

What does *allegorical* mean? It means in the simplest terms an extended metaphor wherein certain things and people represent more than merely people, since they represent prevailing truths. Does the green of Ireland represent (among other symbols and emblems such as the harp) that great impoverished nation? Do the communion wafer and wine represent Christ's body and blood? Or are they merely a cocktail cracker and a sip of jug wine? The first has a mythic significance; the second is merely mundane and devoid of significance. A sophisticated, likely educated, more discriminating person will probably view it in its mythic sense; a fool is likely to see it as trivial and without significance. Some narratives present the same choices. If discriminatingly pursued, they will invite the possibility of comprehension on different levels. Homer's *Odyssey* is one such example. The Greeks regarded Homer (if such a person literally ever existed) as a source of law, theology and probity. Dante's *Divine Comedy* is another comparable document. It is doubtful whether a fool will investigate the pages of either one. An educated reader will immediately recognize that such texts can be apprehended on different levels. Dante, of course, was well aware of this, and discussed it in a few sentences in his famously brief letter to Can Grande. For example, one can always comprehend these two texts on a literal level and perceive them for what they clearly say. There is nothing wrong with this, except that it overlooks a more advanced reading that allows them to be comprehended on a number of other reliable planes, such as to apprehend them as something theological, moral, political, psychological, historical or even comical. The texts will support any of these approaches, and if put to the test, one can justify approaching them through such avenues.

One becomes the product of his reading. If fools read nothing, they show it. Careful readers are edified and enlightened by their reading, and possibly enriched culturally by careful and attentive habits of perusal. There is a sense in which the reader becomes the book and the book becomes the reader. As the British novelist and critic Virginia Woolf explained, each has "his past shut in him like the leaves of a book known to him by heart; and his friends [can] only lend the title." Indeed, the profession of authorship is at once public and intensely private, guarded and confessional, while the pages are subject to unanticipated revelations from readers. Ask not what the author *meant*; he meant what he said, albeit it's admittedly personal at times. Sir James Barrie, whom we probably remember less for his 1891 novel *The Little Minister* than for his theatrical piece entitled *What Every Woman Knows* (1908), provides us a glimpse of the writer's anxiety and literary possessiveness in an address he delivered to an assemblage calling itself The Critic's Circle in 1922. "For several days after my first book was published," he said quite candidly, "I carried it about in my pocket, and took surreptitious peeps at it to make sure that the ink had not faded." So it is that to hold the volume in his hand was to hold it near his heart, as well. As William

Butler Yeats unforgettably advised his admirers, "When you are old and grey, and full of sleep, / And nodding by the fire, take down this book. And slowly read and dream of the soft look/ Your eyes had once, and of their shadows deep." This is hardly counsel a fool would hear, and if heard would accept seriously enough to deliver himself out of the foolish and into the bliss of poetic imagination. It is better not to be a fool.

Even a somewhat unlikely person as French President François Mitterand observed that one loses reality if he is not in the company of his books, which suggests that books are the most intimate of companions and a continuing source of solace, good counsel, and unchanging message and entertainment. Books are not the companions of fools. Robert Farrar Capon (1925), a man of many facets and faces, among them those of a Port Jefferson, New York, Episcopal parish priest, author, gourmet, chef and roving litterateur, remarked, "the values I stand for are not mine. I borrowed them from Socrates, I swiped them from Chesterfield, I stole them from Jesus. And I put them in a book." Well expressed, by Jove, and an apt testimony in support of how we live what we read and depend upon books more than we depend upon lunch. The renowned intellect Desiderius Erasmus, who turned a few pages in his day, tells us that "when I get a little money, I buy books, and if I have any left over I buy food and clothes." But fools read nothing and are nothing. Of course, books demand time, but how better to use that time? Most people we observe merely move from place to place for no clear reason or ultimate end. In the end, they have been nowhere and are going nowhere. A sense of, and commitment to, some worthy end would both solve existential dilemmas and develop intellects. Time is life. Time is money. Both are limited. How shall we use them? Fools never so much as raise the question. But time with good books is never wasted, even though the best of books demand multiple re-readings and reassessments over the literary years. Although the words between the covers do not change, the significance of them does.

Time spent with substantial books is infinitely better than the same time spent with people, since most people are fools and therefore a squandering of time on pursuits that are infinitely unproductive. Roy Blount Jr. is a little of everything: comedian, columnist, musician, actor and peripatetic wise guy. Commenting upon *staying put*, he mused, "a good heavy book holds you down." Darned good advice. "It's an anchor that keeps you from getting up and having another gin and tonic." Point well taken; one cannot but agree. And moreover, as brother Blount says, "they don't make a fuss; they don't make any racket." Somebody also said something similarly on point, namely that books are *quiet*. Precisely; they don't distract you with beastly, uncivilized hideous noise. Anything else? Yes. "They do not dissolve into wavy lines or snowstorm effects. They do not pause to deliver commercials. This is a blessing of no small significance." Anything else? Yes. "They are convenient to handle and completely portable," except of course the good big heavy ones. Bravo. You are dismissed.

Let us, by way of introduction to other pressing matters, now turn our attention to the dreadful word *dult*, seldom used and less recognized, although the OED tells us that it is a variation upon *dolt*, a word and a person with which and with whom we are all too regrettably familiar. It also applies to a *dunce*, or a person who falls to the bottom of his academic class, a fellow taken to be a stupid person condemned to be seated upon a *dult's bench*. We have all heard the term *adult* that derives from the Latin *adulu* that means *to grow up*, which is to imply a certain stage of presumed responsibility, in turn meaning therefore a person of mature judgment and attitude befitting one's ostensibly mature years. It also refers to someone's age, as in *adults only*, implying again that such a person is presumed to behave like a responsible citizen, possessing virtues that insulate him from the universe of goons, whom he perhaps never sees if he can help it, but whose close proximity he is condemned to inhabit. Whereas *adult* is a good enough word, *adultery* is not, having nothing at all do with what one presumes to know as adult behavior. Like adultery, *adulterate* is a pejorative expression that one seldom relies upon, but which refers to something *spurious*, even illegitimate, counterfeit, illegal, unlicensed, unwarranted, debased and so forth. We avoid these words not because our corrupt government forbids them, but because they are wretched, insufferably offensive to the ear as to the mind. One may prefer to soften blows by speaking in *euphemisms*, palliative words intended to fall pleasantly and inoffensively upon one's delicate sensibilities and refined nature.

Nonetheless, the term *dult* dangles above our heads as menacingly as an executioner's noose. We are left with little choice, realists that we are, but to examine it, albeit wearing gloves and surgical facemasks familiar in sterile operating chambers. There are occasions that demand our courageous attention, come what may, to life's less than attractive features, among them revolting language. *Dult!* What, upon scrutiny, does it mean, and why do we detest it? More to the point, the word carries as its meaning dullness, perhaps *dulsome*, the disgustingly heavy demeanor of a dull-witted baboon, an insufferably thick-skulled ape such as one might encounter in a government office that appeals to apparently mentally and emotionally empty-headed buffoons incapable, for example, of savoring an expertly executed *double entendre* or a well-turned *trope* (usually not the literal understanding of a word) that would otherwise send certain sophisticated persons into such riotous merriment that they require clinical assistance before they seize any opportunity to recover their composure. Dults, to the contrary, speak in clichés and offendingly grim monotones that threaten to upset the rhetorical balance of nature. They are as unbearable to see as to hear. We, in turn, limit our discourse to words of but one to three syllables, and to respond to fools, if respond we must, by affecting a dismal monotone of our own. Withal, it's anything but a satisfactory encounter, especially since, while attempting to converse with morons, we are less than comfortably aware that we are not causing ourselves to be understood. To say it with unimpeachable clarity, there are times when we are unsuccessfully attempting to make ourselves understood by a raving fool. Call him, if you please, a *dulwilly*, a rural term some use to identify a Ringed Plover. Call him, if you please, a mere dimwit or, in certain select instances, a *coxcomb*, which, literally, the OED reminds us, is a hat worn by a professional fool, resembling a cock's comb, a fool, a simpleton, a conceited, showy gadfly, vainly crowing his supposed accomplishments. The word may also refer to certain garden plants, a certain kind of lace resembling the fringes of a cock's comb, and a parrot.

But coxcomb appropriately, if distantly, calls to mind dolt, not a pleasant word any way you play it. Let's explore its less than fortunate meaning. We are able to trace the word to the 16th century, beyond which it may find its origins in Anglo-Saxon where in all probability it derived, according to the OED, from such earlier forms as *dol*, *doll*, and *dull*, all of which approximate our serviceable word *stupid*, all of which are quite probably blockheads or numbskulls, about whom we will produce disclosures of the highest significance in later pages. The aforementioned More's *Utopia* (in the Robinson translation) immodestly directs our attention to "thies wyse fooles and verye archdolts," ergo the foolish, foppish and mindless. Dryden's translation of *Troilus and Cressida* (1679) mentions "dolt-heads, asses and beasts of burden," all in the same overburdened sentence. We must not omit mentioning that the rare word *doltify*, which means simply to create a dolt, whereas *doltish* carries an all too obvious meaning, namely thick-skulled, empty-headed and other such unmentionables.

All such language conspicuously allies foolishness to stupidity, whether that stupidity is accountable to heredity, environment, or something else. One cannot always distinguish. For any of several reasons, as we shall see, certain people play the fool (perhaps we all have, at some ill-considered time or another) in the service of amusement and profit. There are occasions, in fact, when it is advantageous to feign stupidity as a means to reach our occasionally nefarious ends. One might, when trapped in the presence of some imbecilic courtroom judge, claim that since one has not read law, nor has any intention of doing so, he cannot be held accountable for the endless monotony and inanity of jurisprudence, anymore than he has not made a study of medicine and therefore cannot be held altogether accountable for any phase of his health. As we all know, courts (moronic though they are) will not admit this defense. Even so, there are advantages in playing dumb. On this precise assumption there was a moronic 1940s radio program called *It Pays to Be Ignorant*, which it undoubtedly does in certain circumstances. It is on this assumption that millions of uncommitted college enrollees openly detest learning and consequently from the lack of it pass the remainder of their doltish lives during which they disseminated their ignorance indiscriminately. *It Pays to Be Ignorant* played upon this raging anti-intellectualism the way another programs called the *Quiz Kids* and *Information Please* (alluding to telephone numbers) attempted to undermine it. However, *It Pays to Be Ignorant* was in effect a fool's self-defense while satirizing the quiz program's ritual of asking contestants seemingly unfathomably metaphysical queries and having them respond with unpredictable explanations. This silly gambit developed out of the vaudeville theatre, hardly a thought-challenging form of entertainment, conceived for the lower rungs of culture, so to say.

CHAPTER 2. ENGINES OF LIMITED COGNITION: DUMB BELLS, DUMB CLUCKS AND DUMB WAITERS

We press on now with our obsessive inquiry into fools and their disarmingly foolish tendencies by examining yet another pitiable side of the question, to wit: the sad plight of the dunce in song, story and sorry human history. Where to begin? A dunce is, when you consider it carefully, fundamentally a *dummy*, be it by chance or choice. Either way, his is not an especially advantageous way to paddle through life, always playing the fool, always the object of derision. *Dummy* has been ever applied through the years to describe a deaf mute, or anyone feigning a deaf mute. The inglorious word *dumb* has, in spite of itself, borne a hefty and inglorious etymological baggage, the contents of which we all would do well to examine with the astuteness of a customs inspector, if reluctantly. The OED, with the queen's endorsement, assures us that the word was in service among speakers of Old Norse and Old English where it meant variously *stupid* and *deaf*, albeit there is neither a fair nor proper relation between those unfortunate significations, except that they address a failure to understand something. It has also been applied to one who, owing to some mental disability, cannot speak well enough to invite comprehension. The word has also been used to describe what we call *dumb animals*, beasts of *limited cognition* in any of the world's great languages, living or dead, and therefore are relegated for use as sustenance and tasks requiring brute force, while the rest of us who converse in perfectly civilized English (for example) survive with impeccably, faultlessly precise mutual understanding. This allows us, we are pleased to say, an astonishing level of common comprehension. It is such that, we imagine, leads us all unerringly ever upward, toward a perfect world, populated by persons who are every inch equipped to appreciate civilized amenities such as multiple definitions, irony, wit and rich ever-endless ambiguity. Fools, we need hardly say, find themselves unprepared to participate in such subtle exchanges of meaning, and are, as a consequence, left stranded in the social desolation that ignorance attends.

Dumbness (to press further on), we've all observed, can in uncertain circumstances be applied to the expression *struck dumb* which is accepted by most to mean that one has temporarily (we should *presume*) taken leave of his senses and finds himself mortified by the extent to which inarticulation has taken him hostage. Yes. There are other implications behind this compelling word. We would be remiss if we did not clarify that *dumb* does not always describe one who does not speak (often a damned good option) or one whose bizarre constitution causes him to posit silence as his message. It may also be directed at those whose taciturn nature forbids much verbal intercourse. By *taciturnity* we mean the disinclination some of us show to participate in verbal exchanges, an instinct such that one may refrain from even commonplace conversation of any nature, be it learned or trivial. *Taciturn*, by the way, comes to us from *tacit*, not a bad word to pop into one's quiver since it means *noiseless*, emitting no sound waves whatsoever. How better the world would be if it were far more inclined toward *tacitura*, i.e., being reserved, saying but little, holding one's tongue. Such may be a service to us all, especially those of us who more prize the written word above the spoken.

To conclude our discussion of *dumbness*, we feel obligated to acknowledge some fugitive applications of the word, among them a *dumb cake*, which is a ceremonial confection baked by maids in blissful silence on (so we are advised) St. Mark's Eve to ferret out marital prospects, more specifically the number and condition of young men unwittingly trapped in the matrimonial sink hole. There are such people as *dumb blondes* in our midst, although we have encountered none in our travels and presume that they are called *dumb* because they have little or nothing of substance to say. There is also a *dumb bell*, which is an apparatus used to support a bell, perhaps a church gong. There are, we are reliably told, *dumb clucks*, although we have never formally encountered many of them, either. We do know, however, that it is possible to be *dumbfounded*, which is to say having gone distressingly numb in the head, or to participate in a *dumb show* wherein the audio portion is deleted, a theatrical presentation without words. One may also encounter a *dumb waiter* which is a dining room convenience designed to assume the role of an intelligent waiter.

Let us now, without fear of recrimination, cautiously approach the expression *dunce*, something that corrals some or all of the numerously hideous characteristics aforementioned. Oddly enough, the term *dunce* originated with a person who was anything in the world but a dunce himself. We refer, obviously, to John Duns Scotus, known to us all as the *doctor sub-*

tilis, the subtle doctor who, as a Franciscan, attempted successfully to rec-
oncile Aristotle and Christianity, and who, closer to our time, has also been
celebrated as the Scottish scholastic philosopher who fearlessly addressed
such sensitive universals as metaphysics, philosophy, ethics and of course
theology. The name *Scotus*, let's have it understood, signified that he was a
Scot. His detractors none too kindly and none too appropriately crowned
him *Dunce*, which may have been suggested by his disciples who were called
Dunse, the meaning of which was later twisted into signifying something like
a *sophist*, which of course in no sense applied to Scotus. By *sophist* we suggest
the Greek term derived from antiquity, denoting a person who presumed to
proffer advice on such high-toned studies as ethics and other contentiously
sensitive intellectual matters—without knowing what the hell he was talking about—but who (nevertheless) advanced speciously unsupported arguments. By *specious* we suggest some outwardly convincing, plausible, but
ultimately advancing misleading and false assertions. From the word *sophist*
comes *sophomoric* and *sophomore*, meaning a stupid person (not always an
appropriate name for a second-year university student, to be sure), one who
is not yet reliably educated and who would be far better advised to keep
his thoughts and his vulgar sounds to himself. Meanwhile, the word *dunce*
has come to signify a *nitwit* who has gone soft in the head, not by hiding his
stupidity but by energetically encouraging it, sometimes ironically through
having passed too many years with his head in a book, the result being that
he is nothing more than what we today call a *pedant* or a *pedantic* person.

Fools, some of them pedantic fools, don't understand what *pedant* means.
We're not saying that any pedants are part of our select circle. No. Nor do
we believe in the slightest that any of our number is in any sense *pedantic*
nor suffering from any other beastly intellectual imperfection. But to get on
with it, we must (with some regret, to be certain) alert our number that perfectly innocent words tend to degrade over the ages; and whereas they were
once articulated in the presence of our civilized companions, this (in certain
regrettable instances) may no longer be so. *Pedant* once denoted some sort of
teacher (before teaching became a moronic career and fell into irretrievably
low repute), but this (we assume) is no longer so. It may be a shortened form
of *pedagogue* that, in its Grecian origin, may have signified (we trust in all
innocence) a trainer or teacher of boys, later broadened to include both genders. St. Paul used the term in the sense of his being a pedagogue of Christ.
We think of it, verily, as a *preceptor*, a remotely suspicious word that brings
to mind a regrettably contemptuous hostility, a dispenser of instruction to
youths who, if they misconstrue a Greek conjugation, are subject to beatings
and other public humiliations. In more recent epochs, pedant has been a term
of intense disapproval, referring to one who flaunts knowledge that he may
or may not possess, and thus does parade his supposed arsenal of information at inappropriate times and places with a mind to affecting a conspicu-

ous display of his learning, while others would much prefer him to desist and disappear. But his motive is to appear wiser and better informed than anyone else. Some have called this fool one who overestimates himself, and in so doing may for example cite learned passages from books he ill-understands because he is ill-prepared to open them, much less read them with comprehension. He is also wont to explain such matters in such scrupulous detail (compare it to any leaf in this volume) as to make himself impossibly tedious. To possess these cloying characteristics is to engage in mere pedantry that, if it has not done so just yet, should be deemed a misdemeanor punishable by burial beneath cascades of spilled books, the contents of which are monotonously laden with information sufficiently mind-numbing as to send its victim into throes of mental agony. Of course, *pedant* contains the root *ped* which, as we all know, denotes the *foot*. Hence (we say this deliberately to divert attention from pedants and their pedantry), *pedantical* directs us quite pointedly to foot travel, or to being in other words a *pedestrian*, a foot person. But its meaning declines from there. When we say that something is pedestrian, by which we mean foolish, commonplace, ordinary, unsparingly prosaic, dull and more than a little monotonous. A person possessing those regrettable characteristics is a blathering dunce and an unseemly bore of the first water. A fool is better represented by his foot than his head.

Hence we return to our example of the common dunce who embraces most, if not all, of the less flattering characteristics we have painfully reviewed in the last less than pleasantly reassuring pages. In our day, a dunce is a person who is (as fools not so astutely call it) intellectually *challenged*, or in other colorful language a *dullard*, a *dimwit*, and a *blockhead*, whose characteristics we will investigate pages from here. We all know, and have possibly donned a time or two, a dunce's cap that had long before become part of the fool's traditionally appropriate wardrobe, sometimes marked appropriately with the letter *D*. There is an old (and we regret to say anonymous) source who astutely observed that dunces "have commonly the best employments... before the mast." That, we take to mean, suggests that a preferential employment for an idiot is on the high seas where, without doubt, someone else is commanding his every move and gesture. We are also assured that inside the British court was to be found a table expressly for use by dunces, and hence called a *dunce-table*. When we read Dickens' *The Old Curiosity Shop* (1840), he directs our attention to a small shelf upon which rests a dunce's cap, a less than subtle clue as to its owner's intellectual limitations. Were we to convene a troop of such people, we might be said to have indulged ourselves in *duncedom*; and if we were to be so honored by having a cone placed on our beans, we might, with some justification, lay claim to duncehood in the manner that others might flaunt their knighthood, sainthood, and so like. By George, stupidity has its rewards, including its ceremonial rituals, rightly claimed by those for whom they are appropriate. As Johnson remarked in one of the *Rambler* numbers, "every man is prompted by the love of himself to imagine, that he possesses some peculiar qualities superior, either in kind or degree, to those he sees allotted to the rest of the world."

Possibly the greatest condemnation of duncehood issued from the pen of Alexander Pope, whose immortal *Dunciad*, the first parcel of which he released to the world in 1728 and which eventually consisted of four books (subsections issued in adjusted versions over the years, the last of them six months prior to the poet's death). The *Dunciad* was rendered in the mock-heroic tradition that derived humor out of burlesquing the great classical epics of world literature such as the *Iliad* and *Odyssey* of Homer and the *Aeneid* of Virgil, thus hilariously transfiguring the sublime into the ludicrous. The result was to satirize by trivializing and rendering foolish something and someone, the rather concealed purpose of which was, and still is, to correct error of one sort or another by turning it into a prolonged jest abetted by humiliating slights aimed pointblank at certain people and objects. There is no object here in our exhuming Pope's satiric targets, except to say that he himself had been the object of other writers' humiliation, most of it born of jealousy on the part of those who fancied themselves part of the British literary forefront. Pope made his way through life with a tubercular spine, possibly the result of unstipulated illness from which he suffered as a boy. Between 1712 and 1714 he produced another mock-heroic piece entitled "The Rape of the Lock," while in the meantime (1713) he proposed to present an English translation of the *Iliad* in six ambitious volumes between 1715 and 1720, followed by a version of the *Odyssey*, to which he contributed only a portion, between 1725 and 1726. This should convince today's skeptical readers that Pope knew a thing or two about classical Greek and the epic mode, and how at the same time he reduced it to mockery by deploying its elegance and lofty themes to the foolishness that he saw in his own time and place. Whereas the *Iliad* derives its name from *Ilon* (another name for Troy), the *Dunciad* derives its from *dunce*. It's all a nasty joke, with a purpose that does quite more than provoke derisive laughter that, if nothing else, established Pope as the leading satirist of his time, which was also a time when taste in English literature placed a high premium on mostly caustic, elegantly witty but still vicious satiric attacks somewhat in the manner of the cynical invective of Decimius Junius Juvenalis whom we fondly remember simply as *Juvenal*, and whom we may, in the fullness of time, regard merely as a testy 1,950-some-year-old bastard.

But then again, satire has its lethal purposes. The objects of Pope's wrath, in a broad sense, are at once personal, in the form of remorselessly contemptuous paybacks to the unkind and foolish attempts of other litt'ry men to undermine, discourage and discredit him personally and his work specifically, and more general: posturing, pedantry and poor taste. Pope, to be quite honest, carried with him what in current parlance might be described as a certain *elegant attitude*, better expressed as an *infinitely refined arrogance*. Said he, "I must be proud to see/ Men not afraid of God, afraid of me." Mind you, we are not necessarily troubled by his outrages, since we believe that there are chaps out there who conspire to abridge our right to verbal excesses. In countries like America, governments would like little better than to muzzle everyone, thereby limiting ordinary discourse funneled through a filtration established by crooked bureaucrats and feculent politicians and (if that not be redundant) tinhorn demigods. Pope was hardly one to submit to such tyranny and, as one of his detractors aptly wrote, he was "a man too independent to be bought and too gifted to be suppressed."

Bravo! But Pope, alas, was of the popish persuasion, which in his place and time precluded his owning land in, or within ten miles of, London. Were that not objectionable enough, Catholics were not admitted to universities nor were they permitted to seek public office. Small wonder that Pope became, if not the greatest poet of his age, at least the satirist with the most wicked of pens. In adulthood his medical perplexities left him a cripple, a condition exacerbated by derision and laughter at a time when, in spite of its supposedly advanced sophistication, fools felt quite free to find humor in his misery, and even used the name *Little Alexander* to taunt him. Johnson recalled that "his stature was so low that, to bring him to level with common tables, it was necessary to raise his seat," adding too that "his legs were so slender that he enlarged their bulk with three pairs of stockings, which were drawn on and off by the maid; for he was not able to dress or undress himself, and neither went to bed nor rose without help." Pope said that fools thought him amusing enough to laugh at him, but in fact he had many an amorous companion. Furthermore, his obviously superior talent as poet and translator inspired an outpouring of his enemies' unbridled jealousy, something to which dunces inexorably resort when they have no other recourse.

Hence it was that Alexander Pope used his *Dunciad* as an engine to make worse dunces of those who were dunces all along. He did, however, establish himself a reputation as a person always prepared to excoriate any fool who appeared in his way since, as one commentator said, "he would damn in one withering line a fool he had claim to." And why not? In the *Dunciad* intelligent people thoroughly enjoyed, and still do, what he called Dullness with a capital *D* and a single *l* to represent Dullness in a way that not only personified it but elevated (ironically) it to the rank of allegory, about which dunces know nothing. But what the devil is allegory? It received mention in the previous chapter and originates from the Latin *allegoria*, which means expressing oneself on at least two levels, the first being literal, the second metaphorical, wherein abstractions may be presented as people. Hence Dullness is not only stupidity; it's a person. Ernest Hemingway said that for a time, he viewed a military battle as a football game between the home team and the visiting team. Allegory, in the sense of discussing two things simultaneously, is nearly as old as the world. Dunces cannot comprehend such a complex thing. In the biblical parable (an illustrative story) of the wise and foolish virgins, we're not necessarily talking about virgins at all, but about something else, provided one can divine what it is. We're discussing one thing under the guise of another. The results? Oodles of them, one of which is that we're playing one narrative off another. Allegorical figures, be they men, animals or things, represent still other things. If someone tells us about a fox in a hen house, we damned well understand the message.

It does not require a superior mind to recognize that Dulness is an allegorical figure appropriately named, since we identify dullness with sluggishness and stupidity, unfortunate attributes found in morons, dolts, dunces and other half-witted fools against whom we sometimes resort to using such disrespectful terms as *dull pate* (dumb head), *dull-witted, dullard* and so forth. We draw upon different but related descriptions depending upon the person and the occasion. And they're everywhere: the work places, the schools, the houses of worship, and the places of business. They infect every bureaucracy we can name, including all block-headed levels of government. Obviously, they are peppered on every television screen. We're surrounded.

Intrepid readers may wish to peruse a remarkable volume called *The Allegory of Love* (a somewhat misleading title) subtitled *A Study in Medieval Tradition*, authored by the Oxford don Clive Staples Lewis and brought out first in 1936, several years after its author was wounded during World War I. "The allegorical love poetry of the Middle Ages," Lewis wrote, "is apt to repel the modern reader both by its form and by its matter." True enough. Allegory, as we just finished saying, is not for dunces, but for persons who (for one reliable example) read this page, and who will be astounded, broadened, rendered incredulous and possibly even entertained by erudition, for it is the delight of everyone not a fool to become as erudite as may be feasible. It is endlessly edifying to read (in addition) Lewis's *English Literature in the Sixteenth Century* (excluding drama), that the author released in 1954. But what is *erudition*? How can it be encouraged by reading Lewis and Pope? Erudition is being learned through a deep acquaintance with the world's finest literature such as the repeatedly aforementioned *Iliad* and *Odyssey*, the Bible and a hundred or so other pieces composed variously for instruction and amusement of the highest order. *Erudite* reaches us from the Latin *erudire* that means to be trained, well informed, knowledgeable, book smart, scholarly. Erudition instantly tells the rest of us that the bearer of such title has unceasingly devoted himself to sophisticated intellectual pursuits well beyond the casual familiarity that may somehow have accrued to the average street fool.

As to Pope's *Dunciad*, it was preceded (to place its chronological and satiric context) by *Gulliver's Travels* (1726) of Jonathan Swift, and *The Beggar's Opera* (1728) of John Gay (1685-1732). Indeed, Pope appropriately dedicated the *Dunciad* to Swift. The eccentric poetess Edith Sitwell crowned Pope "perhaps the most flawless artist our race has yet produced." To say the very least and the very obvious, Pope was immensely and conspiratorially erudite. "I took to reading by myself, for which I had great eagerness, especially for poetry," he wrote, "and in a few years I had dipped into a great number of the English, French, Latin and Greek poets. This I did without any design, but that of pleasing myself, and got the languages by hunting after the stories in the several poets I read, rather than reading the books to get the languages." It should borne in mind that Pope rose in the literary world before the emergence of the earlier cited, latter day *reading class*, something that is ever diminishing, especially in our own day. Hence, he was kept afloat by (as one might say) the *kindness of strangers*, wealthy patrons who were socially wired, allegorically erudite, generous and of course regrettably political. To some degree he rose, as was said in our own time, from Alexander Pope to *Pope Alexander* who wrote elegantly for the educated classes, not for the fools upon whom he took mordantly precise satiric aim.

Two examples of Pope's victims stand out, the first being Louis Theobald, an early editor of Shakespeare's works, having in 1726 presented the world with his *Shakespeare Restored; or A Specimen of the Many Errors As Well Committed As Unamended by Mr. Pope in His Late Edition of This Poet*, referring to a Shakespeare edition prepared by a fellow (afore mentioned *in passim*) named Colley Cibber a year earlier. Theobald had pedantically claimed to have rescued the Bard, arrogantly claiming also that "as there are very few pages in Shakespeare upon which some suspicions of depravity do not reasonably arise." Theobald was also the author of drama and poetry, but nonetheless Pope had christened him *Prince of Dulness* in the *Dunciad*, saying in heroic couplets, "For thee I dim these eyes, and stuff this head, / With all such reading as was never read, / For thee supplying, in the worst of days, / Notes to dull books, and prologues to dull plays;/ For thee explain a thing till all men doubt it;/ So spins the silkworm small its slender store, / And labors 'till it clouds itself all o'er."

And who was Colley Cibber? He was playwright with a rather odd name who authored *Love's Last Shift* (1696), part of his intention being to include the role of a fop that he intended to act himself, just as he had done in a comedy by John Vanbrugh (1664–1726) called *The Relapse* that same year, when he played the inelegant role of Lord Foppingham. True. The parts one plays in public view have little or nothing to do with the actor's off-stage life, and yet Cibber made himself the obvious stand-in for real life absurdity, largely because he tended to prefer ridiculous roles. But in 1739, oddly enough, Cibber became England's poet laureate, in an age when such things actually seemed to matter. He commenced writing verses of dubious merit, whereupon Pope displaced Theobald as head dunce, replacing him with what he variously called *Great Cibber, King Cibber and King Colley*.

So it is that one way to flay one's enemies real or imagined is to roast them alive as idiots, fops, dunces and blockheads. It's a litt'ry man's way of punching them in the nose, only worse. To impugn someone's intelligence is to strike at one's supposedly highest aspect, namely his unimpeachably sterling intellect. Traditionally, as we learn from our reading Plato, the mind is the nearest thing one possesses to sublimity, not to say one's paramount asset, provided of course that one has it and is able to deploy it. Plato shows us that the mind is the gateway to the realm of ideas that lead us toward perfection and, ultimately, bring us through reason and faith (as Dante shows us) toward the ultimate truth and ideality that is, of course, God. The fool, on the other side, is so distanced intellectually from philosophy that such is beyond his ken. Whereas Pope had through no fault of his own half-a-man's body, he had a completely marvelously keen and fertile mind. Others, then as now, and in spite of themselves, carry on with half-a-mind, or at least that's as much as we're suffered to witness. Such persons are identified by various descriptive names, possibly none more appropriate than *halfwit*, which of course begs the question of what a *whole* wit may be but a fully intellectualized, civil individual. Wit appears to us in Old English as *witan*, meaning *to know*. It refers to a person of elevated consciousness, a refined, quick mentality that enables him to express his meanings gloriously well, and aptly. Recall that in the 1548–1549 *Bok of Common Prayer*, the section on the ordering of priests, cries out, "O holy ghoste into our wittes, send down thyre heavenly light." Indeed so, that such benevolent virtues as reason, intelligence and profound understanding may find footing and enlightenment. To have one's wits about him suggests that one is unusually alert, prepared and focused to exercise the withering might of his intellect, and also that he has the creative energy to live cleverly and astutely through his agility. It was Dryden who articulated so elegantly that "Great wits are madness near allied," that in certain occasions seems to be so if we mistake mere eccentricity with madness. Dickens, again in *The Old Curiosity Shop*, refers to one's "living by his wits—which means by abuse of every faculty that worthily employed raises man above the beasts," a reference to exercising one's intellectual ability in concert with his innate genius and extraordinary acumen say, in rapier-keen adroitness and astounding cleverness or, need we also say, an innate ability to solve intricate problems rationally. Wit may on occasion also imply such niceties as prudence and (with seeming nonchalance) solve dilemmas well beyond the comprehension of any flaming fool, and possess a special genius that operates through an uncanny association of random thought, unexpectedly to dazzle ears that behold it.

Oh, to possess wit! Oliver Wendell Holmes, a scholar in both medicine and jurisprudence, said it: "We get beautiful effects from wit—all the prismic colors—but never the object as it is in daylight." How so? Some of us appreciate the witty, offhand remark, others in a sort of *jeu d'esprit* at the feet of learned men and other presumed paragons of perilously unfathomable talent and extraordinary genius. They may be found as near as one's fireside. The leading English novelist William Makepeace Thackeray (1811–1863) addressed that point in his *Vanity Fair* (1847–1848), saying, "go on Ann. You're the wit of the family," she being the one with a certain confluence of refined humor and powers of observation in concert with the infinite possibilities of our mother language. All this is completely lost on fools, but it can at times occasion a beastly war of wits, a dazzling combat of wondrous thrusts and parries.

One of our favorite wits is Robert Greene who in *Greene's Groatsworth of Wit* (1592) jokingly observed the preponderance of "so many epigramists [and] wit-worms." One may also hear the expression *to wit*, that is a different way of saying something like *namely* or *that is to say*, sometimes replaced by the Latin *videlicet*, or simply *viz*. Wit may also be used to express a measure of sanity, mental soundness, ingenuity, banter, and sometimes *persiflage*, which is frivolous nonsense and raillery, light hearted repartee that toward the end of a long session may leave any near normal person at his *wit's end*, which means in a state of destitute bewilderment, utter mental exhaustion, dangerously perched on the edge of irretrievable mental damage that may demand professional attention. It need hardly be said that the term *wit* has gone unnoticed and uncommented upon, if only because persons of uncommon intellect trade upon it, and so many species of fools, those who throughout history have been obviously *witless*, are wanting in wit. The playwright William Congreve (1670–1729) who, through the voice of his character Witwoud in *The Way of the World* (1700), wittily pronounces that "a wit should no more be sincere than a woman constant; one argues a decay of parts, a t'other of beauty." Shakespeare's Dogberry in *Much Ado About Nothing* ambiguously observes, "a good old man, sir, he will be talking; as they say, 'when the age is in, the wit is out.'" Dryden too in his "Absalom and Achitophel" wrote with characteristic wit himself, "Of the false Achitophel was first, / A name to all succeeding Ages curst. / For close Designs and crooked Counsels fit, / Sagacious, Bold and Turbulent of wit." Later in literary history comes the remarkable Samuel Johnson, about whom rakish James Boswell (1740–1795) wrote one of the world's extraordinarily great biographies. Johnson commented upon Lord Chesterfield (Philip Dorman Sanhope, 4th Earl of Chesterfield, the same chap who in turn wrote a treatise the purpose of which was the education of young men; said Johnson of him, "this man I thought had been a Lord among wits; but, I find, he is only a wit among Lords!" Speaking of the Mermaid Tavern in London, the playwright Francis Beaumont who in collaboration with John Fletcher wrote some 52 plays and quite a mess of letters, penned a few lines of light verse to fellow playwright Ben Jonson, exclaiming "what things have we seen, / Down at the Mermaid! Heard words that have been/ So nimble, and so full of subtle flame, / As if that everyone from whence they came/ Had meant to put his whole wit in a jest, / And had resolved to live a fool the rest/ Of his dull life/."

Wit! What is there to compare? There is an excruciatingly funny *song*, actually a toast (as we call it) anonymously left to posterity: "Here's a health unto his Majesty.../Confusion to his enemies.../ And he that would not drink his health, / I wish him neither wit nor wealth, / Nor yet a rope to hang himself." Best of all was Pope's comment on wit as expressed in his "Essay on Criticism." It reads, "True wit is nature to advantage dress'd;/ What oft was thought, but ne'er so well express'd." That said, take pity, dear reader, on the lowly half-wit (we are not, let it be understood, *not* referring to our handicapped brethren but those who, through the customary channels of heredity and [especially] foul environment, have been guided into the less than wonderful world of half-wits or [quite possibly] have gone there of their of their own volition to join forces with others of their pitiable number). The OED calls such a person "one who is only half a wit; a dealer in poor witticisms," or obviously "one who has not all his wits," i.e., a half-witted person, that [*sic*] does not add much to our sympathetic understanding of dipwits, great numbers of whom we've all had to confront in some fashion or another. One commonly finds them among elementary school teachers, clerks, functionaries, bureaucrats, fifth wheels and gatekeepers, all of whom have been further described as "lacking and deficient in (common) sense."

A gatekeeper, obviously, is one who possesses huge authority over a gate, and to enhance this authority he may possibly be attired in a uniform (suggesting counterfeit military rank) laughingly suited to a dunce. But there is more to be said about such a person who, left to his whim, can, and does, create all sorts of mischief for the rest of us. We find him as a person literally guarding a gate or other passage and deeming it his self-determined professional role in life to prevent people from proceeding where they wish to go, are well-advised to go, entitled to go, by all rights ought to go, and so such. The gatekeeper, all the while attempting to exercise the bewilderingly burdensome trust placed in him, has as this role to stand like St. Peter (or whoever it may be who patrols the entrance to paradise), except that he guards a gate that may well lead nowhere. Police and such like dim witted personalities love to impede all they possibly can, but to no apparent purpose except to delay travelers and bring a halt to anything they can find a way to stop, which seems to suggest that they, having for some reason been prevented from going much of anywhere, have devoted themselves to placing such restrictions upon others. Police love to obstruct traffic for no rational purpose except that it permits them to create the impression that they're doing something useful by ordering citizens around and wasting their time. They particularly enjoy distributing orange cones on highways so to reduce four lanes to one, effectively bringing motor traffic to a standstill for dozens of miles, entirely to no purpose. The usual pretext is that there *is road work in progress,* when it seldom is.

One commonly finds gatekeepers in medical offices where they stand guard between patient and physician, so as to keep the two separated for as long as possible while the patient dutifully supplies the same information currently on file and in triplicate, although no one will ever read any of it. Ridiculously enough, the basic idea is to prevent the sick and injured from receiving attention, something the gatekeeper thoroughly enjoys because he fancies himself even wielding the authority over health matters, while he detains others from going about their business. Clerks in automobile license bureaus thoroughly enjoy exercising their real or invented authority over citizens by showing cause why they are not to be accorded driving licenses, license plates, evidence of automobile ownership and other noisome bureaucratic requirements that have brought said citizens to such dismal offices in the first place. The motive is always the same: to exercise imaginary authority and to control others by detaining them and wasting their time. Such rubbish is similar to insurance issuers who, for a year or more, refuse to honor the contractual obligations they themselves drafted and into which they freely entered. They, in turn, are rather like admissions officers in universities who make it their business to turn away more-than-qualified students. Such people are half-wits behaving like what they are: control-personalities attempting to prevent anybody from doing anything, were that possible. Certain literary agents and editors do what they can to impede good manuscripts from publication, although predictably enough they know little about books, nor read any with even minimal comprehension. Consider officious issuers of building permits who attempt to prevent anything from being constructed, or health departments that close restaurants for the wrong reasons. This reminds one of legislators who make a career out of telling the public what opinions it must embrace and what language it may use, or instruction manuals that answer all the questions except the obvious ones, or tell bankers how to manage banks and physicians how to practice medicine. A gatekeeper's post is at his (or somebody else's) gate. There they ideally practice their calling in jails, prisons and other houses of detention that are excellent settings for imposing their gatekeeping upon essentially helpless individuals, be they criminals or not.

In *Howard's End* (1910), a tedious novel by E. M. Forster, a woman ruminates over a gateway that, if not guarded and barred, leads one to his existential way amid interminable confusion, chaos and clamor. "Like many others who have lived long in a great capital, she had strong feelings about the numerous railway termini," we are told. "They are our gates to the glorious and the unknown. Through them we pass out into adventure and sunshine, to them, alas! we return." But if one can do no better than obstruct such gateways, it signals that he is the prisoner of cosmic impasses himself. Security guards, in all probability, aren't much more than uniformed blockheads who, were they not blocking gates, might well be moving through them and infinitely well beyond. By *blocking*, we mean unobstructed obstructing. We place blocks in front of automotive and aircraft wheels to prevent their rolling. In football, popularly known as *fuppall*, blocking means attempting to prevent one's opponent from advancing through the line of scrimmage and into an end zone. Once accomplished, there is little to do but do it again— and again. The game does not allow a player to carry the ball off the field, out the exit gate and into oblivion. To be called a *blockhead* means that one's head is little more than a block of wood, possibly a dead, branchless tree or a butcher's block upon which one dismembers a carcass of meat, chopped and sliced, or a block upon which a helpless and humiliated slave is made to stand while being auctioned. A blockhead has a head with nothing in it besides wood, or nothingness. He has little to no intelligence, which goes a long way into making him a fool as he lacks feeling, judgment, sensibility, sense of decorum, or capacity for reason. Nicholas Udall in his comedy *Ralph Roister-Doister* (c. 1552) with which we are all quite familiar, carried a remark reading, "Ye are such a calfe, such an asse, such a blocke." Doister is a preposterous prancing buffoon who, in his own estimation, is irresistible to women. Shakespeare uses the term similarly, as for example in *Julius Caesar*, saying, "You blockes, you stones, you worse than senseless things." So does the Scottish dramatist Robert Tannahill, shouting, "the greatest dunce, the biggest block," or (as they say) an enormous chip off the old block (head), one of whose great satisfactions in life is putting himself in others' way by obstructing sidewalks, congesting traffic by "blocking on't."

Blocking others, as in football, is to make an effort, at least, to stop inertial force. This is not necessarily a good thing, especially when the force has a purpose behind it that may be useful, even beneficial. Or maybe not. To *knock someone's block off*, i.e., *knock one's head off*, is a barbaric way to settle a dispute, whereas a *block and tackle* is something mariners might use to lower a mate (attired in a diver's apparatus) into water. In carpentry, a block is merely a section of wood glued so to secure a joint. There are also children's blocks with which to build, learn numbers and begin ABCs. A block may be a large hunk of anything one pleases, such as shares of equities or whatever one regards as a monolith, such as a lump of stone or a city block that, as a series of buildings without intervening spaces, may represent concrete and steel locked together like a ship's freight. We also find it used as *block buster* and *block busting*. The best way of confronting such fools is not necessarily to block them at all. Should they be unavoidable, the best way to proceed is with extreme adroitness so not to make a spectacle of oneself amidst fools and blockheads. One effective yet quite regrettable strategy to avoid such miscreants is never to say anything that might be construed as comical, by which we mean even distantly amusing. In these particular circumstances, it's best to stay well clear of anything that a passing knave could interpret as funny, witty, laughable, droll, risible, ironic, whimsical, absurd, jesting, farcical, zany or (heaven help us) slapstick, peculiarly odd, bizarre or facetious. It won't work, simply because fools of any stripe, albeit they may themselves seem quite funny, seem not to recognize mirth in others, probably because the recognition and appreciation of humor presumes a modicum of intelligence, something that that's conspicuously difficult (if not impossible) to discover among blockheads whose minds (what they have of them) are impossibly clouded, literally, in such a way that the appreciation of common humor, not to say humor in its more sophisticated manifestations, is all but impossible. In short, comedy is out of the question. It's not even something that one ought to consider when attempting to communicate with blockheads, who, we all learn sooner or later, hopelessly outnumber us. "Tis for the honour of England," says Congreve's character Fainall in *The Way of the World*, "that all Europe should know that we have blockheads of all ages."

The infinite potentialities of our language have given rise to a plethora of other cognomens that we may deploy when we attempt other descriptions of fools. Among them is *dope*, not the sort of thing one would choose to be called, and yet for a fool it is not altogether inappropriate when circumstances warrant it. Any chemist would prefer to call it *dioxyphenylalanine*, a crystalline amino acid prescribed for Parkinson's Disease that, for all we know, is untreatable. Pharmacists know it as *dope*, perhaps *dopa*. Chefs know it as *doop*, a culinary sauce used in dipping, and in its generic sense as a thickish fluid devoted to the service of extraordinary dining, or even as a lubricant similar to common motor oil. Henry Mencken finds its origin in a Dutch word meaning *sauce*. In America, the term *dope* is sometimes used loosely to apply to any drug that seems to call for one. *Scientific American* once described *dope* pleasantly enough as "a preparation of pitch, tallow, and other ingredients which, being applied to the bottom of the shoes, enables the wearer to glide lightly over the snow softened by the rays of the sun," and it has also been applied (both literally and figuratively) over the running surface of skis, the better to breeze over snow banks with the misleading sensation of well-being. *Dope* also applies as a light finishing coat to the cloth surface of old airplanes and even as light coating applied to some model aircraft to promote and preserve a taut surface. There are also dopes used as an enhancement for fuels, but alas, it has its foolish applications as well, some not worth a pocket full of piss.

We return to some commonplace vernacular, in search of approximate synonyms, although all synonyms are approximate. Commonly speaking, a *dope* is a stupid person. How better to express it? Jackass? Moron? Dimwit? Dunce? It often suggests someone hopelessly under the trammels of a narcotic, probably an illicit one that perchance contains opium in its syrupy rendering, long preferred by contented legions of opium puffers worldwide who consume it in that elusive form. The desired effect is to deliver the smoker into a stupefying trance that, we are reliably informed, is not in one's best interest if he is committed in the slightest to what dunces call a *healthy lifestyle*. The use of dope became public knowledge well before 1922 when a publication called *Public Opinion* warned "the cabarets in Constantinople are a meeting place for all the world's dope purveyors." *Room at the Top* (1957) by British novelist John Braine (1922–1987), whose name and work has usually been identified with a literary movement called *The Angry Young Men*, applied *dope* in its more current sense: One bloke asks, "Who's Alice?" Another responds, "You've met her, you dope." It may well refer to a person, or an animal, with a mind frazzled by some kind of vile chemical. Race horses have been occasionally and surreptitiously administered something known to all stable boys as *dope*, intended to enhance chances of winning, or possibly losing, what some idiots call *hass* races. Dope, as some may recall, was falsely rumored to be an ingredient of Coca-Cola, so to enlarge upon its famous flavor. The word has also been used to mean information, as in *giving someone the dope*, the nature of which may well be intentionally spurious. Dorothy Sayers, creator of the detective Lord Peter Wimsey, referred to "a dope addict's dream," induced by some impurity that results in making a fool all the more foolish, i.e., dull-witted in the manner of our friend Dopey Dilldock, a silly name that turned up in that aforementioned 1940s radio program called *Can You Top This?* Other pejoratives such as the archaic *dope fiend* (meaning one shackled in narcotic transport); *dope peddler* (better known in our enlightened day as a seller of illicit narcotics, a pusher); *dope sheet* (which advises one upon which horses to wager); and *dope out*, which may mean to cogitate, whether that cogitation may be reliable or not.

There are other fool names that employ the suffix *head*, among them *pinhead* that ostensibly means what is says: the head of a pin or anything that suggests it, such as a person whose head, for some good and sufficient reason, terminates in a point, in other words another fool, another bean brain. The Indiana vernacular playwright and essayist George Ade, partly in whose honor the Purdue University football palace receives its name, was to be sure no pinhead, but did mention one in his *Forty Modern Fables* where he wrote, "is it not sad to see a pinheaded Rake dissipating a large fortune?" By *rake*, Ade was referring to a *rake hell*, an old and cherished expression for one who possesses loose morals, someone of dubious virtue given to loose living, possibly a man of libertine inclinations such as snake oil salesmen, although the term has seldom been applied to women of dubious honor. William Hearth, the satiric painter and engraver whose sense of derisive humor led him to prepare sets of plates depicting contemporary foolishness, developed his *Rake's Progress* (1733) consisting of eight related pieces, namely 1) Tom Rakehell preparing his father's funeral, 2) Rakehell's setting himself up in lavish style, 3) his ordering night-long entertainment, 4) his early signs of debauchery and his decline, 5) his having been saved from going to debtors prison for his recklessness, 6) his continued gambling and squandering of his inheritance, 7) his sitting dumbfounded in debtors prison, and finally 8) his ending in a madhouse. The term *progress* does not here suggest progress as it is usually construed. It means instead to make one's way on a journey, to travel. When we hear mention of the *queen's progress*, it refers to her journey, possibly through her cherished foothills, usually by moving forward, proceeding, advancing, rather than retreating, back-paddling or back-pedalling, and so forth. Tom Rakehell can hardly be said to *progress*, unless we mean marching to the rear, digressing. Hence, we observe the ludicrous downfall of a rake and a fool.

Among the fools one encounters in normally convivial social intercourse is the common *chucklehead*, not necessarily (we hasten again to emphasize) the sort that one immediately detests on sight. All the same he is a significant component in a diverse nation such as ours that accommodates various kinds of *goons* and *idiots*, the latter of which once again cries out in desperation for further explication. *Idiot* is not what one could call a *fine old word*, one that has a cherished place in our endlessly fertile and yet idiosyncratic vocabulary. Nevertheless, one must come to terms with *idiocy*, in the manner that one would *come to terms with* a deflated tire. The Greeks came to terms with idiots in a rather different light, their being the uneducated, morbidly stupid persons of the sort we know by the dozens. In a gentler light, one may at his own pleasure view idiots merely as common men, which is to say, without feeling any professional calling to rescue a place for them among those generally assumed able to *know*, and perhaps be understood. Or he may be charitably viewed as a *dope*, an *ignoramus*, a person not yet (at least) schooled in *philosophy*, to say it diplomatically and without a trace of malice. Let us suffice to think of idiots merely as unschooled, ill-informed chaps, and let it go at that. In 1698 an unidentified person with admirable directness wrote, "I confess myself an Idiot, understanding no other Language than Turkish", for which we trust he may have been thereby culturally limited and directed to disappear in peace. A somewhat more strident person (also unidentified) had the audacity to say, frankly, "It would be safer to ask the judgment of a young lad or country idiot...than those lubricous wits and outworn Philosophers," a view that, frankly, we endorse, but only privately. The OED, putting the matter quite forthrightly, advises us that an idiot is, pure and simple, "a person deficient in mental or intellectual faculty as to be incapable of ordinary acts of reasoning or rational conduct." Bravo! It continues, it can be "applied to one permanently so afflicted as to be distinguished from one who is temporarily insane or *out of his wits*, and who either has lucid intervals or may be expected to recover his reason." Gilbert and Sullivan in their *Mikado* (1885) pay homage to "the idiot who praises, with enthusiastic tone, All centuries but this, every country but his own."

Points well taken, we are obliged to submit, but add too that others have viewed the idiot as what some describe as a *natural fool*, something we take to mean a fool by birth rather than one who, as we have so often heard, *makes a fool of himself*. Both are fools nonetheless. No less than Algernon Swinburne, who made a career waging war on common morality, counseled us that "an idiot or natural fool is he, who notwithstanding he be of lawful age, yet he is so witless that he cannot number to twenties, nor can tell what age he is of, nor...who is his father or mother, nor is able to answer to any such easier question." Well put, we feel obligated to submit in response. There are occasions, we regret to point out, when the word *idiot* finds deployment as a verbal grenade. In Dickens' historical narrative *Barnaby Rudge* (1841, one character shouts, "You idiot. Do you know what peril you stand in?" Accordingly the idiot may obviously be a source of amusement, as we shall see later in these turgid pages. If one derives laughter from the prospect of a handicapped person, an idiot may be just such a hapless target: a poor chap deficient in intellect, and having to become an object of low comedy in the minds of others who (following Aristotle's remarks on comedy) apparently view themselves as appreciably more intellectually equipped to extract pleasure at the prospect of an impossibly pitiable idiot. Wordsworth, to the contrary, wrote with sympathy in his lengthy poem entitled "The Idiot Boy," citing both the lad and his bedraggled mother, appropriately named *Betty Fog*, but such sentimental expressions of feelings are not unusual among poets of a frowzy romantic disposition. Elsewhere, slapstick comedy derives from persons feigning mental disability. We are reminded too of William Faulkner who, in *The Sound and the Fury* (1929), borrowed his title from Shakespeare's *Macbeth*: "a tale/ Told by and idiot, full of sound and fury,/ Signifying nothing."

All this is the merest preparation for approaching the *chucklehead*, the mere thought of whom calls to mind a severed head lost in feckless, possibly morbid, laughter that is intended, without question, to advance the lowest sort of serial mockery. The term *chuckle*, after all, is the vehement, convulsive laughter one may anticipate from an idiot. Samuel Richardson in his *Pamela, or, Virtue Rewarded* (1740), directs our attention to "such Liberties of Speech as they would scarcely chuckle at." The OED expands upon the word, calling it laughter "in a suppressed manner...to make or show inarticulate signs of exultation and triumph, sometimes referred to as gleeful exultation." What then is a chucklehead? Predictably, he's markedly quite similar to a blockhead, a bit like an idiot, reminiscent of a moron and yet comparable to a halfwit with a modicum of the jackass and a dollop of the dunce. The prolific British scholar George Saintsbury commented upon what he called "an amiable but, to tell the honest truth, rather chuckleheaded young English squire" of the sort who, we daresay, are not unfamiliar. Mark Twain was acutely aware of chuckleheads, and in point of fact singled one out in his ambiguously titled *A Tramp Abroad* (1880), commenting quite unabashedly that "with the native chuckleheadedness [excellent choice of words, say not?] of the heroine of romance, she preferred the poor and obscure lover." We happen to like the sound of that, because it strikes us as impossibly absurd.

So do the recent problems surrounding South Carolina governor Mark Sanford, his peregrinations, his wife and his mistress, all of whom prompted one Republican *strategist* to ask, "how did these chuckleheads end up running my party?" The mere mention of chuckleheads, surrounded as we are by them, calls inexorably to mind dunderheads who at this writing propose a new world order, a foolocracy, dedicated to the noble advancement of stupidity, heavily underwritten by the United States government that is itself swimming in unvarnished bureaucratic idiocy to the tenth power of inanity, and devotes itself the laudable business of wasting taxpayers' money as if it were so much confetti. A foolocracy, as any fool knows, is simple (and foolishly) a government of jackasses for the promotion of fools and their foolishness. Moreover, its imperial intention is the encouragement of inanity and outright moronic passion enthusiastically to encourage the high cause of idiocy the world over. In better words, it advocates pissing one's life away with folly, living merely day-to-day, devoting no thought to one's existential perplexities and how best to resolve them. There, simpletons reign in robes of stupidity, and moronic pinheads are elevated to high posts of moronic public adoration for the ninnies they assuredly are. The magnificence of their doltishness is well upon us, so much so that the weaker among us have joined their ranks, fallen into place, and are strutting down a thoroughfare in ceremonies of mindlessness in such a way that stupidity controls our ballot boxes and public schools. Their music fouls our radio bands and eardrums, their rubbish fouls our streets, their hideous taste has captured our television broadcasting.

Dunderhead, let it be understood, derives from the word *dunner*, an expression that in turn refers to a loud, unceasingly offensive racket so hideous that persons of quality find it intolerable, largely because it occasions a sort of deathly vibration that portends an Armageddon. The OED does not fail to note that *dunner* has its onomatopoetic implications, suggesting essentially that it sounds like what it means, namely a ghastly reverberation, offensive to any who possess ears. It may also be taken to mean a *blow*, or deafening explosion that augurs or possibly announces what the OED calls "a ponderously stupid person; a blockhead" (something to which we have accorded some attention), a numbskull, the meaning of which some take as a dull-witted person with a hard, even impenetrable, reinforced head, in other words a common dolt. A *humskull* (derivation of *numbskull*) is unmistakably just that: the *noddle* or *noggin* (if you please) of a dullish person, a nitwit. We are all reminded that Laurence Sterne (1733–1768) in his roguish *Tristram*

Shandy directs out attention to a fallen world populated with "blockheads, numskulls, *doddypoles*, dunderheads and other unsavory appellations." *Doddypole* is not, we submit, an expression one hears every day. It has its origin in *dotty*, which in common exchange means *feebleminded*, *goofy*, *eccentric*, even *crazed*. *Dunderheadedness* tends to imply gross stupidity, as used for example in an 1870 remark published in the *Saturday Review* that reads, "this dunderheadedness of crime which is brought home to us by reports like these," etc. Another application of dunderhead turns up in, of all places, in the *Knickerbocker's History of New York* (1809) of gay blade Washington Irving where we hear "a dunderpate like the owl, the stupidest of birds." There is also such a thing, we regret to report, as a *dunderwhelp* (a dog) that Fletcher used in 1621 when he shouts, "what a dunderheaded whelp."

This inevitably puts us in mind of a *dupe*, which, taken as a verb, means to make a fool of someone, if he is not been a fool all along. *Dupe* usually refers to a deluded person, one who, out of sheer stupidity, allows himself to be lured into additional stupidity, someone who is so easily misled as to be recognized as a *flaming idiot*. Swift, in his *Tale of a Tub* (1704), commented that "those entertainments and pleasures we most value in life, are such as dupe and play the wag with the senses." What he probably meant by *wag* is *tail-wagging*, better still *tongue-wagging*, which is to possess a certain talent for verbal deception or simple minded practical joking. *Wag* eventually came to mean a mischievous person who, as was once remarked, *played the wag*, so to become a trickster, a wise guy, a joker, the better to press his foolery upon fools. Swift, by the way, is best identified in the popular mind today as the author of the highly deceptive narrative *Gulliver's Travels*. It was he who put the *gull* in Gulliver, *gull* meaning (besides a wide-winged webfooted marine bird) to delude, in the sense of tricking someone, especially if that someone happens to be a simpleton, a dupe or other foolishly unsuspecting, credulous, blazing jackass, its ideal victim. To say it another way, to gull is to swindle, mislead, and defraud one's prey. The predator is of course a fraud in the form of a cheat, a trickster, and impostor, a confidence man. One is also immediately reminded of the adage *Si mundus vult decipi, decipiatur*, a piece of advice that tells us if the world must be gulled, let it be gulled. This especially makes sense if one sees the world as a place peopled with a gaggle of gulls, hats in hand, waiting patiently to be bamboozled, swindled, cheated, fleeced, raped and robbed.

Foolishness obviously invites such abominations. As we are so often reminded, there is a fool born every minute, sometimes expressed as there being a *sucker* born every minute, as Phineas Taylor Barnum, the politician and showman (lies therein a difference?) is alleged to have remarked. At any rate, the well-worn maxim "never give a sucker and even break" may (or may not) allude none too kindly to a child or other young mammal before it is weaned, but it has other implications such as a country bumpkin who is a naïve, trusting inexperienced gull, possibly a greenhorn, simpleton and any other bumptious imbecile. Even Sherlock Holmes, in one of Arthur Conan Doyle's mysterious tales, says to our incredulous surprise, "I'll see this sucker and fill him up with a bogus confession." *Bumpkin* may derive from the Dutch *boomken*, meaning *little tree*, but it also refers to some pint-sized clown whose demeanor would suggest that he is an ideal mark for a scam artist. *Country* adds insult to injury by implying that such a person comes from the rural innocence of the backwoods rather than from the depraved city. It refers to the supposedly street smart (we won't say sophisticated) urban sharpie overwhelming the wide-eyed agrarian from the open and presumably unsullied countryside of daisies and doodlebugs.

It is one of life's inescapabilities that one may be unfortunately referred to (surely in error) as a *tom fool*. It's a tolerably innocent, even inoffensive expression, and yet one that merits close linguistic review and possibly even painstaking scrutiny, inasmuch as one cannot distinguish its innumerable implications at first blush. There is no predicting what an apparently off-hand reference may conceal behind its back. Such it is here, since the expression has come to denote a mentally handicapped individual, what others prefer to call (less delicately) a *half-wit*, something that we viewed antiseptically in certain pages preceding this one. There is evidence that *Tom Fool* originated at least as far back as the Middle Ages when we discover mention of a figure named *Thome Fole*, also known as *Thomas Fatuus*, the Latin for *foolish fire*, an eerie light that ominously overhangs a marsh at night, although it also refers to something that deludes, that leads to misdeeds that arise out of our misunderstanding. The Latin *Tom* has long been used in the British Isles to refer to a prostitute or any other sexually permissive female. In *King Lear* when Edgar says that *Poor Tom's a-cold*, it brings to mind a mentally ill person, as for example Tom Bedlam, Bedlam being, as it was, a primitive excuse for a mental hospital. Accordingly, "Tom Fool" is said to have designated a person too deranged to declare his designated name. It also evolved (while we're on the subject) into what we know as a *Will O' the Wisp* and silly names like *Dick Fool* and *Jack Fool* who are nothing but common buffoons who, among other hopelessly ridiculous things, accompany Morris (aka morice, Moorish) dancers. They are therefore the butt of vile jests that modesty precludes our disclosing. We should not omit to say, however, that the noun *buffoon* (a designation central to our inquiry) refers us to the verb *buffoon* which means gutter jesting and coarse ridicule. It will come as no surprise that Lord Byron speaks of his having *buffooned merrily*, his being the rather licentious figure that he assuredly was. Buffoonery in the 16th century partly assumed the form of purveying merry tales, the lascivious nature of which we also prefer not to disclose. Buffoonery today is a rather disgusting term, decidedly inappropriate for mixed company, especially affecting persons of quality.

As to *morris* dancing, the less said the better. The OED reminds us, however, that is, or was, or possibly still is, "a grotesque dance performed by persons in fancy costume, usually representing characters from the Robin Hood legend" especially "Maid Marian and Friar Tuck," therefore "any mumming performance." Hugh Latimer, a salty chap of 45 whose sermons have been painstakingly preserved, remarked on "such fellows [who are] more meete to daunce the morrice daunce then [*sic*] to be admitted to preache." Such thought as this gave rise to the *morris bell* that dancers tied to their costumes. Hearing this reminds us of Juvenal's stern exhortation: "Comes now Gaditarian with his troop of naughty songs, and wanton pranks of much applauded dancing girls that stoop and rouse desire with undulating flank." If we consider such spectacles as *mumming*, the word deserves some thorough explanation. Historically, a *mummer* is one who participates in a dumb show which, we also remarked, is a speechless part appended to a theatrical play, and has also been called *silent acting*, although at times it has been anything but silent, and was sometimes involved with allegorical figures to whom we painstakingly referred earlier. One such performance appears in *Hamlet*, where it is spoken of as a *play within a play* that may or may not have an ostensible connection to the outer drama. Shakespeare said that dumb shows were for the purpose of entertaining *groundlings*, meaning those who occupied the pit, or *ground* of a theatre. Such were presumed to be fools, as suggested by their lack of artistic discrimination and their inability to recognize drama as an aesthetic and intellectual spectacle. Shakespeare also commented ruefully in *Hamlet* that groundlings, for the most part, are "incapable of nothing, but inexplicable dumb shews and noise," adding too that some "shall bite [their] tongues, and in dumb shews Pass the remainder of our days...." Accordingly, the term *mummer* meant one who *mutters, mumbles* or *murmers*—which is the next best thing to remaining silent. Pope, in his *Dunciad*, referred to them as "Peel'd, patch'd and pye-bald, linsey woolsy brothers Grand Mummers! Sleepless some, and shirtless others." It was their wont to satirize and ridicule religious ritual by attacking Catholics. If being a mummer means that one remains *mum*, then the word also may relate to *mummy*, consisting of unsightly, desiccated flesh.

Mummery, far from dead, survives in Philadelphia where locals proudly trace the origins of their comedy to 440 B.C., the good old days when the Roman festival of Saturnalia flourished and everyone had a hell of a good time celebrating Saturn in December when, history tells us, there was nothing but uninhibited merrymaking and (better still) licentious abandon that we seldom enjoy in our own time. Today, the fun begins appropriately on Broad Street in south Philly and ends at the City Hall. Locals regard it as their *Mardi Gras*, an occasion for indulging themselves in comic abandon, string bands and fancy brigades, investing new life into *dancing fools* the world over. Such celebrations appear even in Second Samuel 6:45 where we're told (in the *New*

English Translation) that "They took it [a cart] with the Ark of God upon it from Abiminadab's house on the hill, with Ahio walking in front. David and all Israel danced for joy before the Lord without restraint to the sound of singing, of harps and cymbals" as if engaging in an ur-form of the *Mummer's Strut*, its having been described as those with "their backs arched, executing cross-over steps forward and back," in the Philadelphia manner while "snapping in time, nodding mischievously to the music." Have they perchance been tippling? Playing the crowd? In Philadelphia, at least, we're assured that mummery is *a way of life* that has historically been encouraged and (with some reservations) generally applauded. Be reminded that Robert Burton's *Anatomy of Melancholy* (1621) encourages "dancing, singing, masking, stage-plays, howsoever heavily censured by some severe Catos, yet, if opportunely and soberly used, may justly be approved [since] there is a time for all things, a time to mourn, a time to dance, a time to embrace, a time not to embrace and nothing better than that a man should rejoice in his own works."

The *dancing fool* has therefore traditionally been an expression of endearment, since there is little to no foolery in the exercise of Terpsichore unless, as with the Philadelphia mummers and even the Morris dancers, it becomes an intentionally comic spectacle intended to entertain and celebrate with foolish derision. In the Biblical sense, the fool became as much as anything impious and even vicious because of his failure to observe rigorously the teachings of the church, including the requirements of Christian living as illustrated, for example, in the parable of the wise and foolish virgins, known also as the *parable for the ten virgins*, that advances several moral messages, central among them the consequences of good and poor judgment in Matthew 25: 1–13. Simply put, a parable is a didactic anecdote (i.e., instructive, carrying a precept, a command, a moral or practical lesson) that one might refer to as *Christian* (because they are more often than not ascribed to Jesus) allegory. On the surface of this parable we are advised that there were ten girls, five of whom were foolish, the other five prudent, who set out to meet a figure described only as a *bridegroom*, who has yet to show up at a wedding, possibly because no one got him to the church on time. The wise virgins are sometimes interpreted to be *bridesmaids* (although there is no bride mentioned), who not only filled their oil lamps but also packed a refill with them on the chance that they might need it. Sure enough, the bridegroom arrived late, when all ten of the girls had dozed off until midnight, when they were notified of his arrival, at which time the foolish virgins had insufficient oil and asked the wise ones for replenishment, only to be briskly refused and told to purchase it elsewhere. The bridegroom arrived (for the second time), and those who had sufficient oil attended the brideless wedding ceremony which was enacted behind a closed door, whereupon the foolish virgins showed up and asked that the door be opened to allow them passage, but were refused admittance (by a gatekeeper, of course) just as they had been earlier. This time, however, the bridegroom tendered the refusal, saying, "I decline; I do not know you." Indeed, apparently he does not know *any* of them, including the wise virgins inside the ceremonial chamber. The parable concludes by advising, "keep awake then; for you never know the day or the hour," an obviously ambiguous bundle of messages, as was the first line of the parable that reads, "when that day comes, the kingdom of Heaven will be like [meaning similar to] this."

All this is wide open to interpretation, some of it skewed one way or another according to which translation one examines. The conventional, and obvious, reading shows us that we must be prepared; but for what? Probably the Second Coming. And who is the bridegroom, but the presumed narrator, Jesus himself, although the bridegroom is never identified and Jesus is never mentioned. Even so, to some readers, Jesus is remarking in a rather veiled anecdotal way about his pending appearance and the uncertainty of its timing. Meanwhile, the story posits two sets of fools: the five who were out buying oil when the bridegroom arrived, and the fools who were not wise enough to pick up on the story's rather unlikely parallels, such as equating a wedding ceremony with the Kingdom of Heaven, and the groom as the savior of mankind. Ergo, it's all about being shut out, excluded, refused entry. It is aimed pointedly at fools, those who are asleep at the switch, imprudently low on provisions, tardy to the party and (as they say): a day late and a dollar short. They are obviously inadequate, as compared with those who are both wise and prepared. Of course, there are any number of possible interpretations; one could imagine it is intended to present theological matters in an anecdotal narrative form apt to deliver meaning to the theologically unsophisticated, but this seems absurd since the parable does more to disguise significances than to elucidate them. Mark Hendrickson in the February 20, 2009, issue of the *Catholic Exchange* suggested that "in this parable there was no redistribution of property from the prudent to the imprudent." He also astutely observed that "the foolish virgins weren't charity cases, unable to fend for themselves," but rather "they simply didn't make the necessary effort to succeed." Allegories, after all, allow for generously variant readings. One could also argue that the real winner in this interesting exchange was that clever "he" who sold these fools their oil at, as we say, *top dollar*. Seldom mentioned, however, is the signification behind lamps and the light they emit. Light usually represents enlightenment, truth, and ultimately goodness. Its opposite is darkness that represents obscurity and ultimately evil. Dante's hell is illuminated only artificially by fire, and is otherwise known as the *realm of darkness*. Most certainly, representations of evil worsen as we join Dante and his part time docent and psychopomp Virgil as they descend to hell's pit. By contrast, Dante's paradise is bathed in light, and God's own presence finds its symbolic representation in the form of an illumination so brilliant that it, at least initially, blinds those who attempt to behold it.

Fools, as we know, are best identified as ignorant, or in some instances ignorant-appearing. The foolish virgins we've observed are in danger of running out of oil which means running out of light which means running out of brains and thereby running out of luck. Notice too that intelligent persons are often described as *bright*, which tells us that they are enlightened, informed, closer to the truth than others, particularly those who exist in darkness. It has even been suggested that the wise virgins are actually the virgins they are purported to be, and that the foolish virgins are whatever people become when they're no longer virgins, the possible *meaning* being that it's preferable to be pure than impure, better to be more worthy than less worthy. The purported occasion, after all, is a wedding, albeit, as we have said, one without a bride, possibly because there were no virgins available. That same Mark Hendrickson, this time writing for the *The Center for Vision and Values* (February 18, 2009), suggests that they were in an oil mode, if you know what that means. Those who lacked it were too late for the party. This parable is tantalizing because some of its features seem to make no sense, not merely because it's a brideless wedding, with its tardy bridegroom and a gaggle of ten virgins. In the opinion of some, Jesus is here unaccountably rendered as a woman, although we cannot explain why. We can only suggest that the Bible is an apt example of folk literature, meaning that it is the product of oral rather than printed origins, and that it is the work of many hands, some of which have presumed to modify, add, delete and otherwise manipulate the narrative, for what purpose we shall never know. For the nonce, and for our thematic purposes, let us say that, among its tangled messages, it is addressing fools and the result of their foolishness, which is to be excluded, overlooked, locked out, ignored, rebuked and thereby insulted by a person who functions as a gatekeeping door-slammer.

There is no question that in biblical times, as in ours, fools are welcome only by other fools, and maybe not at all. University admissions officers, so much as it is within the scope of their influence and guesswork, attempt to keep fools out of the academy, an institution ironically long since overrun by hoards of idiots in faculties and student bodies. It is also within their authority to decline promising candidates and accept others who, after four or more years, are awarded with a bachelor's degree, pursuant to which they present themselves as sufficiently foolish. We once met a fellow who, in the knowledge of this paradox, did what he believed a favor to himself by *not* enrolling at a university at all. Granted, that was a chancy thing to have done, or, as it were, *not* to have done. Entering a university these days carries with it the additional problem of paying for it, and also the additional burden of dodging, evading, undermining outsmarting and outwitting its moronic features such as fraternal societies and institutional efforts to stifle freedom of expression, both of which over recent decades have done universities and their students (what relatively few there are) immense damage by dispatching some of those students out into the world to perpetuate the high cause of stupidity, especially those who resolve to invent a career out of government (dis)service. In America it is challenging to find anyone who is not a fool. This begs the question of how then to deal with it and them. One possibility is to join them, although it is safe to assume that anyone who has read this far is (as we've been saying) hardly an idiot. One needs, however, to come to terms with social conditions as they are, rather than as we might prefer them to be.

One option (and a damned fine one at that) is to become a *hermit*, assuming that one has not long nurtured hermetic tendencies beforehand by doing such things as evading matrimony, living alone and taking direction from within rather than from without. Being, or becoming, a hermit is entirely possible and entirely effective, if only because it presents one the opportunity to delete any number of life's stupidities (weddings, dinner parties, support groups, committee meetings and all such rubbish), and live far better for having done so. Foolishness is where you find it, and quite often one can (to borrow a favorite computer expression) *delete* it. Examples: If you're sickened by politics in our District of Corruption, *delete* it from your huge mental inventory by not suffering politicians (is there a more disgraceful occupation?) and by deleting them by any (legal, of course) means possible. One can also delete organized religion, or if one pleases, *religion* itself, with the possible exception of extracting from it what intellectual properties it carries with it. One can easily delete the menace of television simply by withdrawing its power cord, or better still, by hurling the television out a window, providing that there's no one below to catch it and (believing it a bountiful gift from God), immediately power it up for the purpose of poisoning his mind and promoting his foolishness. One may also detach himself from almost anything encouraged by the United States government or all such organizations animated by *pooled ignorance* into which no intelligent person would care to jump unless (out of a broad sense of humor) he finds it a source of uproarious amusement. This may not be possible, since fools, even in their clownish manifestation, are seldom amusing. Suppose, probably out of insecurity, one still wants desperately to join something. Let us count the ways. Affiliating is not always the problem it appears to be, so long as one remembers that he is not to be governed or even influenced by it whatsoever. Since many of these moronic clubs are variously secretive, exclusive and altogether mystifying, we can neither endorse them nor find fault, although they do attract the more chronically curious among us, at that. They may or may not offer some promise of comfort or perhaps an illusory satisfaction of belonging to something. It hardly matters what. One can, of course, be altogether solitary, which by all odds is the best option.

Randomly, but in alphabetic (we almost said *diabetic*) order, we have accidentally run across a wide selection of groups that (who can say?) may deliver more than they promise, and may inspire more than routine interest among the randomly fastidious. Let us begin with the famous Arctic Brotherhood (pursuant to whom, according to *Genealogy Research's Complete List of Fraternal Organizations*, all one needs to do as a condition of membership is "to go to a meeting, sing the song [sounds like a hell of a good time to us], promise to look for gold and spread the word";; Angelic Order [ordure?] of Fairy Belles; American Order of Owls; Ancient Order of Zuzimites; American Stars of Equity; American Self-Endowment Association of America; Albany Zonave Cadets; Black Knights of Moldess; Camels of the World; Catholic Total Abstinence Society; Fairest Among Ten Thousand; Fraternal Order of Pineapple; Grand Chapter of the Ancient and Venerable Order of Hasodim; Grand Court Order of Calanthe; Hermetid Fraternity; Hooded Ladies of the Mystic Den (which is, or was, an "auxiliary of the Ku Klux Klan"); Honorable Order of the Blue Goose; Ladies of Abraham Lincoln (is there something that Honest Abe wasn't telling?); Ladies Independent Order of Reindeer; and that's just the beginning.

Many of these, like college fraternities and sororities, demand and foster obedience through team-centered activities more appropriate to fools who have difficulty regulating their own lives. Those who submit are obliged to fall in line and follow directives aimed at the less sophisticated and less educated who are handed code words, secret handshakes, access to allegedly privileged information and other nonsense. Allegedly the ten most esteemed of them include Skull and Bones, better known (although they trade in fraternally dark secrets that appeal to certain kinds of personalities) as the *Brotherhood of Death*, that has appealed to some Yale undergraduates who have been clamoring to join since its 1932 inception. Another favorite is the Freemasons that supposedly dates back to 1717 and embraces such mystic symbolism as the compass and the square, whatever that may signify to the uninitiated. Of course there is the ritual secret handshake that some find fascinating. A particularly popular choice is the Rosicrucians with their array of secret significances and their historic documents relating to an alchemist named Christian Rosenkreuz who is believed to have played a role in a *chemical wedding* (whatever that may have been) between a king and a queen who lived in a *castle of miracles*. There is also a group calling itself the *Ordo Templis Orientis* that owes it mysteries to a chap known in mystic circles as *the great beast*. A *perennial favorite*, as fools call it, is the Hermetic Order of the Golden Dawn that appears to involve occult rituals directly traceable to documents allegedly containing magical rites. There are those to who feel drawn to the so-called Knights Templar, commonly known as "The United Religious, Military and Masonic Orders of the Temple and of St. John of Jerusalem, Palestine, Rhodes and Malta."

We move on to "The Illuminati," a popular secret tong originating from a coterie of fellows who called themselves, in all modesty, *Perfectiblists*, while putting away their schnapps in Upper Bavaria. The less than well known Bilderberg Group, from what we can learn, has no members *per se* but instead attracts a select coterie of *influential* folks who converge now and then to discuss matters forbidden to the rest of us that have never been discussed before, nor will any of its attendees spill the beans, if you get our drift. The inquisitive may instead find The Priory of Sion alluring, although we have been advised by a party who prefers not to be identified that the priory *doesn't exist.* We have been furthermore advised that there is a lunatic group out there who, despite their denials, believe that their members are direct descendants of Jesus. We come lastly to the Opus Dei, believed to have been a secret group that grew out of the mystic chambers of the Catholic Church that, on the other hand, takes a dim view of any such thing within its purview.

Such is the profound secrecy that some of us (we'd prefer not to specu-late for fear of offending any fools) find enticing, since the ho-hum reality of ordinary life can become insufferably humdrum, so much so that we take enthusiastic refuge in joining others who treasure irrelevant secrets that we hold in common. We prefer to think of this mystic passion as our *veil of secrecy*, without which we would consider ourselves wanting an identity. We include beneath this veil of secrecy a private jiffy bag, a padded pouch, a secret service dedicated to collecting intelligence and trading in espionage well beyond the comprehension of common fools. As Henry James wrote in *The Figure in the Carpet*, "Vermeer's secret, my dear man—the general inten-tion of his books: the string the pearls was strung on, the buried treasure, the figure in the carpet." We can scarcely take others to task for their irresistible attraction to secrecy while we crave it ourselves, and maintain a *secretaire*, an odd piece of furniture where one's private papers, his darkest secrets, can be stockpiled in the illusion of privacy. A redundant term, private secretaire, as we prefer to think of it, is a person trusted to maintain our confidences in utmost discrete confidence.

Have we not all observed ardent affiliative enthusiasm and longed to join in and join up? Have we not also ascribed to ourselves such things as pursu-ing futile quests resulting in our squandering time and energy? Have we not all told, ample times, well-rehearsed yet pointless jokes that, though entirely well intentioned, were (we must come clean on this) ill-timed and (shall we say) ill-considered and that were furthermore asinine (meaning ass-like) and in the end merely preposterous? As we have amply seen, a fool is most likely identified by his deficiencies in the company he keeps as well as his faulty judgment in matters of taste and critical acumen. In the selection of pointlessly secret societies, fools are quite able to persuade others to accept the proposition that they're not fools in the slightest. It was John Donne, the English poet of "metaphysical" inclinations, who warned us "who are a little wise, the best fools be." Some are astonishingly crafty at convening the illusion of sagacity, conveyed often through the art of oratory, unveiling their elocutionary acumen before university classrooms, courts of law, pulpits of perfect holiness and even congressional halls of the world's lowest caliber of corruption at the highest volume of congressional fraudulence. Such impostors are, when appropriate (which is almost never) called not merely fools, but *damned fools* and fools hopelessly beyond redemption.

They are not (allow us to emphasize) to be confused with *idiot savants*, who, unlike politicians, occasionally have an abundance to offer themselves and others. Let's examine the expression. The OED calls a savant *a man of learning*, whereas a *savante* is sometimes taken to mean, suspiciously enough, *a woman of leisure*. Hugh Walpole, the New Zealand-born novelist, wrote of a certain Madame de Rochefort, "her manner is soft and feminine as though a savante, without any declared pretensions." The savant is sometimes construed (we can't say why) to be engaged in scientific inquiries, but more often regarded as someone absorbed in other futile avenues of learned research. The French *savant* means *learned one*. An idiot, aside from its strict psychological definition is, by contrast, "a person without learning; an ignorant, uneducated man; a simple man; or clown" elsewhere expanded so not to exclude "a person so deficient in mental or intellectual faculty as to be incapable of ordinary acts of reasoning or rational conduct," sometimes called a *natural fool*, a person born with mental complications.

What then does the oxymoronic (self-contradictory) expression *idiot savant* mean? In psychiatry, it denotes a mentally handicapped person (sometimes pronouncedly so) with an unexplained extraordinary talent such as the ability to play the piano beautifully or perhaps to excel at chess or higher mathematics. It all begs the question of how *epistemologically* such a person *knows*, and from whence his knowledge originates without benefit of education and, in some regrettable instances, without literacy. Idiots savants have demonstrated the arcane ability to determine, without recourse to any printed source, on what day of the week a certain date will fall fifty years ahead, or did fall fifty years behind. We are told that the idiot savant is, in about fifty percent of instances, *autistic*, the meaning of which in psychiatry being one *morbidly* self-absorbed and out of reach with *reality*, whatever we take that word to mean. The word *autism* derives from the Greek word *self* plus an *ism* suffix. *Morbid* in this context comes to us from the Latin *morbidus* (to die), pertaining to disease, more likely affected by disease or other pathological circumstances. Savants are six times more prevalent among males for reasons no one can explain.

Today's *idiot savant* has been subsumed by the more euphemistic and accurate *autistic savant*, that became partially the subject of a 1988 film called *Rain Man*. Removal of the pejorative *idiot* from idiot savant has mostly removed the stigma of idiocy. Nevertheless, is the idiot savant in any sense an idiot or a fool? The emphatic answer is no, unless of course we take account of the common tasks that such a person seems unable to perform. This raises the inevitable dilemma of how to evaluate the foolish-appearing who are in significant ways anything but foolish and obliges us to revise conventional notions of what it means to be a fool. He may appear to be an idiot, a block-head, a dimwit, a dolt and a dunce, even when he demonstrably transcends those less than accommodating designations. An autistic savant is different from the rest of the population in that he dwells mysteriously in a region of his own. If the savant is not autistic, then chances are he's something else, such as a victim of a brain disorder, a brain injury or even mental retardation that causes him to dwell in what's become known as an *island of genius*.

Darold Treffert, M.D., who is a clinical professor in the Behavioral Health Department the University of Wisconsin's medical college in Madison, published a leading article on the subject, titled "Savant Syndrome; An Extraordinary Condition," in the May 27, 2009, number of *Philosophical Transactions of the Royal Society*. Dr. Treffert notes therein that "no model of brain function, including memory, will be complete until it can fully incorporate and explain this jarring juxtaposition of severe mental handicap and prodigious mental ability," emphasizing too that "more progress has been made in better understanding the condition in the past 15 years than in the prior 100." He continues by citing some of the astounding capabilities of such autistic savants. Among them were identical twin brothers able to calculate days of the week on calendars 40,000 years both back and forward, and another A-S victim who can within 90 seconds determine how many hours and seconds a person survived if he lived 70 years and 12 hours, allowing for 17 leap years (the answer: 2,210,500,800), not a shabby performance for someone formerly presumed an idiot. Dr. Treffert concedes, by the way, that calendar calculators are few in number and exceedingly obscure as a skill. I-S people, for reasons no one comprehends, may similarly be gifted in music, being able to master as many as 20 instruments; they are most often known for piano performances. For those more attracted to the practical arts, the preference trends toward sketching, painting and sculpture. Those who are inclined toward mathematics, while they may lack the ability to solve simple arithmetic problems, execute *lightning* calculations, including the ability to compute prime numbers. Dr. Treffert further reports that others can calculate distances without using instruments, and can comprehend subtleties of map-making. Other autistic savants have mastered multiple languages, exhibited extraordinary sensory discrimination in smell, touch, vision and *synesthesia*, commonly known as a *concomitant sensation*, better explained as describing one sense through another such as the color blue by way of musical imagery. No ordinary fool could explain the color of a skunk's odor, but there have been idiots savants able to judge the passing of time without benefit of clock and calendar. Others have developed what Dr. Truffant calls *prodigious memory* that includes obsessive preoccupations with, and memorization of, music and sports information, license plate numbers, maps, historical facts, or the distinctive sounds of vacuum cleaner motors. Later he cites the case of a "53-year-old male who has memorized over 8,600 books and has encyclopedic knowledge of geography, music, literature, history, sports" and so forth.

They're talented idiots, if one prefers to call them so, but not the sort whom we have examined earlier. Nonetheless, some characteristics of the autistic-savant place them in the popular mind as foolish, such as their disturbing inability to communicate with others, their inability to solve problems, balance a checkbook, and in some cases their potential for becoming enthusiastic over junk television or other inanities such as silly, fatuous, pointless jests, hoaxes and widely disseminated inconsequential matters such as Academy Awards, Nobel Prizes, Miss America contests and soap operas (which captivate so many fools of every stripe). On the other hand, they may well possess the sort of madness that leads them obsessively toward *fool's errands* that may appeal to so-called *wise fools*, or *fool sages* and what has been called the *ardent enthusiast*, all of which, on the surface of it, are harmless but still present to them an attractive opportunity to pursue phantoms of their own devising. Such idiosyncratic preoccupations may leave the impression that (if it's anyone's business) one is puttering aimlessly, something that of course perfectly normal people never engage in, and moreover find preposterously foolish. Of course, unlike normal people, the autistic savant operates within his own territory, lending credence to two maxims, the first of which says, *a fool has few friends* (something that we regret to hear), and the second, *a fool laughs at his own jokes*. William Blake, the madcap visionary, poet and illustrator, observed in his "Marriage of Heaven and Hell" (1793) that "a fool sees not the same tree that a wise man sees," and (perhaps accordingly) developed an idiosyncratic poetry uniquely his own (granted, that may be said of nearly everyone who is poetically inclined, but even so...) that generations of poetasters have interpreted as the product of a fool and lunatic, but at least, as Shakespeare recorded in *Romeo and Juliet*, "children and fools speak true."

Perhaps so, but one cannot depend upon it. Foolishness, as we usually define and recognize it, is unfortunately part of the cultural mix and cannot be thwarted without resorting to unusual measures, the first of which being not to associate with it, so far as may be possible. This can be accomplished by refraining from visiting public places such as houses of worship, houses of ill-fame, houses that Jack built, houses of lords and such like, including motion picture theatres, raucous taverns and parties of all kinds: dinner parties, political parties, homecoming parties, going away parties, welcome home parties, get lost parties, poker parties, hunting parties, search parties, drinking parties, card parties, pool parties, Tupperware parties, rush parties and so such. One might be similarly advised to avoid matrimony and parenthood, refrain from joining anything, but instead to sleep alone, dine alone, drink alone, celebrate alone, clean house alone, bowl alone, go broke (if necessary) alone, go fishing alone, travel alone, urinate alone, go crazy (if that be a final resort) alone, enjoy life alone and die alone.

But one must not grow fat alone, because it is ruinous to one's health and because Obesity and Stupidity are the most intimate of allegorical friends. The probability is that anyone who allows himself to grow fat is stupid, which is to suggest that he is somewhat or a great deal on the foolish side. An article entitled "Obesity Doctors Are Weight Biased," published in the September 1, 2009, *Psychology Today*, reported what we might have assumed, that "the psychologists, physicians and researchers who treat the overweight" apparently take a dim view of their pudgy patients, and why not? Moreover, another study published in *Obesity Research* similarly reported that *health professionals* obviously (and responsibly) enough, "did show a fat bias," meaning that they justifiably associated rotund people with laziness and stupidity, and identified them with pejorative words such as *moronic*, and *worthless*. The Centers for Disease Control estimated that 61 percent of U.S. adults were overweight in the year 2000, and that 20 percent were deemed clinically obese. Opinion is divided between those who believe that obesity is one cause of stupidity, whether stupidity encourages obesity, or both. An actively debated article by Kate Melville in a site called *Science a Gogo* entitled "Obesity Linked to Stupidity" (August 26, 2009) argues that "a person's risk of cardiovascular disease, type II diabetes and hypertension is known to be linked to obesity, and now researchers have established that being overweight can also affect a person's brain." Melville cites a Paul Thompson article in the *Human Brain Mapping Journal*, claiming that "obese people had 8 percent less brain tissue than people with normal weight, while overweight people had 4 percent less tissue." Moreover, a *Health Cognition Study* concluded that "in looking at both grey matter and white matter of the brain the researchers found that the people defined as obese had lost brain tissue in the frontal and temporal lobes, the areas of the brain critical for planning and memory, and the anterior cingulated gyrus (attention and executive functions), hippocampus (long term memory) and basal ganglia (movement)." Furthermore, "overweight people showed brain loss in the basal ganglia, the corona radiata, white matter comprised of axons, and the parietal lobe (sensory lobe)." Thompson, a UCLA professor of neurology, commented that "the brains of obese people looked 16 years older than the brains of those who were lean, and overweight people looked eight years older." Said co-researcher Cyrus A. Raji, "along with increased risk for health problems such as type II diabetes and heart disease, obesity is bad for your brain." Furthermore, an article entitled "Long-term Obesity is Linked to Loss of Brain Tissue," by Robin L Brey, M.D., turned up in the peer-reviewed *Neurology* dated 2004 by the American Academy of Neurology, and posited that whereas "nearly 60% of adults in the US and 50% in Europe are classified as obese or overweight," there is "a risk factor for diabetes and high blood pressure...conditions [that] can cause damage leading to loss of brain tissue" and conceivably be "linked to poor cognitive function," observing also that "researchers are not sure what the real relationship is between being overweight and loss of brain tissue. It is also possible, however, that being overweight 'causes' diabetes and hypertension, which in turn 'causes' loss of brain tissue. It is also conceivable, however, that being overweight 'causes' brain loss independent of these other conditions."

Obesity has nothing to recommend it, and those who bring that condition upon themselves are, to put it more or less diplomatically, pronouncedly foolish. Obesity carries with it other attendant characteristics, all of them hideous. Commenting on precisely that, a person calling himself *Jackbenimble* contributed a December 8, 2007 article to a group calling itself *Progressive U*, titled "Poverty, Stupidity, Obesity and Food Stamps," having ostensibly to do with his alarming visit to a Wal-Mart store on the first day of a month when its customers besiege the premises with their WIC/Food Stamp Cards. Apparently *WIC* means in bureaucratic circles "women, infants and children." "The first thing one realizes," says Jackbenimble, is [the] reason these people are poor; they are barely functional and probably don't have the intelligence to hold a job. It was amazing to watch them try to use their WIC cards," which, he explains, "they don't seem to have figured out." The second thing he notes "is the prevalence of obesity," observing, however, that "Americans in general are over-weight," and that a Wal-Mart store is "as good a place as any to maintain it," since "these folks paying with a WIC card make the rest of America look like anorexic supermodels." Ironically, Walmart shoppers appear, if anything, like "they are getting too much food." One of his conclusions is that "poverty, stupidity and obesity are all closely related and that food stamps are part of the problem and that food stamp reform is part of the solution."

True enough; what we're witnessing is a subculture of fools whose every foolish gesture begets another miserable choice. In all likelihood they come out of poverty, a circumstance quite beyond their control, but they know no other way to fumble through life than to depend upon governmental redistributions of public wealth, and any other source of universal charity, since this has become a way of life for at least two generations. From their point of view, this is life as it ought to be: awaiting the next welfare check from that government's eternal willingness to embrace deficit spending and its encouraging everyone to become hopelessly dependent upon working Americans and profitable businesses for their survival, whose earnings are confiscated and then metamorphosed by stages into programs like WIC, then food stamps for the benefit of those who have made a mockery out of everything they touch, such as public schools that have in turn made a mockery out of intellectualism by sending forth hopelessly uneducated schoolteachers (to put it redundantly) who believe they can teach anything to anybody. Hence the proliferation of WIC card carriers who drop away from such dubious educational opportunities, find themselves mostly illiterate, as were the schoolteachers who may have been certified by the state's *teachers* (without the apostrophe) *colleges*. WIC people then set about producing the next generation of WIC recipients and lifting additional welfare from working people's pockets. As *Jackbenimble* correctly says, they fumble through life "filling their bellies with frozen pizzas, TV dinners and anything else that is not nutritious." This, needless to say, inexorably results in health problems or what fools call *issues*, obesity among them, that the government addresses in the same manner that the government addresses everything else, which is badly. If obesity usually does result in mental and other impairment, as health researchers suggest, then with the mismanagement of a moronically bureaucratic government partly elected by fools, conditions will deteriorate in such a way that WIC people and others like them whose lives are totally worthless to themselves and to society will inherit the earth. Hence, they usher forth another generation of WIC people who will continue to reproduce an infinite population of fools whose talents are limited to reproduction and the consequent reckless proliferation of stupidity. Such keeps society amply supplied with what used to be called its *underclass*, that of idiots who live upon the reluctant kindness of strangers who (chances are) have bothered to get an education (a real one), earned niceties such as a high credit rating, a decent job, or (better yet) a place in one of the profession, thereby becoming a benefit to us all, and deservedly earning a pile of money that the government means to confiscate for the purpose of issuing more WIC cards and other cycles of waste.

As someone (we're not certain who) asked recently, "were you born stupid, or did you take lessons?" Foolishness, let us be aware, is not entirely the property of the lower classes. As any sociologist will attest, social class is the product of several circumstances, and not limited to income; it pivots upon cultural aspects implicated variously with civility, taste, education and cultural superiority derived from discerning judgment, self-respect, responsibility and all such wondrous things, not excluding wholesome health habits and the ability to manage money shrewdly. There are upper class people with little money, and lower class people with buckets of it. Be he wealthy or poor, a fool (by whatever subset he goes: blockhead, fop, moron, nitwit, dummkopf, jackass, dunce, and so forth) remains a fool, something that not only does not become him, but does not benefit the rest of us. That is also why, incidentally, fools have earned little more than reluctant toleration from others, if that. In recent years, fools, with encouragement from a foolish government and foolish banks, have accepted mortgage loans that even a fool ought to have seen would never be repaid. The world financial catastrophe this occasioned not only brought the American economy to its knees but threatened economies around the globe, whereupon the American government (such as it is) merely printed more money and incurred extravagant debt out of which it will never extricate itself. Even if it were to do so, it would rapidly mishandle wealth and drive the nation back into debt. This is the work of malicious political fools, far worse than ordinary dunces and blockheads, whom one is rather obliged to confront. History has nothing good to say of them, and their examples of egregious incompetence are endless.

Earlier we mentioned Edward Young, credited with inventing the bromide "a fool at forty is a fool indeed." One commentator (we will conceal his name) has none too kindly said he "was the author of many more or less feeble lyric poems, now never read," but (we will add) he has been, nonetheless, rightly remembered for having written the eerie *Night Thoughts on Death and Immortality* (1742–1744) and thereby qualified himself for inclusion in what some classify as the *graveyard poets*, seeming to suggest those who devote their nocturnal hours to composing poems in and about cemeteries. Elsewhere we find that "a fool always finds a bigger fool to praise him," and Shakespeare's no-nonsense, daggered remark, "a fool doth think he is wise, but the wise man knows himself to be a fool" that has more than a modicum of merit to it. Consider too that "one fool praises another" or Emerson's famous paradoxical pronouncement that "a foolish consistency is the hobgoblin of little minds," that he may have invented to mask his own inveterately contradictory tendencies. "A fool always talks when he has the least to say," makes some sense, as might Pope's polished iambic pentameter "fools rush in where angels fear to tread," or this expert little remark on fools conceived by the great Oliver Goldsmith, the ubiquitous omni-talented literary man whose novel *The Vicar of Wakefield* (1766) is great fun and an amusing literary adventure for everyone not a fool. Goldy is believed to have written that "fools who came to scoff, remained to pray," possibly the influence of his father (a curate) and of Goldy's own failure to arrange a cozy preferment in the Church of England.

There are truckloads more nasty maxims applying to idiots, such as "dead men and fools never change their minds," and "a fool believes anything," "foolish is as foolish does" or "a fool demands much, but he's a greater fool who gives it." That's a nice one, but this is better: "if all fools wore white caps, we'd all look like geese." Try this sartorial one for good measure: "a fool and his foulard are soon parted," or similarly, "a fool and his money are soon parted," or maybe "a fool and his words are soon parted." Not bad; say what? If you think not, be reminded that "arguing with a fool shows that there are two." Be reminded that "a fool can ask more questions in a minute than a wise man can answer in an hour." Loads of other such mighty maxims play fools off against wise men, forming a dichotomy that runs through the onionskin pages of the Bible, as we have seen. Consider: "a fool says what he knows; a wise man knows what he says," or perhaps "a silent fool is a wise fool."

There are a number of other such pronouncements afoot. It's been suggested that "a fool's treasure is his tongue," although we've had many a nitwit make surprisingly good use of his tongue; we've also heard that "a fool is like other men as long as he is silent." Here are two of a kind, illustrating that chips off the old block nonetheless remain chips: "a fool despises his father's correction, but he that regards [apparently takes seriously] reproof grows prudent," versus "any fool knows more than his father." There's the old "once a fool, always a fool," whereas "an educated fool is dangerous," not to say exceedingly annoying. Some of these maxims that rail against fools are themselves foolish, as for example "a fool laughs at his own folly" and "a fool laughs when others laugh." Another received opinion is that "a fool's bolt is soon shot," that pertains to bad timing that counsels us to hold our fire until the propitious moment is upon us. Similarly, "a fool may talk, but a wise man listens," presumably to one who is not a fool, and "a fool's mouth is his destination," and yet "a fool might be counted wise if he kept his mouth shut," amply illustrated in certain other unusual instances.

Occasionally, other foolish phrases may appear more opportune, but the possibilities are all but limitless. Here, for example is a sententious one that may be fitting for some *emergent situations*: "a fool says I can't; a wise man says I'll try," although the message might just as well be reversed. There is a relatively moronic adage telling us that "any fool can earn a penny [except some of the fools we know], but it requires a wise man to spend it," which also may be read in reverse. A more sedate criticism that may best be perused while one has his belts tightened: "a fool's vexation is presently known; but a prudent man conceals his," advising us, one may suppose, to play our cards *close to the chest*, which is similar in spirit to counsel that reads, "any fool can spend; a wise man puts his cash under a mattress." There is a relatively stupid maxim that tells us, "every fool wants to give advice," or "live as a fool, die as a fool," sometimes rendered as "live a fool, die a fool," as if there is nothing one can do to redress his stupidity. Other conventional wisdom allows for contradiction, for example, "never joke with a fool," on one side, and "no fool, no fun" on the other. Whereas it is "a cunning part to play the fool," taken as theatrical advice, nonetheless "foolish is as foolish does."

Many of the foregoing maxims are part of Anglo-American folk *wisdom* (such as it is) that originates from familiar *adages*, a word that in turn comes from the Latin *adagium*, i.e., *proverb*. And what is a proverb but a short, pithy saying. That's what. It may make no sense, and yet boneheads persist in repeating it. Sometimes they do this because it's alliterative, and inane, things that idiots adore and even crave. This is not to suggest that there is no meaning attached to such mottos, but it's likely to be some dumbassed, bromidically sententious piece of foppery that is ordinarily presented as *common sense* that is, more times than not, mere nonsense. Another one, and quite on the mark, holds that "according to the philosophic adage: *omnes stulte insaniunt*, all fools are out of their wits." The alleged *poet of love*, his excellency Barnabe Googe who is not much read anymore, nevertheless put it quite aptly when he proclaimed, "as the Proverbe in Englande is, set a Knave on horsebacke, and you shall see him shoulder a knight," however that may be received in our day. His *Book of Proverbs*, nonetheless, comes to us as poetic, not to say didactic, sections of the Old Testament into which we have at some time or another all unavoidably poked our inquiring noses. In any case, to be *proverbial* is to cruise at leisure through fields of metaphoric stupidities, especially those concocted by dimwits. With knowledge of enough proverbs, one could speak almost entirely through them, although one would sound at times oddly like Moses.

All this demands supplementary elucidation. When we say *metaphoric* we mean referring to one thing by referring to another. For one dreary example, be reminded of the foolish old saying, *your eyes are stars*. If one were to say *your eyes are like stars*, it is also a metaphor, but more specifically a *simile*, meaning that we use the comparative words *like* or *as*. Aristotle, in his *Ars Poetica*, tells us to "raise language above the commonplace," and that "the greatest thing for a poet is to be a master of metaphor." Metaphors, including similes, trade in analogies, which are comparisons between two or more things. Fools don't understand a great deal about metaphors and the like, unless they belong to what in foolery is an elite, if ridiculous, subclass we know as *educated fools*, great numbers of whom inhabit offices in universities where they pass their days engaged in primarily two things: promoting absurd ideas mired in oceans of irrelevancy, and attentively sitting at meetings that purport to address matters of insignificance, most of them being contradictory and above all counterproductive. By *alliterative*, we mean the repetition of consonant and vowel sounds as in *Piers Plowman*, where we find, to our amazement, the following utterance: "In a somer seson wan soft was the sonne," which is sort of like "Peter Piper picked a peck of pickled peppers." By *bromidic* we refer of course to *bromide*, but not in the chemical sense (a compound of bromine with an organic radical or perhaps an element), but in the sense of persons whose remarks are *bromidic*, that is to say trite, *platitudinous*, commonplace, soothing (like a snort of potassium bromide), tiresome and idiotic because every idiot repeats certain accepted sayings with the ardor with which he might say his rosary. To be linguistically trite is to be given to repeating insufferably commonplace observations such as "it's a nice place to visit, but I wouldn't want to live there," or "Christmas comes but once a year," among other inanities commonly voiced by sententious jackasses. The problem with triteness is its stale, thoroughly mindless repetition of something that was once possibly quite fresh—but not for long. Today such gibberish is merely *hackneyed*, a word that over time has signified many things, all of them worn out, possibly vulgar and now cloyingly commonplace.

We've been calling some of these rapier-sharp anti-fool statements maxims, that is a form of *axioms*, self-evident *ipso facto* pieces of information that mathematicians, for one, rely upon as containing what they believe to be incontrovertible truths and principles upon which other assumptions rest. The OED calls a maxim a *proposition*, especially a sententious one (that is to say gurgling over with somebody else's cosmic wisdom), presumed to be unassailably intelligent, cogent, pompously full of itself, generously spilling out aphorisms, definitive judgments on all matters living and dead, and the last word in verity, certainty, well beyond contradiction. Hence a maxim is something of such honor that we should all rise from our seats and render our full, respectful and sympathetic attention in the knowledge that we stand well within the ultimate light of sublime truth. Maxim, after all, denotes *maximum*. This brings us to Richard Mulcaster, hardly a fool, whose pronouncements we can all attest with pristine certainty convey an unnerving veracity. Some of us revere him for celebrating the English language as self-evidently superior to all other tongues, be they ancient, modern, western, eastern or otherwise. So it was that Mulcaster himself memorably told the world that there are in our midst "certain universal propositions which they that be learned in the Laws of England and likewise the Mathematical, do term maxims." We comprehend this perfectly and have no intention of challenging its flawless truth.

Accordingly, but with a certain reticence to which we confess, we return to our fools and to what greater minds than ours have pronounced upon them. Hold fast. Let us now examine our friend the fool in context, by which we mean its sources, spoken, written, imagined, and even rectally trumpeted. Certain biblical passages, as we have amply witnessed, roundly condemn fools (although if one searches scriptural passages, he can defend bloody near anything). One can always *take words out of context*, as idiots say, for the purpose of committing deliberate deception, especially if it is aimed at fools who read virtually anything (if they read at all) literally, although they are in peril of misreading anything, even if they try not to, which is less than doubtful. *Context*, to judge by its origins, means, *to weave*, or, if you please, *to weave together*, which is today in the usual context a text that becomes a series of more or less coherent thoughts, or so they are assumed to be. Suppose the text of a litt'ry review reads, "This filthy excuse for a book is the remotest thing in the world from a *masterpiece*," only to have advertising claim that the aforementioned reviewer called the book *a masterpiece*. That is the not too creative use of surgically excised passages out of context, which we may ourselves be about to do. At the very least, however, the following excerpts, even if they tell us close to nothing, provide a slight contextual interrelationship. For example, Martin Luther the German lawyer believed that he had experienced an epiphanous spiritual *experience*, after which he determined to become a priest and (one might well suspect) began to stew about his chances for salvation. By *epiphanous*, we refer of course to *epiphany*, a word that no fool can possibly define, nor would care to. It means (if we may construct a definition of our own), a sudden, miraculous *appearing*, such as is celebrated in the Christian celebration of Christ's appearance before the Magi. More recently, however, epiphany means a glorious *manifestation*, a moment of enlightenment, such as readers of this book have all experienced, as when someone quite unexpectedly beholds amid the fog of confusion a sudden magnificent realization heretofore shrouded in the murkiest darkness. In any case, it was Luther who referred to one who, to the contrary, "remains a fool his whole life long," and hence remains mired in the darkness that ignorance (and evil) represent. Luther's thought puts us in mind of Proverbs I-26:11, vulgarly referring to how "a dog returneth to his vomit, so a fool hath said in his heart [i.e., not out loud for all to hear] there is no God." Shakespeare, as we have seen, referred to fools with some frequency, declaring things like "now, the Lord enlighten thee! Though a great foole," and "all our yesterdays have lighted fools/ the way to dusty death," pointedly a "triple pillar of the world transformed/into a strumpet's fool," as well of his disdainful advice never to "suckle fools and chronicle small beer." Fools, as we shall see illustrated, are everywhere, and easily infiltrate our literature, for example with Milton's "paradise of fools," Pope's "never failing vice of fools" and Byron's declaring that "fools are my theme."

Fools, it would appear, are *everybody's* theme. Among the *time-honored* (as idiots say) favorites that carry a certain *practical* purpose, for example: "he is a fool that kissed the maid when he may kiss the mistress," suggesting that it's foolish to settle for less than life can deliver. Another is of the same ilk: "it is a foolish sheep that makes the wolf its confessor," or in still plainer language, "fools are those who unburden themselves to the wrong people." Another folksy morsel of advice holds that "fools grow without watering," advising the rest of us that idiots, like dandelions, spawn and multiply plentifully and without encouragement. Consider also the shop-worn observation that "we are fools to one another," inferring that opinions differ upon who is the fool and who is not.

It may interest a few to be reminded of Henri IV of France, whom some remember as the rascal who put his weight behind the Edict of Nantes (signed in 1598) that, liberally enough, accorded Protestants the option of retaining their Protestant ways in France that, then as now, was predominantly Catholic. What has that to do with fools and foolery? Just this: Henri had the colossal effrontery to call James I of England "the wisest fool in Christendom" — he who didn't much bother his mind about having his mother Mary, Queen of Scots, on orders from Elizabeth I, beheaded 20 years later. According to one source, James I "is thought to be the author of a number of fine poems" which, we confess openly, makes us think a great deal better of him. The reasons behind Henri's calling James I a fool are (to be quite open about it) uncertain, except that he did not revere him a great deal. We have no difficulty with that; we too hold certain persons in less than august esteem. That sort of thing happens in monarchs and monopolies the world over.

In deference to Abraham Lincoln, the oft-quoted Franklin Pierce Adams, a cigar-puffing radio wise guy and newspaper man, declared with a certain indomitable authority that "you can fool all of the people all of the time," which might be a slight hyperbole (an exaggeration not intended to be taken literally), albeit the most philosophic of breakfast table maxims share that tendency, as for example when Freddy Lonsdale confidently announced to the world that he wasn't a *bloody fool*. We're inclined to take his word for it, but he did author a number of comedies for the musical stage, among them *Aren't We All?* (1923), *The Last Mrs. Cheyney* (1925), *Once Is Enough* (1938) and *The Day After Tomorrow* (1950). Even if one weren't a fool, as Rudyard Kipling (1865–1936) observed, "it takes a very clever woman to manage" one, something that we're not inclined to quarrel over. Kipling, who authored *Wee Willie Winkie* (c. 1887) entertained certain reservations (shall we say) about women, although he married an American of that gender, and lived more or less happily afterward in Vermont, but he was buried nonetheless in Westminster Abbey. It was, we feel confident in asserting, his *destiny*, about which the American writer with the unlikely name of Ambrose Bierce called "a Tyrant's authority for a crime and a fool's excuse for failure." Bierce (his even more unlikely middle name was *Gwinett*), sometimes went by the (less likely still) penname *Dod Grile*, although he had been called *Aesopian*, after Aesop (6th century B.C.) who, as everyone knows, traded heavily in fables, those usually involving irrepressibly talkative animals whose inclinations run toward satiric anecdotes with certain moral purposes concealed behind them. We remember them redundantly as beast fables, such as might have been written by Kipling, Joel Chandler Harris and George Orwell. Bierce called his animal tales *Fantastic Fables* (1989). Such things as these are of course didactic, although Bierce defined *educational*, in his *Devil's Dictionary* (1911), as "that which discloses to the wise and disguises from the fools their lack of understanding."

On the subject of fools and animals, we turn at last to Samuel Butler, a man of simple tastes who assured us that "the greatest pleasure of a dog is that you may make a fool of yourself with him, and not only will he not scold you, but he will make a fool of himself too." Being as he was in equal parts an author and a sheep farmer, Butler rather meant what he said about the joys of living contentedly among the lower animals that, incidentally, reflected his abiding interest in evolutionary theory. He too was anything except a fool. Although he was in his youth directed toward an ecclesiastical career, he thought better of it and became a little man remembered affectionately for his novels entitled *The Way of All Flesh* (posthumously 1903) and *Erewhon* (1872), that being the word *nowhere* spelled backwards—an appropriate title for a utopian subject.

Like so many other major world authors, Mark Twain was interested in fools (he humbly listed himself among them) and their foolery, as if to suggest that they populated most of society, for example in the pages of *The Innocents Abroad* (1869), *The Adventures of Tom Sawyer* (1876), *The Gilded Age* (with Charles Dudley Warner, 1880), *A Tramp Abroad* (1880), *The Prince and the Pauper* (1882), *The Adventures of Huckleberry Finn* (1884), *Following the Equator* (1897), *Pudd'nhead Wilson* (1894) and The *Mysterious Stranger* (1916). In Huck Finn he wrote, "hain't we got all the fools in town on our side? And aint that a big enough majority in any town?" It's a damned fine observation, to which he added, in *Following the Equator*, when he assigned fools to a worldwide, universal purpose: "let us be thankful for the fools...but for them the rest of us would not succeed." In *Life on the Mississippi* (1883) he mused, "if you send a damned fool to St. Louis and you don't tell them he's a damned fool, they'll never find out." Said he in *A Connecticut Yankee in King Arthur's Court* (1889), "there is nothing different about a king than there is about a tramp, after all. He is just a cheap and hollow artificiality when you don't know he's a king. However, reveal his quality, and dear me, he takes your breath away to look at him. We are all fools." Even in his *Autobiography* (posthumously 1924) Twain wearily conceded, "Ah well, I am a great and sublime fool, but then I am God's Fool and all His work must be contemplated with respect." In an 1885 letter to his wife Olivia he confessed that "if all the fools in this world should die, lordy how lonely I should be!"

The outrageously outspoken Norwegian playwright Henrik Ibsen was not nearly so sanguine about the existence of fools, but then Ibsen was a man of strong and certain opinions, seldom wavering in his views. *En Folkefiende* (An Enemy of the People) that appeared in 1882 held that "the majority never has right on its side. Never, I say! That is one of the social lies that a free, thinking man is bound to rebel against. Who makes up the majority in any given country? Is it the wise man or the fools? I think we must agree that the fools are in a terrible overwhelming majority, all the wide world over." Indeed, one need not be altogether paranoid to imagine a foolocracy so overwhelming that it will in time envelope the globe, if it hasn't yet done so. We recall that Bertrand Russell, the British mathematician and social activist, won a Nobel Prize before Nobel Prizes became a laughing stock and booby award accorded to crooked left-wing politicians. Of course, Russell presumed himself to be what he viewed as *rational*, something that may or may not be supported by subsequent philosophic opinion. One must be reminded that the perception of what is sensible is always contestable, even among minds presumed to be rational as well. Even so, as Russell speculated, the result is more likely to be foolish than wise.

CHAPTER 3. IMPRUDENCE AND ITS IMBECILIC IMPLICATIONS

We find ourselves uneasily obliged at this juncture to examine another aspect of fools and foolery not hitherto addressed, partly because of its sensitivity and the seriousness of its implications for fools and those who, whether they will it or not, are obliged to have some truck (trafficking, trading) with them, probably out of necessity and possibly out of obligation. It addresses the indelicate matter of *impudence*, a word as offensive to hear as it is distasteful to investigate, but investigate we must, in the name of thoroughness, by exploring its regrettable sociological history, its etymology and its implied threat to us all. Imprudency (not to be mistaken for *impotency*, or for that matter, *impudence*) is nonetheless a primary aspect of foolery that begs our sustained attention. The OED tells us that the term comes to us through the Latin *imprudentia*, meaning (to be quite forthright) *shamelessness*, especially as it bears upon Immodesty and its despicable comrade Indelicacy. By shamelessness we commonly mean, as the OED says, a certain "painful emotion arising from the consciousness of something dishonoring, ridiculous, or indecorous in one's own conduct or circumstance," adding incidentally, "a thing which is shockingly ugly or indecent, or of a disgracefully bad quality." One might also put it less decorously as a feeling of *guilt* over something that one knows to be *improper*, and in some hideous cases, *disgraceful* or quite unabashedly *awful*. *Shameless* means that we are without a sense of shame, and therefore unable to experience fully the guilt over having committed some regrettable act. Shakespeare, in *A Midsummer Night's Dream*, forthrightly asks, "have you no modesty, no maiden shame?" The less poetic among us stubbornly persist with more commonplace expressions such as *a great shame*, *an awful shame*, *a darned shame*, and so forth. Shame may be deployed in proper circumstances as a noun that refers to the thing (or in some regrettable circumstances the person) occasioning disgrace.

Sir Philip Sidney, if mem'ry serves, had a character remark in his *Arcadia* (begun in 1580) that "I should become a plague to my selfe and a shame to womankind." In more common parlance, it is something repugnant, something indecent, possibly in conspicuously *poor taste*, quite possibly a disgrace of extraordinary proportion. If one *takes shame* (we seldom hear that these days) it simply means that he assumes responsibility for it. That's quite all it means, and no more. To be *put to shame* means causing shame to present itself. To be *shame faced* tends to suggest that one feels somehow embarrassed; as one unidentified moralist pronounced it, *past shame, past grace*. Alas, *Proverbs* 3:35 assures us that "the wise inherit honor, but fools he holds up to shame." Even François Rabelais in his *Gargantua and Pantagruel* (1532–62) advises us to "speak the truth and shame the devil."

And to what do fools attribute their shame? To *immodesty*, that's what. Modesty implies moderation, which is to say (among other points) to eschew exaggeration, importunity and excess wherever they may be discovered. Moreover, it discourages one from becoming variously arrogant, overbearing, vociferous and imposing. It implies as well a sense of *sublime decency*, self-effacement, a sense of humility, possibly even chastity and other forms of civil self-control. To be immodest is to forgo all such virtues, or to say it in a different light, it may well turn one in the regrettable directions of pretension, forwardness, and (to reassert our word) *imprudence*. Take it any way you will; it's thoroughly disgusting and therefore best suited to fools, as is the notion of indelicacy, one of the earmarks of foolery.

What, then, is indelicacy? Just this: it is the absence of propriety (which means that one is improper, incorrect, inappropriate) and it means that one in all probability lacks good taste, good social (and otherwise) judgment on a number of fronts. As a result, his manner bespeaks a prevailing crudity, coarseness, offensiveness and perhaps indecency. As Samuel Richardson wrote in his *Pamela, or Virtue Rewarded* (1741), "these, gentlemen, the very best of them, are such indelicates." All such regrettable features bivouac beneath the name and nature of imprudence, a thoroughly imprudent word, and yet one reserved for our references to fools. Imprudence carries a sense of recklessness about it, a tendency toward intolerably regrettable nastiness that encourages foolery, and its habit of botching each opportunity, misreading every situation and seizing every inappropriate course of proceeding. The damage that accrues falls to one's betters to correct and control in unique ways they can best devise. The larger problem with imprudence has been the subject of scholarly investigation by a group calling itself *Summa Theologica* and made generously available through a party known as *New Advent*. It gingerly raises questions that persons gifted with extraordinarily inquiring minds may find intellectually challenging and (in special cases) theologically troubling. Consider, for example, the overwhelming question (since it directly involves fools and their foolery) of whether, and if so, and with what justification, we may (with clear heart and due penitence), address the matter of whether or not imprudence may be regarded as a sin. The answer?

No. We quote: "For every sin is voluntary, according to Augustine (*De Vera Relig.* XIV)"; whereas imprudence is not voluntary, since no man wishes to be imprudent. Therefore imprudence is not a sin." Case settled. Next? Is imprudence a special sin? Answer: No. Next: Whether precipitation is a sin included in imprudence. Answer: No. Imprudence is opposite to the virtue of prudence; whereas precipitation is opposed to the gift of counsel, according to Gregory, who says (*Moral* ii, 49) that the gift of "counsel is given as a remedy to precipitation." Therefore precipitation is not a vice contained under imprudence. That, we presume, puts an end to the discussion and therefore any subsequent comment, unless of course one wishes to address (and we don't advise it) the question of "whether thoughtlessness is a special sin included in prudence." We'll be honest about the matter: we've (in fact) scratched our head for decades (every bit that) and abandoned it, quite frankly, for want of intelligence. Allow the record to show, however, that keener minds than ours have resolved the matter in such a way that it, too, will remain closed to subsequent debate and creative cogitation. Consider: it would seem (mind you, *seem*) that thoughtlessness is not a special sin included in imprudence. Like it or not, the reader is entitled to know about two remaining *issues* (as dunces today generally refer to them) pertaining to prudence or the lack of it, which so bedevils the lives of fools. The first is "whether inconstancy is a vice contained under prudence." This, we submit, is more an organizational query and therefore not in the highest rank of concern. Even so, we shall find a way to dismiss it from further examination. It would *seem* (there's that word again) that inconstancy is by no means a vice to be considered under the general term *imprudence*, but even so, "perseverance in matters belongs to fortitude"; that jolly well puts the matter to rest.

Finally (we are nearing an end) the matter that lastly challenges our capacity for reasoned solutions to metaphysical conundrums is just (and only) this: "whether the aforementioned dunces arise from lust." We were afraid that the matter would somehow demand our opinion, but we privately hoped it would not, and frankly felt ill-prepared to entertain it. But here goes: it would seem (yet again) that the term vexes us because it merely opens more streams of cogitation, capitulation and (quite frankly) consternation that the aforesaid vices do not arise from vice, and we feel an immediate sense of relief to have philosophically traveled this far, namely: we are prepared to say that *envy is not a distinct vice from lust*. As a sort of parting shot, we should suffer the reader one more thought from *Secunda Secundae Partis*, namely, that "carnal vices destroy judgment of reason so much the more as they lead us away from reason."

Our subject, lest it be forgotten, is the existence of fools and their impru-dent behavior that merely contributes to their being all the more foolish, and therefore a problem to themselves and to those of us who, we trust, are in no sense foolish. Accordingly, allow us to direct attention to a particularly illuminating article published in *The Western Criminology Review* (7 [3], 41-55, 2006) the work of Bruce J. Arneklev, Lori Ellis and Sandra Mellicott, entitled "Testing the General Theory of Crime: Comparing the Effects of 'Imprudent Behavior' and an Attitudinal Indicator of 'Low Self-Control." We warn the reader, however, this protracted study hinges precariously upon the slippery term *tautological*, that may cause some readers to pause, if not to seek psy-chiatric assistance. Let us examine the word this way: its *etymological* origin (*etymology* comes essentially from the Latin *ethimolegia*, which is to say the origin of words, with attention to their evolving manifestations and transi-tions) reveals that it means, and perhaps always meant, *taut*, which in turn means to *tangle, tighten*. More specifically, tautology refers to the needless repetition of the same declaration, such as has been readily evidenced in these pages. Example: "*It's visible to the eye.*" It cannot literally be visible to much else, such as *visible to the foot*.

The *WCR* article posits that criminal activity is partly the result of "low self-control [and] self-repeated imprudent behavior (e.g., drinking and gambling)." Moreover, they eventually assert that "the primary difference between imprudent behaviors and analogous (criminal) behaviors is that while the former are not illegal [nor, as we have seen, are they apparently immoral, either] they (apparently) provide immediate benefits amid...distal [remote, distant] (though not illegal) consequences." All of this doesn't have much surprising to say until the authors address *Imprudent Behaviors*. Here they cite their effort to discern the consequences of those behaviors, remind-ing us all the while that those consequences, while not illegal, remain dis-tal and are, notwithstanding, still of some urgent social concern to us each. Specifically, they asked respondents whether they do such foolish things as drink, smoke or "eat things they feel like eating (without being concerned with how consuming them affects their health) or whether they indulge in other imprudent activities such as failing to wear seat belts, [or] gambling" and furthermore "if they had been in an accident or injured themselves so severely in the last year that they had to see a doctor." Such people would in all likelihood live what we would safely call *foolish lives*, meaning in part that they ignore ordinary dangers and behave as if there is *no tomorrow*, which for them may be a glaring reality. Whereas most of the respondents admitted to no criminal behavior, they did concede that they were foolhardy enough to relegate themselves to habits that in all probability would compromise their chances of surviving and prevailing in wholesome, productive and respon-sible lives. In other words, they had succeeded in becoming their own worst adversaries.

More specifically, the authors addressed a table of *Low Self-Control* items that lead to nowhere except toward imprudence that in turn lead to the formation of what we without hesitancy call poor *life choices*, foolish options that ruin lives and compromise the commonweal. Among them is the failure to consider one's future when it compromises one's current pleasure and therefore compromises longer-term goals, if indeed such people have any. Fools tend to view life in the short run rather in the longer run, opting for what brings the greater pleasure today, without thought of tomorrow and its vile prospects. The authors also address what they call *simple tasks component*, which means the avoidance of things perceived to be *difficult*, in favor of something perceived to be easier to accomplish. A risk-taking component involves an unwillingness to assume problems perceived to be *chancy*, in favor of something perceived to be less *risky* and, in the end, less rewarding than something demanding more risks. There is resistance to subjecting oneself to tests that may or may not establish the limits to one's ability to persist and perform, two features that can determine success. There is also a tendency to opt for the physical over the intellectual, meaning that one might prefer to select for what one presumes to the easier of the two, which (oddly enough) they judge to be the physical. The authors also address what they call *Physical Activities*, a consideration that not only tends toward the physical but for what they call being *on the move*, rather than to sit frozen in one place and cogitate. In other words they much prefer being somehow in motion rather than motionlessly engaging in ideas. Such people, the authors determined, have a higher capacity for physical energy than others of their age. There is also what they called *a self-centered* component that means a desire to *look out for myself*, disregarding the problems that this causes others that in turn means a disinclination to be sympathetic to other people's dilemmas and other people's delicate feelings. This means among other things a tendency to reflect only about one's own ends rather than other peoples'. The authors also identify a *temper component*, a tendency to overheat easily and to attack others rather than attempting to resolve differences through a morbidly protracted and *monotonous* discussion.

A similar table divides into such telling and highly significant considerations as the aforementioned smoking, eating, drinking, and gambling, including such items as accidents and the aforementioned controversy over seatbelt use. In a rather Dantesque manner it examines crime participation in the form of such matters as fraud and theft. Turning to *Social Consequences Measures*, it scrutinizes the quality of one's friendships (whatever that may mean), in conjunction with *Life Satisfaction, Marital Status*, educational attainment and income as they pertain to low self-control as a predictor of imprudent behavior commonly observable in idiots. Low self control, the researchers discovered, means fewer *quality friendships* that we assume to mean associations with persons *worth knowing*; less likelihood of marriage;

and less involvement in religious controversies — all which may be assumed more advantageous rather than disadvantageous, in our skeptical opinion. However, they are also apt to have low *educational attainment*, never a good thing. Ironically, however, the authors determined that imprudent behavior "results in higher economic status," simply because "imprudent behavior requires income" to carry it off with any authority.

Hence, the study concludes, a paucity of *self-control* (conceding that the term remains somewhat ill-defined) blurs sociologists' ability to predict outcomes. What is conspicuously absent in all this obfuscation is the role of personal responsibility for selecting and pursuing sensible *life choices*. We are rather led to think that that such people under discussion in the study are somehow inexorably *doomed* not to assume management of their foolish lives and redress them for the good of society. This leads us back to old theories of, and surrounding, *determinism*, meaning that such ridiculous lives described here are governed not by free will but by forces so great as to be irresistible. Assuming that people of sound mind can and must control themselves from within, then their failure to do so consigns them irretrievably to the social gutter. Determinism, to the contrary, posits that a person is at the mercy of heredity and environment, both of them immensely powerful forces over which one cannot prevail because he is at the mercy of circumstances over which he exercises *no control*. We refer to such things as one's innate intelligence, the color of his skin, his gender, his talents (if any), his physical attractiveness (if any), his handicaps and his proclivities toward certain diseases that have been genetically programmed since the moment of conception.

Further to complicate his destiny are environmental circumstances, many of them also well outside his control, others not. Among them: on which side of the railroad tracks one is born; how wealthy or impoverished his family happens to be; how much or how little one is opportunity availed, and where; how much and what quality medical care is available to him; the amount of encouragement and discouragement to which he is exposed; into what social class one is born; what cultural advantages (if any) he has at his disposal; how much or how little good counsel he has available and whether he has duly considered it; and whether he has defiled his body with tattoos, ghastly punctures and other dermatological outrages, grotesque facial hair; what sort and how much spiritual commitment one has, what sort of diet one chooses or can afford; how widely or narrowly traveled one is; how much or how little leverage he is prepared to exercise over his destiny; how well groomed and dressed one wishes to be and can afford to be. In short, thousands of such details unite to form who a person is and what his chances in life may be, even after he's tried (perhaps) to prevail over the hereditary circumstances that were in place before he had a chance to be born—or aborted. It's all up to chance and accident, so compelling theories of determinism insist. We have earlier discussed existential questions that suggest to us that we can introduce meaning into our lives, virtually at will. Does one need to be, or become, a fool?

To be sure, the average bloke, even at Princeton University, recognizes imprudence when he (or in this instance *she*) sees it. Camille Framroze, writing for the April 8, 2009 *Daily Princetonian*, prudently asks, in her article entitled "Imprudent Princetonian Priorities," what an "average healthy adult need[s] to survive." The answer is as simple as it is perfectly obvious: "food, water, shelter and seven to nine hours of sleep." Well and good. She then asks what the average Princetonian requires, but this time the answer is somewhat more complicated, and needlessly so, consisting, as it does, of "one square meal a day, shelter, A's, four to five hours of sleep, significant involvement in three different student groups and water." One might also add that since bicycles are *de rigueur* on American campuses, one must, if he is to conform and survive, learn how to cycle prudently or know how nimbly to dodge those who don't. There was an arresting piece in the July 21, 2009 *Ottawa Citizen* written by Robert Sibley, entitled "The Psychology of Imprudent Cycling" having to do with fools on bicycles. We can just imagine. Whereas in the military, soldiers "keep a good distance apart when on patrol," he writes, would it not be prudent elsewhere to observe that same protocol, such as among ordinary citizens who are advised to ride single file? We'd have to agree that yes, it would, and let it go at that. Moreover, one would do also well, and be on the prudent side, if he would restrain himself from sleeping in rubbish containers. A computer site called *Overlawyered. com* reported that a problem of that pernicious sort developed in Florida. In a May 16, 2007 piece headed "Sleeping in a Dumpster Proves Imprudent," Walter Olson patiently explained that a 44-year-old chap "went to sleep in a trash bin, which was really a bad idea." We might have presumed so. It came to pass that "garbage collectors emptied the container into a truck," with the poor chap pummeled and crushed each time the truck compacted a fresh load of rubbish, thereby breaking his legs and ribs. Olson, a fellow equipped with a legalistic frame of mind, speculated upon whether the victim, should he seek legal representation, could make much of a case in his own defense, inasmuch as sleeping in a dumpster is, after all, an act of trespassing, besides the fact that if one makes a practice of sleeping in heaps of stuff that are intended for the compactor, chances are that sooner or later he's going to be inadvertently compacted.

David Phelps of the *Minneapolis Star Tribune* speculated in his July 5, 2009 article called "Imprudent Posts Online Can Sabotage a Job Search" that the "electronic *faux pas* once considered the legacy of college students and 20-somethings who would post beer-sodden pictures of themselves and friends on *My Space*" was not the most prudent thing to do, in the longer perspective. Nevertheless with the rabid popularity of *Facebook*, *Linked In* and

Twitter, employers are learning that grownups, as Phelps says, "can be just as knuckleheaded as freshly scrubbed college grads when it comes to leaving digital impressions. The result is that prospective employers don't reward imprudent job candidates." He concludes by reminding even those who are, if taken at face value, adults, that "every tweet, every post is being actively indexed by different search engines. It's going to be available in perpetuity."

In a related matter titled "Probe Finds Kozinski's Sexually Explicit Photos Were Judiciously Imprudent," Debra Cassens Weiss, writing for the *ABA Journal* on July 2, 2009, reported that "a federal judicial council had admonished Judge Alex Kozinski for maintaining erotically explicit material on a personal website, concluding with an ethics investigation spurred by a June 2008 *Los Angeles Times* article, noting that the judge's computer contained "a photo of a naked woman on all fours painted [imprudently] to look like a cow[,] and a video of a half dressed man cavorting with a sexually aroused farm animal." The chief presiding judge prudently explained that "at the time he [the defendant, presumably] wasn't aware [that] the website could be [not so prudently] accessed by the public. The panel found all this "judicially imprudent," not to say foolish. The opinion, just as foolish as the incidents upon which it was judging, commented that there had been a not-so-prudent "disregard of serious risk of public embarrassment." The judge again prudently explained this time that "he had downloaded many of the files without viewing them." We understand perfectly. After the "judicial counsel prudently found that the offending material had since been removed and destroyed," everyone felt considerably relieved. "Accordingly," we are apprised, all agreed with the utmost judicial prudence that "this proceeding is properly concluded."

A similar case was cited in *Democratic Underground* on March 20, 2008, by an unidentified scrivener on the subject of *imprudent curiosity*, wherein he asked how anyone could have been dismissed for that supposed infraction, speculating that it applied to such imprudent matters as "illegal wiretapping, spying and all matters of civil rights violations we are increasingly subject[ed] to by this [unidentified] illegitimate, lawless administration." The controversy involved an interrogation wherein someone imprudently submerged a detainee's fool head under water, for the laudable purpose of determining how long he could survive without breathing. The reporter referred to the incident as "just a case of imprudent curiosity." So it was, and was again in an item published by a source ambiguously called *Pink Slip* that brought to our attention the plight of an "imprudent employee" who managed to lose $1.4 billion on the Asian futures markets, a mere imprudent procedural accident exceeded only by another lad who lost the bank he represented $7.18 billion by imprudently "placing bad bets." According to a report carried in the *Malaysia Star*, the fellow's motives were, to say the least, *totally irrational* and just a bit *imprudent*. It was uncertain, said *Pink*

Slip's January 25, 2008 article, whether the fellow "wanted to continue with a career in banking or seek fame and fortune elsewhere."

An unsigned article in the October 15, 2007 *American Papist* called "JP2's [John Paul II's] Flair for the Dramatic and Imprudent Vatican TV" has to do, oddly enough, with the late pontiff's somewhat unlikely reappearance in an imprudent majestic ball of ecclesiastical fire. The Vatican TV director claimed that he [His Holiness] had indeed, and that it occurred near the pope's birthplace in Katowice in the northern part of that country on (as it happened) the second anniversary of his death. A chap who took photographs of the miraculous occurrence said (in Polish), "It was only afterwards when I got home and looked at the pictures that I realized that I had something." He ran the photography past this brother and sister, and after that his bishop, who supposedly pronounced with holy certainty that "Pope John Paul had made many pilgrimages during his life, and he was still making them in death." But the supposed reappearance of the pope was, still, as they say, open to question, and opinion remained anything but unanimous. One priest opined that the photo merely encouraged what he called *pseudo-mysticism*, and that, yes, it was imprudently "based on nothing more than emotional spiritualism."

In other theologically imprudent news another holy quarrel broke out, this one reported as "Psychotic Imprudent Ignorant Presumptions" in the February 5, 2007 copy of a lesser known and possibly seldom perused publication called *Ex Pente Costal Thoughts*, composed by an imprudent fellow identifying himself as *Lutherius*, whose passion it was to rescue victims of Pentecostal teachings and thereby set them free. "It usually takes from 7-10 years to recover from the bad effects of extremely emotional religion," Lutherius explained. More specifically, he found extreme fault with "Pentecostal preachers [who] assert things with authority where they have total ignorance on the subject." He cites as an example of this nefarious carrying-on his having heard "several preachers say that the wine Jesus offered during the Last Supper was really grape juice," and accordingly they "use this [grape juice?] to justify their ban on drinking, and [then] have the pure ignorance to say that the Bible is against drinking." We begin now to comprehend the full thrust of his learned argument, to which he rightly adds by way of footnote that "just because some preacher has some history of 'white trash' in his family...this gives him justification to lie that the Bible prohibits the use of alcohol in any way." Points well taken, we feel compelled to say. Lutherius further suggested that "speaking in tongues is the initial evidence of receiving the Holy Spirit, because the Bible never says so." This is manifestly obvious to us all, and, by Jove, we could hardly agree more. He continues, ever more dangerously, to assert that one miscreant had the gall to attack something called *Spongebob Squarepants*, astutely arguing that "sponges are asexual animals, [and] were enlightened to promote homosexuality." Those who assert such nonsense, he contends, are "a bunch of ignorant jerks for preachers trying to shock their audiences with strange assertions with no evidence," another point, if we may say so, well raised. Lutherius then complains that "when they have to yell and scream to keep your attention, you know that your preacher is too ignorant to come up with an interesting sermon—usually because he's never gone to a seminary!" Bravo! As to Lutherius, he kindly lets us know that he is (to no one's surprise) "now a Lutheran."

We all understand that imprudence, manifested in the form of foolish thoughts and foolish acts, can be the result of our exposure to stupidity and foolery, against which we are at times inadequately fortified to defend ourselves. Determinism, recall, is the notion that human behavior is anything but free and, to the contrary, is the product of our heredity and environment, two forces that hold us inexorably in defenseless bondage. One might consider, to the contrary, that one's will can be deployed in the service of existentially overhauling our lives, on demand. Were it any other way, one's existence is entirely predetermined, leaving an individual to do what little he can with what little he's got, or (as it were) with how much he's got and how well he can harness and deploy it to appreciable advantage. *The Stanford Encyclopedia of Philosophy*, referring to *causal determinism*, characterizes it as "the idea that every event is necessitated by antecedent events and conditions together with the laws of nature," cautioning too that "there is no agreement over whether determinism is true (or even if it can be known true or false) and what the import for human agency would be in either case." Determinism, if such there be, is so monstrously influential that it precludes what some call *free entry*, or what others call *free will* which means the option of one's exercising his will, his own choice, and therefore permitting himself to be driven from within instead of from without. This raises the moldy question of whether humans are free in the first place or whether they have rather few choices and options, if any. Exercising free will means taking charge of one's life. One might ask himself if he is reading this book as an act of free will or whether someone or something (we can't imagine what) has compelled him to it.

Fools have no notion of what determinism is, but they nevertheless embrace it, assuming that life has handed them only so much, and there's nothing that can be done to redress it. Fate has left his mark, and there is no object in fighting back. To be a fool means in part that one has given up controlling his life because he has no education, no influence, no money, no job, no income, no luck, no future—to all of which for most people most of the time there can be no remedy. They can acquire a real education, but fools are not interested in learning, nor committed to it, nor ambitious enough to pursue it with the necessary alacrity to succeed at it. Certain young people at about the ideal age of 18 begin a bachelor's degree at a decent university, and begin to study such things as the so-called *arts* and the *sciences*, all the while enrolling in such nonsense as *education* courses that are intended for school-teachers who are not much interested in learning anything, including how to teach nonsense to children. Such people leave universities with a mind duller than the one they had upon entering.

Money is out there if one pursues it with sufficient determination in concert with adequate preparation. Wealth can be acquired in legitimate ways. Wealthy people save and invest. Fools get and spend. To earn the most, one combines what he likes to do with what he's paid to do. Robert Frost (1874–1963) said in best in his "Two Tramps in Mud Time":

> But yield who will to their separation,
> My object in living is to unite
> My avocation and my vocation
> As two eyes make one in sight.
> Only when love and need are one
> And the work is play for mortal stakes,
> Is the deed ever really done
> For Heaven and the future's sakes.

The essential message is *existential*, in that one must decide upon a purpose, a calling of the sort that he can do for pay what he would have done *for no pay*. The term *avocation* signifies something diversionary, something that calls a person away from his usual work obligations (assuming that he has any) toward something he would far rather be doing. This stands in contrast to one's vocation, something that some fools don't happen to possess. It is his primary calling, his bread and butter, such as fixing cars or pouring cement or digging graves. All of these fulfill needs, but they may or may not satisfy his existential yearning. Granted, it is far better to perform something useful, something utilitarian, than to do nothing except be a fool and a good-for-nothing. To do something useful presumes that one possesses certain skills, such as how to dig holes with a shovel, along with the willingness to do it. *Voc*, after all, is an abbreviation of *voce*, meaning *vote*, a vocal command, but to do what? To *stand and deliver*, something that many of our fools are quite unable to accomplish. Fate and determinism be damned, it is a sense of achievement that dangles precariously in the balance. People of accomplishment continue accomplishing despite armies of detractors, most of them fools, who preach and warn of failure, the main feature of fools' lives. In its Latin origin (*fatum*) fate means something like *that which has been spoken*, a doleful sentence sent from *on high*, but portending nothing very good. In its Greek original its meaning tends more to suggest a person's *lot* in life. *Lot* carries lots of meanings, among them a games of chance as in *Lotto* and *lottery*, a quantity of wood or almost anything else, a chore (as in a position in life, expressed as *his lot*), something given to a person by Destiny (divine providence, luck, fortune), a division of a whole, a piece of land, for instance, possibly a gambling loss sometimes referred to as a *bad lot*.

Hence *fate* is often used to describe a person's *situation* in life, his state of affairs as measured any number of ways, among them financially, spiritually, vocationally, avocationally and so forth. Historically, people have viewed fate as something (for better or worse) that has been handed, awarded, gifted by the gods, presumably for having pleased (or in some cases displeased) one of their number. Often enough it is a sentence of doom. In mythology, *fate* refers more generally to destiny, in the sense of something destined to happen, be it to whole civilizations or to a single person. Destiny, so far as it can be determined, has come to mean something *unalterably predetermined*. Mythic characters such as Oedipus, in the Greek drama, can do nothing to thwart destiny, and are left to witness its horridly inexorable unfolding. The Greeks envisioned three allegoric figures classified as Fates, those being Clotho, Lachesis and Atrophos, whose assignment it was to spin the thread of human destiny. They were also furnished with shears with which they might, with a deft snip or two, trim destiny at their inscrutable discretion.

The farmer and poet Hesiod, best identified by his *Works and Days*, claims that they were daughters of Night. Fate is elsewhere presented to us as a single allegorical figure. Shakespeare deferentially refers to the goddess Fate in *The Tempest* ("stand fast good Fate to his hanging") and John Milton cites it as well in *Paradise Lost*, saying things like "when everlasting Fate shall yield to fickle Chance." Fate has been credited with predetermining events, and has as well been a word used to describe someone's or something's disappointing end or dismally final result, as in *his fate*, or *its fate*, and so forth, that quite often is catastrophic, as in the common expressions *seal one's fate*, a *fate worse than death* or to *decide one's fate*. But if indeed Fate is predestined, it portends the worst, such as ruin, destruction, annihilation, and other such abysmally awful things. Palm readers have long purported to foretell one's fate by searching the face of his hand; crystal ball scrutinizers have purported to do essentially the same thing by gazing into a mystic globe, since Fate, they apparently presume, guides and controls mortals toward momentous and inevitable destruction.

Fools have traditionally bought into the principle that they are in the hands of forces who, or that, exert total dominion over them, and therefore assume that good fortune, in the form of Luck or Chance, may or may never come to them. Moreover, they tend to regard successful people as being merely *lucky*, the recipients of a benevolent, if fickle, presence represented in mythology as a maddeningly moody woman deservedly named Fortune, the personification of good luck and all such bonanzas, a force that brings happiness and good times, wealth, and all manner of niceties, but does so depending substantially upon how she happens to be disposed at a certain time. Her nicely appropriate avatar is the wheel, a roulette wheel, and a wheel of

Fortune. By *avatar*, we mean not so much as a human-appearing incarnation of an idea or deity, but as a display of her symbol, her manifestation. Fortune distributes life's lots as may befit her mood, the politically unfashionable explanation being that she (being a woman) is therefore subject to alterations of mind. Shakespeare (once more) was aware of this and alluded to it in *Henry VI*, saying that "Fortune's malice overthrows my state," etcetera. Loosely speaking, Fortune involves chance, happenstance and accident such as may befall anyone at anytime. However, it frequently involves wealth or the lack of it, by her allotting and thereby controlling its distribution.

Boethius (c. 480–524) in his *Consolatio Philosophiae* (*Consolation of Philosophy*) composed in prison where he was confined on trumped-up charges, accords Fortune the same treatment, complaining that "with success false Fortune favored me/ One hour of sadness could not have thrown me down, / But now her trustless countenance has clouded, / Small welcome to the days that lengthen life. / Foolish the friends who called me happy then." Dante cordially invited Fortune to make a cameo appearance in Canto VII of his *Inferno*, the first of three sections in his Divine (as we now call it) *Comedy*. Dante, recall, is a character in his own drama of salvation, guided most of the way by the elegant Roman poet Virgil, author of the *Aeneid*. Here, Virgil explains to his ward (in the Musa translation), "your knowledge has no influences on her," since she has a mind (unpredictable though it is) and will of her own. Virgil continues, "She provides for change, she judges and she rules/ Her domain as do the other gods their own. / Her changing changes never take a rest," as if to say that she may just as well be changing her clothes as changing her mind. "Necessity keeps her in constant motion," similar to a gaming wheel, "as men come and to take their turn with her" as if to consort with a prostitute. Dante continues, "and this is she who is so crucified and cursed; even those in luck who should be praising her, revile her and condemn her acts." *Conventional wisdom*, as some call it, has always carried a burden of suspicion toward Fortune, but others know better. The Romans had a number of good things to say about her, perhaps because they, at least for the nonce, surmised themselves fortunate.

Who, we ask, had a better grip on the maxim than our noble Roman forebears? Some of their better known utterances bearing upon wealth are inclined to favor Dame Fortune, to wit: "*Fortuna favet fortibras* (fortune favors the brave) and similarly, *fortes fortuna ic vat* (fortune helps the brave)—presumably to grow braver. There is also *audaces fortuna iluvat* (fortune favors the bold) and the more neutral *fortuna caeca ese* (fortune is blind) and by all means *fortuna amicos parat; in opia amitos probat* (fortune prepares friends; abundance teststhem), or our sentimental favorite, *vitrea est; turm cum splendet frangitur vitrea est; turn cum splendet frangitur* (fortune is glass; just when it glistens, it shatters). Yes. Fortune has been a favored topic among other maxim makers, one of whose more challenging opinions is that she does indeed favor fools, something that, at first glance, seems exceedingly doubt-ful. Fortuna *favet fatuive* is one early expression of that persuasion. Compare the Latin *fatuus* with the English *fatuous*, the meaning of which is *foolish*, inane, absurdly silly and besotted, the last of which means infatuated, stupefied, intoxicated by some vile person or substance, resulting in mental or even moral idiocy. Milton, in his *Comus*, a masque (religious theatrical entertainment) aptly illustrated in 1634, citing a "swinish gluttony, with besotted base ingratitude."

That said, there are predictably different versions of the *Fortuna flavet fatuous*, among them that *Fortune can exalt fools*, meaning that fortune can elevate, glorify and elate idiots, which must surely be some ironic jape. Another version tells us that *Fortune favours Fooles as old men say*, which may be taken ambiguously to suggest that since the men are old, then they must know more, or perhaps that the only people who believe this are fatuous old men. Still others say, "because Fortune favors few fooles this yeare, wee must tarry longer to play our game," suggesting that we must not leave life's gaming table prematurely. Sir Thomas Browne noted in his orthodox *Christian Religio Medici* (1643) "that contemptible Proverb, that fools only are fortunate," something he found absurd. To the contrary, if Fortune is partial to anyone, she is hardly a fool. We have noted that she favors those who earn their way, such as the bold, and those who stay the course while threatened by obstacles, and who pursue fortune and other forms of reward. Chaucer's friend John Gower enthusiastically reported that "Fortune unto the bold is favorable to helpe," which makes more sense. The English printer and editor William Caxton speculated that fortune comes to those who are *hardy*, which is to say able to take the bad times with the good, as did biblical translator Richard Taverner who wrote on or about 1552 that "Fortune helpeth men of good courage." Whereas Fortune may not favor fools, others have depicted her as altogether blind and consequently unprepared to identify those to whom her favors flow. We find that sentiment in Greene's pastoral romance *Pandosto* (1558) where he recorded that "Fortune although blind... sent them...a good gale of wind." Shakespeare too in his *Merchant of Venice* said interestingly that "so may I, blind fortune leading me, miss that which one unworthier may attain," and again in *Henry V*: "Fortune is painted [b]lind with a muffler." So too did Ben Jonson the poet and dramatist record in his *Poetaster* (1601) that "all human business doth command without all order; and with her blind hand she, blind, bestows blind gifts."

Every fool may have his fling with Fortune, although he will in all likelihood thwart the opportunity, for it is *received opinion* that "fortune knocks once at least at every man's gate." All but forgotten Elijah Fenton, himself one of Fortune's favorites, who tried his luck at being someone's secretary, at teaching school and finally as a steward, dwelled in England's literary shadows, but is nonetheless alleged to have said that "fortune once in the corner of our life dothe put unto our handes the offer of a good turne." Espousing a somewhat different point of view is the conviction that Fortune is *variant*, meaning simply that she varies, which is obvious enough. Gower observed that she "hath ever been may-be and may-not." Alexander Barclay's version of the *Ship of Fools* (about which we will have some subsequent observations), asserts, "Fortune euer hath an incertayne end." Some, as other quipsters have observed, don't so much as open a door when Fortune calls. Thomas Skel-eton's *Don Quixote* (1605, 1615) contains a cautionary passages that reads, "it is not fit that whilst good luck is knocking at our door we shut it." So too a message from an unidentified author astutely advises that when "fortune smiles on thee, take the advantage," something that fools are less likely to do. There are a great many morsels of advice on fortune, among them, that "man is the architect of his own fortune," which is to say that one makes his own luck, and (among American proverbs) the belief that "a change of fortune hurts a wise man no more than the change of the moon," as well as the some-what contrarian opinion that "a great fortune is slavery," along with the wry counsel that "better a fortune in a wife than with a wife," which asserts that a man will do better to marry a fortune than to bring a fortune to a marriage, for to do the latter will pour fortune into a funnel.

More usual is the advice that Fortune comes to him (but not to her) who seeks it, and that rather than seeing it at the end of a rainbow (as roman-tics envision it) Fortune lurks behind some obstacle, and that she assists the person who strikes out in search of it—or her. Such a person endorses the usual bromides about fortune; among them that it is far easier to lose than to acquire, usually expressed as "fortune is more easily gotten than kept," and all such. One of the lesser heard mottos is "Fortune is like price; if you can wait long enough, the price will fall," and "Fortune is not often on the side of the fainthearted." As to the fools who have nonetheless managed to raise a fortune comes the admonition, "Fortune is the good man's prize but the bad man's bane," facilely assuming that a *good* man is wise, a *bad* man foolish. Equally moralistic (and what people enjoy hearing) is the assumption that "Fortune is the companion of virtue," earnestly recommending that persis-tence and patience are among life's virtues that will in the end yield gener-ous rewards. Paradoxically, there are those who actively avoid Fortune for reasons only they can explain, except to say that they may feel neither equal to, nor deserving of, it.

If all else fails to make sense, one can always claim that "Fortune knows neither reason nor law," which in summary tells us that good things come to us altogether at random. It would be far more accurate to say that fortune and luck happen, to put it allegorically, when Preparation meets Opportunity. Then do good things *occur*, and not accidentally. One then has more than the impression that luck, chance and fortuity are anything but random. When Fortune presents herself, popular opinion is pleasantly surprised, if mystified. Another piece of counsel advises that "when Fortune smiles, embrace her," something that possibly a few fools might also do out of gratitude and relief, and yet (irony of ironies) most fools seem to turn their backs to Fortune and her companion Opportunity, rather than following the careworn advice that "when Fortune Smiles, take advantage," something that most of us would be quick to do, mindful that (to put it more existentially) "every man is the architect of his own fortune."

The adage "Fortune is the companion of Virtue" carries more than a little veracity with it, asserting that the virtuous should be the most likely recipients of Fortune. Virtue, after all, at least implies a person of higher mindedness, so much so that it may ally itself with the divine and the supernatural, suggesting a sense of celestial comprehension well beyond the mundanity of ordinary life. In a lesser sense, a virtuous person may be assumed to have acted within elevated levels of morality and rectitude. Do fools embrace virtue? Hardly, given that it addresses the highest standards of moral excellence. Virtue comes to us, like Fortune, as an allegorical presence in feminine form. The expression *woman of easy virtue*, as we all know, refers to a person of compromised standards, if any standards at all. Among men, virtue may take the form of the gentleman, by tradition identified with valor, grace, courage, commodiousness, accomplishment and such like, none of them identified with fools to whom the expression *gentleman, principled, honorable* and so forth, mean nothing. The classical gentleman observed the marks of gallant conduct including stringent morality and the principle rendered in Latin as *ipsa quidem pretium virtus sibi* (virtue is its own reward), a maxim attributed to the fourth century Roman poet Claudian, and reiterated by Thomas Browne. Others, to be sure, have endorsed the idea of virtue's reward, variously "virtue is the only true nobility" (possibly so), or "Virtue is a jewel of great price," maybe "virtue never grows old," and predictably "there is no virtue that poverty destroyeth not," meaning, we take it, that poverty has such potency that it can destroy righteousness.

Any examination of virtue is pointless without a closer look at vice and its relation to foolishness. The OED primarily refers to vice as a "depravity or corruption of morals; evil, immoral or wicked habits of conduct; indulgence in degrading pleasures or practices," which is as ideal a place as any to enter the wonderful world of depravity. Horsemen call an animal's bad behavior a *vice*, although that may strike us as inappropriate. As with the allegorical qualities of Virtue, Fortune, Goodness, Chastity and such, Vice too finds an allegorical home as a person who prances about with that regrettable name and nature, meaning as it does some unfortunately flawed aspect of a person's identity. The name is also applied, as the OED reminds us, to a blemish or other physical defect, including deformity and weakness. This was especially so in human history when mental and emotional handicaps were emblematic of evil, and consequently punished. Vice has also been deployed to include what's been called a *spoiled* or a *vitiated condition*, refer-ring to something impaired, ruined. To *vitiate* means to corrupt morals, pro-mote low moral standards, ruin (as a verb) by rendering impure, to render something inconclusive, unsatisfactory, incomplete, imperfect, and so like. *Vitiate* therefore feeds into, and thereby contributes to, vice which is usu-ally associated with imperfection. Accordingly, a *vice ring* is a posse involved in criminal activity in such things as illegal gaming, importuning and other such activities. A *vice squad*, as any fool knows, addresses such things as vice rings, with a mind to neutralizing mischief.

Vices are not clear cut; their list depends upon one's point of view, including such as perhaps smoking, drinking, wagering, attending theaters and movie houses, reading books unapproved by one's betters, overeating, viewing television and anything else that may be considered decidedly not in one's highest *interest*, as if it requires an outside authority to resolve such things. Such may be regarded as vices to some. Other people's vices, of course, apply to others. Many of our friends and chance acquaintances remain quite absorbed in them. Yet it is as indefensible as it is alluring. Pope's *Essay on Man* (1733) is not an essay as we know it, but a long discursive poem in four epistles (letters) the likes of which modern people rarely peruse. In the second epistle he writes, "Vice is a master of so frightful mein [demeanor, aspect, appearance], / As to be hated need but to be seen;/ Yet seen too oft, familiar with her face,/ We first endure, then pity, then embrace." Such are the enticements of Vice, here represented by a woman too seductive to be ignored. Pope's saying that (in spite of her frightful appearance) she still demands to be seen, reminds us of Milton's *Areopagitica* (1644), an eloquent oration elegantly defending freedom of expression. One of its often cited pas-sages reads, "I cannot praise a fugitive and cloistered virtue, unexercised and unbreath'd, that never sallies out and sees her adversary, but slinks out of the race where that immortal garland is to be run for, not without dust and heat. Assuredly we bring not innocence into the world, we bring impurity much rather, that which purifies is trial, and trial is by what is contrary," suggesting that no one may claim to be free of vice until he has indulged in it, and then (if he can find it in himself to do so) turned away from it. The passage from the *Essay on Man*, to the contrary, suggests that to taste evil is to be enthralled by it, and thereby enslaved by it. As the supposed fool Feste says in *The Twelfth Night*, "I hate ingratitude more in a man/ Than lying vain-ness, babbling drunkenness/ Or any tainte of vice whose strong corruption/ Inhabits our frail blood."

Of course, vice is not exclusively a fool's defect, nor is it his only defect, wanting, as he is, evidence of having been tutored, instructed and educated, itself a term understood to mean a person who has been schooled long enough to appear civilized, instructed how to think clearly and having been gener-ously introduced to the more significant and challenging regions of study, encouraged to develop intellectual skills such as the ability to read, write, and jiggle numbers. Such a person, one might assume, holds some respect for the mind and its infinite possibilities. Intellectuals ought surely to know how to marshal evidence to support an argument, a contention, a theory, and so such. They are to be considered among the aforementioned *reading class*, the requisites for which are to read with comprehension in more than one language, and possess some understanding of the world's great books bearing the world's great ideas. It has been suggested above that the definition of an intellectual is one who cannot read a book without a pencil in his hand, the idea being that the discriminating reader cannot but participate in the reading experience without elaborating, quarreling, expanding, elucidating in some cases and deleting sections of what he's read. Such a person is likely to be a *professional reader*, one who does more than read; he participates. Such habits of mind are likely, but not necessarily, to rescue him from the terrors of foolishness and prepare him to meet life better and more effectively through the informed ability to reason, compose and speak as may be necessary for citizenship in a civilized world, if such can be found. All persons are, in the end, self-educated and self-regulated. Albert Camus observed that the intellectual is one whose mind watches itself. George Macaulay Trevelyan who is today identified with his *History of England (1826) as well as his British History in the Nineteenth Century* (1922) held that "disinterested curiosity is the life-blood of real civilization, *disinterested*, meaning not *uninterested*, but rather *impartial*, unbiased, unprejudiced and so like. Without such intellectual advantages, in Shakespeare's words (from *Love's Labors Lost*) one "hath never fed of the dainties that are bred in a book; he hath not eat paper, as it were, he hath not drunk ink." One might add as well that (in the words of someone whose identity goes unrecorded), such a person has not, as we say, *bathed in the waters of philosophy*. Samuel Johnson, long bathed in those scintillating currents, remarked that the intellectual is one whose mind is continuously searching. "Curiosity," he wrote in *The Rambler* (1750–1752), "is one of the permanent and certain characteristics of a vigorous intellect."

The learned person is a delight to civilized life, and of course a threat to anti-intellectuals who are woven tightly into the fabric of common, street-fool culture that harbors a paranoid suspicion toward citizens with advanced learning, of whom a goodly number are fools who have received what they know from universities and sermons. Others have profited far more from their private inquiries, their immense curiosities, and their ceaseless quests of erudition, the significance of which deserves, nay demands, some attention. An erudite person is generously read in fields that arrest his attention, which is to say those that capture his mind. He is his own man who has directed his life to the disciplined, scholarly approaches life and its passions.

The road out of foolishness, if such there is, comes well paved with a rigorous and sustained program of learning shepherded by those who are qualified to direct it. Of course most fools are hardly in a position to learn anything, owing to a variety of circumstances which may preclude anything of the sort. One may be emotionally unequipped, whereupon the possibilities of education end then and there. One may be intellectually unprepared, but that remains an uncertainty until one places himself behind the ponderous wheel of education and prepares to lean his shoulder to it. That can be intensely rigorous, as well it should be, so much so that certain people may be unwilling or unable to carry education very far. Many people have not the financial resources to pursue it, although history shows us that most students are financially handicapped most of the time, since university studies are themselves a full time occupation that pays nothing now, and does so, if ever, in the dim future and in uncertain amounts. Government distributions, in the meantime, foster the impressions that, if education is free (let us suppose), it must not be worth anything. If it is not worth anything, then it is hardly worth pursuing. That is the position taken by armies of would-be college students who take their limited (if any) university days so lightly that they squander them on Greek letter secret societies and all such rubbish instead of devoting themselves to vital intellectual tasks. The financial return that education brings is somewhat beside the point (although it can be reassuring when one's debt rises). Education's true dividend arrives when a raw university recruit (let's call him) mutates into a relatively enlightened individual of some remote use to himself and society, rather than becoming (or continuing to be) a common dunce.

Ironically, learning comes at a cost in things other than dollars. It demands time, of course, but the time is profitably spent. It also means that, as a person of some learning, the university graduate will find himself (and to his profound surprise) variously marginalized, excluded, passed over and overlooked. This is the result of being better educated than most of the population and therefore acrimoniously distanced from it. Being better educated than most comes with certain social consequences that are, if one considers it, a small (and often amusing) cost that attends not being a fool nor consorting with one. But learning is always its own reward, although it tends to drive one (or be driven) outside the common herd and into a life of extraordinary independence, if it comes to that, as it should. The 18th century literary pundit known to us only by the pseudonym *Junius* wrote, "learned...you are, and quick in apprehension," a splendid complement to advance and to hear. It is eventually possible, if one feels the irresistible need to join whatever he may be inclined to join, or invited to join, a so-called *learned society*, if one takes that to mean what it says. Ordinarily it is a somewhat eccentric colony of scholars who, through their arcane passions, derive comfort in others sharing at the same time bizarre (but not necessarily insignificant) exercises of intellect and its related inclinations. There is little harm, if any, in doing so; and in some odd way, they make life on this planet a little better for most of us who celebrate the life of the mind and who are covertly troubled by the morons in our midst.

There has always been some lingering suggestion that knowing (as they say) *too much* leads one inexorably down the dreary road toward misery and damnation. Conversely, as has been intimated earlier, there is some suggestion that to remain ignorant is, paradoxically, the wiser way. That interesting dilemma is first introduced and best illustrated in *Genesis*, where a number of highly engrossing things transpire in a relatively brief narrative, among them a parade of circumstances with which we are all dismally familiar. The sequence begins in *Genesis* 2:5 when (again, in the *New English Bible*) the Lord, having created Adam "from the dust of the ground," breathes life into the first of the miserable human race and then (as we all know) places him in "a garden in Eden away to the east," in the middle of the world's first orchard where he also placed the Tree of Life (most significantly for our inquiry) also known as *the tree of the knowledge of good and evil*, whereupon he advises Adam that he is quite free to "eat from every tree in the garden" with the notable exception of one, that being (of course!) the tree of the knowledge of good and evil. Here, if we may mimic the language of the Bible, *beginneth the first bold gesture of anti-intellectualism on the face of the globe.* One message (and justification) is this: if you know too much, it will destroy you, symbolically rendered as "on the day that you eat from it, you will certainly die." It may not be altogether quite that dire, but as *Genesis* goes on to say, there are penalties for being too damned curious for your own good. Example: there will henceforth be what today we know as *the battle of the sexes*, which means (as millions of years have amply taught us), that men and women do not get along harmoniously most of the time, even though God himself has previously opined that *it is not good for man to be alone*, which, as George Gershwin reminds us in *Porgy and Bess* (1935) is one of those things that you're liable to read in the Bible that ain't necessarily so. In any event, Eve's munching on the fruit of the knowledge of good and evil, has, among other awful things, "put enmity between you [Adam, God help him] and the woman." But that, as we also know, was merely the inauspicious beginning of misogamy. Other notable (perhaps inevitable) problems: that women will suffer the agony of childbirth; that they will be *eager* for their husbands (whatever that may tell us), and that their husbands shall be their masters, a penalty that rubs some people the wrong way. It gets worse. "With labor you shall win your food," hence the obligation to toil for one's bread and beer all the days of one's life, or until some corrupt government awards him with a welfare check.

"The Serpent," whom we take to be the Devil, drops it in Eve's ear (she being the world's first wife) that it's perfectly acceptable to nosh from that tree, and that, moreover, it won't kill her, and that (here's where the trouble really begins) her eyes will be opened and she will be *like the gods* (but what gods are these?) in the knowledge of good and evil. Is there a problem here? Yes. Eve understands that if she knows too much, the aforementioned *eternal curse* will be set in motion and, among other things, that the human race will labor to sustain itself from this point forward. Ergo, if you know too much, you're in competition with the gods (whoever they may be), and that's not a good idea. In Milton's 17th century England, girls were usually not schooled beyond the age of nine. The essential point here is that if you want to glide blissfully through life with relative ease, by of all means remain stupid. Become a fool, if that's what it takes. Do not lust after knowledge, do not enroll in a university, do not crack a book, peruse papers or listen to scholars. In a word: *remain dumb and barefoot*. Here begins the great anti-intellectual tradition and the mythic origin of fools in such arresting forms as idiots, blockheads, morons and all such riffraff. In the meantime, the Lord says (in so many words), *you've had it*. He then casts Adam and Eve out of Paradise. It's a sad story, we'd all agree, but in a mythic sense it explains quite a few things, chief among them the misery that life is, and why in the Middle Ages the prevailing opinion was its being a *veil of tears*, far more to be suffered than savored. As some nitwits, with a certain astuteness, say, the human race has become *sadder but wiser*. They're sadder because they know too much, and what they know isn't pretty.

Learned people, when appropriate, are referred to rather cynically as the *literati*, because they have patiently devoured shelves of *good* books, remembered every syllable and are consequently laden with knowledge. It then remains to be seen what, if anything, they do with it. Being among the *literati* assumes that one is safely above foolishness, but one cannot be certain, since some of them verge on it at times. One may hide in books, of course, because he's unable to confront *reality*, however that is to be construed. It is a curious experience to encounter a person who has become (as it were) *lost in literature*, for all that may imply, and thereby qualify as part of the esteemed aforementioned *reading class*, which means what it says: a class of people who read serious books, take them seriously and are prepared to comment astutely on their contents. Not just any book, mind you, but the more learned, more sophisticated, more challenging ones that, more than attracting the literati, also attract those we call (and not without a dollop of cynicism) the *intelligentsia*. It is difficult at times to ascertain quite how intelligent the supposed intelligentsia is, knowing as we do that their number includes imposters, posturers and outright idiots. We are informed, by the way, that the word *intelligentsia* comes benevolently to us by way of pre-Revolutionary Russia where it was applied (appropriately or not) to persons of advanced intellect coupled with bodacious book learning. The playwright Anton Pavlovich Chekhov amused himself by cynically depicting such people, all the while finding them innocuous and tendentious,s in, for example, *The Cherry Orchard*, composed in his final year. The English novelist Aldous Huxley referred in a letter to resident English smarties in Florence as a "queer collection: a sort of decayed provincial intelligentsia." Nikolai Berdyaev, the Christian existentialist and Russian exile, wrote that "life is moving toward utopias [something that may offer comfort]. But perhaps a new age is opening up before us [we earnestly do hope so] in which the intelligentsia and the cultured classes will dream of ways to avoid utopias [what!] and to return to a non utopian society, to a less 'perfect,' freer society."

Possibly so, but the term *learned*, which of necessity we would have to identify with the intelligentsia, has been applied to animals trained to perform what appear to be intellectual feats such as comprehending incomprehensible manuals that come boxed with electronic gadgets. A true learned person, however, is he who has acquired his learning through decades of diligent application, although to anti-intellectuals he may be a fool. Learned people, at least those of the correct gender, have been rightly called *men of learning*, suggesting that the depth of the inquiries into the arcane have on occasion been received by common people (none of them fools, of course) as rightly remarkable and praiseworthy. Learned people have intellectually lit the way for other intelligent, if less erudite, citizens through their sometimes unusual revelations about all conceivable phases of civilized life. Dryden used the word in an ingeniously poetic context in his *Essay of Dramatic Poetry*, referring eloquently to Shakespeare, saying, "those who accuse him to having wanted [needed] learning, give him the greater condemnation: he was naturally learned [which today means *innocent of libraries*]; he needed not the spectacles of books to read nature; he looked inwards and found her there. I cannot say he is everywhere alike; were he so, I should do him injury to compare him with the greatest of mankind." Hence, Shakespeare, a man without a library card, became a natural genius so intensely accomplished that he needed only to search his soul for the form and substance of his unparalleled mastery of our language that today is habitually under siege by dunces whose stake in life is to sully and defame it.

Speaking of belittlement, the reader's attention is respectfully directed at lines 612–618 of Pope's *Essay on Criticism* where the poet, consumed by anger at the reckless ways of modern literary critics, unloads his acrimony to say:

> The Bookful Blockhead, ignorantly read,
> With Loads of Learned Lumber in his Head,
> With his own tongue still edifies his Ears,
> And always List'ning to Himself appears.
> All books he reads, and all reads assails,
> From Dryden's Fables down to Durfey's Tales.

These uproarious lines place us immediately in mind of Joseph Trapp, not the sort of name or personality that would, even in a fool's parlance, *ring a bell*, or to be quite honest, ring anyone's bell. Be it understood, however, that Joseph Trapp was a high church man who warned us long ago that "the nature, folly, sin and danger of being righteous over-much" would inexorably lead us all down a disastrously hypocritical road from which we might never retrace our foolishly arrogant steps. Trapp, introduced earlier as Oxford's first professor of poetry, composed verses in both English and Latin, although, to be quite honest, he (like everyone else) had his detractors, among them Jonathan Swift. Trapp colorfully deployed the designation *learned* during an interesting exchange of correspondence with George I, who had the colossal audacity (effrontery, impudence, insolence) to solicit a donation from Trapp's extensive library. Consider it: a man's *library*. What has a man to show for himself but a library? His dog? His footman? Trapp, we can assure you, was hardly a garden variety bloody fool. This, of far more than commonplace interest, was Trapp's eloquent response captured, stripped and shackled in iambic pentameters:

> The king, observing with judicious eyes,
> The state of both his universities,
> To Oxford sent a troup of horse, and why?
> That learned body wanted loyalty;
> To Cambridge books, as very well discerning
> How much that loyal body wanted learning.

Some elucidation is here necessary, and we will attempt in some modest way to comply. First, *effrontery*. What does it say except what it says? It says something close to *unblushing, shameless* and (in its original sense) jutting one's forehead in an arrogant sort of way. It means approaching someone in an *insolent* manner. Insolent? It has to do with certain haughtiness, arrogance, contempt, overbearing indifference for the feelings of others. It's a perfectly awful word that exactly applies to some of the fools it is our extreme displeasure to encounter, often in the disgusting form of gatekeepers whom we have earlier examined with a certain insolence of our own. Even so. Impudence is another such unpleasant expression, this one inferring a person's crudeness, his shameful immodesty, disrespect and errant effrontery. Nevertheless one packs the word in his quiver as one dart in the arsenal of his verbal reproaches that he holds in readiness and reserve for haughty fools and foolishness in all its blockheaded manifestations.

But to return for a moment to Trapp and his pentameters: did they elicit (draw forth, bring out, extract) a response? Yes. It arrived quite unexpectedly from none other than Sir William Browne, the physician and poet. His response is as continues:

> The king to Oxford sent a troup of horse,
> For Tories own not argument but force:
> With equal skill to Cambridge books he sent,
> For Whigs admit no force but argument.

Well said, and we might also suggest that we put the whole matter to its eternal rest, and get on with it. Our point is simply this: that few to no fools engage themselves in intellectual jousts, and fewer still have at their disposal a rich lexicon of perfectly good (and occasionally serviceable) words culled from our momentous language. Much less do they understand when and how to bring them forth, take meticulous aim, and fire them mercilessly.

We will never appreciably reduce the numbers of fools the world over, but our efforts may serve to limit their numbers for our sakes and for other more or less intelligent and reasonably learned brothers and sisters in future ages. Our efforts may avert the continuance of overt (at least) foolery, and warrant in some modest ways a better future for civilized individuals yet to be born. To that specific end, we have the Libertarian Party, which is the third largest in the thoroughly disgraceful and enormously corrupt American political spectrum, but which by far is the least political of them all. It is not composed of fools but by more or less rational citizens and has been a speck on the political map since 1971. Libertarians purport to be massively in support of "free markets and civil liberties," both of which would improve American civilization and which therefore will never be seen. As one mere signal of the utter decay into which our *District of Corruption,* has mired itself, one civil libertarian recommended that Nobel Prizes, that have been reduced to mere convulsive belly laughs, be, in their faded grandeur, announced on April Fool's Day, every bit appropriate to the mock sententiousness with which such Swedish booby prizes are ceremoniously awarded. Said Libertarian National Committee chairman William Redpath, "Unlike the gullible people who listened to 'The War of the Worlds' in 1938 and thought Martians were attacking the United States, when I heard this morning that Barak Obama won the Nobel (sometimes called *no ball*) Peace Prize, I changed the channel in disbelief," recalling that a panel of Swedish dunces had handed the absurd award to a momentous imbecile named Albert Gore who had actually been an American vice president, and "whose [bogus] global warming theories he will not defend in open debate."

"Do you think," asked George Bernard Shaw, the Irish dramatist, critic and social wit, "that the things people make fools of themselves about are any less true or real than the things that they behave sensibly about?" Were one to pose that question to those who ceremoniously and gratuitously distribute Nobel Prizes to some who are nothing more nor less than glaring jackasses, the answer would have to be an emphatic no. Having once made a worldwide reputation for themselves as fools, their reputation (if ever they enjoyed one) has been deservedly destroyed. The world can support only a limited amount of utter stupidity before declaring war on it. We are reminded that Bowles *Mike* Pearson, the Canadian-born diplomat, said of Dean Acheson (1893–1971), the US Secretary of State between 1949 and 1953, "he did not suffer fools gladly; he did not suffer them at all."

Unlettered Steve Jobs, the co-founder of Apple Computer and another company known as Pixar Animation Studios, in 2005 delivered a commencement address to about 4,712 supplicants to be graduated from Stanford University with bachelors, masters and doctorates, along with another 18,000 or so passively serious spectators. His remarks fell into three subsections, but his central message, captured in four memorable words: *Stay Hungry, Stay Foolish*, begs for interpretation. It was a moving address that, on the surface of it at least, paradoxically advised graduates to stay lean and (if necessary) stay undernourished in pursuit of the dreams that a university graduate ought to entertain. In still other words, it means to hold tenaciously to one's sometimes illusory ambitions at nearly any cost. When he advised graduates to *stay foolish*, it may have struck a few listeners as amusing, but the real message was to embrace tenaciously one's creative imagination even when it may, and probably will, strike others as absurd. A fool, in his foolishness, is ill equipped to say with any authority what is foolish, since he is mired in it himself. Others may erroneously declare something foolish while dreamers (of the right stripe) have transmuted what appear to be foolish ideas into bonanzas, as Jobs himself managed to do.

We know that some of the world's geniuses have been taken for nothing more than idiots. Carl Sagan, who made a hefty and not especially foolish reputation for himself as an astronomer and astro physicist, proceeded to write with authority on such things as extra terrestrial intelligence, the evolution of knowledge, science as romance, forgotten ancestors, life, death and his personal search for God. He cautioned that, as to questions raised by geniuses and fools, "the fact that some geniuses were laughed at does not imply that all who were laughed at are geniuses. They laughed at Columbus, they laughed at Fulton [Robert Fulton (1765–1815), the portrait painter, crafty inventor of torpedoes and submarines and the first commercially successful steamboats), they laughed at the Wright brothers. But they also laughed at Bozo the Clown." Swift, we must recall, reliably told us that "when a true genius appears you may know him by this sign: all the dunces are in confederacy against him." Accordingly, Jobs appeared to suggest that genius flourishes amid the derisive laughter of morons who accuse him of their own foolishness. Hence the paradoxical advice: Stay Foolish.

Jobs told his Stanford audience that he never before attended a college graduation, having never been graduated from anything except a high school. His mother, an unwed graduate student, placed him for adoption on the assumption that a family of college-educated people would rescue him. It did not happen. He was to have been adopted by an attorney, but when he turned out to be a boy, the family decided to wait for a girl. He was subsequently adopted by a couple consisting of one person who was never graduated from college and another never graduated from anything at all. Nevertheless they spent their savings sending him to Reed College in Portland,

Oregon, out of which he dropped within six months because of insufficient money, and also (as he told the Stanford audience) because he "couldn't see the value in it." Like other disadvantageous events in his life, dropping out at the proper time "was one of the best decisions [he] ever made." Moreover, he recalled, "I was very lucky. I found what I wanted to do early in life. Woz [Steve Wozniak] and I started Apple in my parents' garage when I was 20. We worked hard, and in ten years Apple had grown from just the two of us in a garage into a two billion dollar company with over 4,000 employees." By the age of 30, however, Jobs was fired by what had been his own company. "I was out," he remembered well, "and I was very publicly out. What had been the focus of my entire life was gone, and it was devastating." What then? "I didn't see it then, but getting fired from Apple was the best thing that could have happened to me. The heaviness of being successful was replaced by the lightness of being a beginner again...it freed me to enter one of the most creative periods in my life," to which he added, "I'm convinced that the only thing that is true for your work is true for your lovers."

"About a year ago," he continued, "I was diagnosed with cancer. I had a scan at 7:30 in the morning, and it clearly showed a tumor on my pancreas. I didn't know what a pancreas was. The doctors told me that this was almost certainly a type of cancer that is incurable and that I should expect to live no longer than three or six months. My doctor told me to go home and get my affairs in order, which is doctors' code for 'prepare to die.'" It came to pass, however, that the cancer was not fatal after all, and that it required only surgery. Jobs later judged himself as healthy once more, claiming (characteristically) that "death is very likely the single invention of life." What existential advice had he for Stanford graduates and anyone else with ears? "Your time is limited, so don't waste it living someone else's life. Don't be trapped by dogma, which is living with the results of other people's thinking. Don't let the noise of other's opinions drown out your own inner voice." Jobs lastly cited a popular counter-cultural beanbag called *The Whole Earth Catalog* that, in its final number, carried a wistful back cover photograph of what appeared to be an early morning country road that, Jobs explained, was "the kind that you might find yourself hitchhiking if you were so adventurous." The inscription read, "Stay Hungry, Stay Foolish." This is a reiteration of the Frostian advice, cited earlier, that one must allow his avocation to become his vocation. What strikes us about Steve Jobs, fool (of the right sort) by reason of his own indomitable optimism, was his self-assuredness and his astonishing ability to transform failures into astonishing successes. Fools (the real ones) have not such indomitable courage, since they are bent on failure and bubbling over with excuses.

They have accepted W.C Fields' earnest advice that says, "if at first you don't succeed, try again. Then quit. No use being a damned fool about it." Fields fashioned a brilliant career out of playing misanthropic, drunken idiots. His grandson Ronald J. Fields edited a biography entitled *W.C. Fields By Himself* wherein he clears (with assistance from Ed Stephen) some of the murkier aspects of his grandfather's tempestuous life and bumpy career, including allegations that he had but four years of education, that he fled his Darby, Pennsylvania, home at 11 after his drunken father struck him over the head with a shovel, that he purportedly lived for a time in a hole, during which he stayed alive by stealing food and clothing. None of these assertions will apparently withstand investigation. By 13, however, he had learned to play pool and juggle. One of the things he juggled was money, since he is alleged to have opened a bank account in every town he ever played. By the age of 23 he played next to actress Sarah Bernhardt at Buckingham Palace, and next to Charlie Chaplin and Maurice Chevalier at the Folies Bergères, after which he joined the Ziegfield Follies (two institutions about which we will have more to say by and by). The word *follies* expressly beams light upon the mephitic activities of fools. *Uncle Claudie*, as he called himself, was no fool. He eventually appeared in 36 Paramount films, and finally betook himself to Universal where he prepared his own material.

One point of all this is the need, nay requirement, for inner direction and Emersonian self reliance, since men like Jobs and Fields (to cite but two) are instances of up-from-nowhere nobodies who, in the old American way, clawed their way to wealth and prominence despite handicaps such as a bulbous nose and a lack of university education. Say what one will, this is not a fool's way of approaching life's manifold miseries, cosmic uncertainties and pernicious disappointments. Perhaps, depending upon one's point of view, all such quests are, in the end, futile and pointless as a game of checkers. Fools believe it to be precisely that, and are unwilling and unable to pursue what appear to be impossible ends because their Weltanschauung (from the German *Welt*/world and *Anschauung*/view, hence *world view*) is absurd and therefore a manifestly foolish journey. The contemporary novelist Dean Koontz, by the way, has remarked that "humanity is a parade of fools, and I am at the front of it, twirling a baton."

Koontz is not the only baton-twirler out there. Foolishness has always had its public celebrations, and one of the more *perverse* (meaning distorted, corrupt, subverted) of celebrations is of course April Fools Day, so-named for an April Fool, meaning someone dispatched on ludicrous mission, sometimes known as a *bootless errand*, a pointless quest. The game is to dispatch someone on a wild goose chase, the object being mere trickery with a mind to making a fool of him, if indeed he was not a fool beforehand. The *Britannica* assures us that (to no one's surprise) April Fool's is celebrated in April, but not necessarily on the first of that month, and that it celebrates something patently stupid, namely the jolly custom of playing so-called practical jokes. Why *practical*? Apparently because they're *in common practice*. It's what people do. It is not theoretical; it is practical as is the *practice* of law and medicine, what attorneys, and physicians regularly do, an habitual activity, something hardly out of the ordinary. We are told that April Fools Day is also something not out of the ordinary, but has nevertheless an obscure history that resembles preexisting rites such as the *Hilaria* of Roman origin and the *Hobi* celebrations in India. It also resembles a ritual of French origin at a time when the Gregorian calendar moved New Years Day from March 25 to January 1 in 1582, thereby suggesting that those who celebrated the new year on or about April 1 must be fools. Still another theory holds that the April celebration, close as it is to the March 21 vernal equinox, is the time when people are likely to be fooled by sudden and unexpected weather. The *Britannica* further tells us that there are cultural variations such as the French habit of attempting to make a fool of someone they called a *poisson d'avril*, an April fish, meaning a young fish, easily snagged. Even now, French children surreptitiously attach a paper fish to unsuspecting victims. In Scotland the habit is called *Gowkie Day*, meaning *gowk* or *cuckoo*, suggesting *cuckold*, a man whose wife has been adventuring behind his back. April fool celebrations, of course, take on any number of forms of trickery such as misleading newspaper headlines, laughable reports of Martian invaders, absurd rumors and anything else that may mislead the *gullible*, a word (cited earlier) that derives from *gull*, not the marine bird, but what the OED calls a "credulous person, one easily imposed upon, a dupe, simpleton, fool." Taken as a verb, *gull* means to swindle some unsuspecting knothead through fraud, deception or any other means of practical trickery. It licenses fools to make fools of everyone else, as if to suggest (to invoke two cherished bromides) that there is always *safety in numbers* and that *misery loves company*.

There are those fools who find uproarious hoaxes amusing; others find them irritating in a world filled to capacity and beyond with *conundrums* (puzzling circumstances, unanswerable questions) enough. The word *hoax* is apparently a shortened form of hocus (as in *hocus-pocus*) that in turn is an old time word for a conjurer or juggler, but moreover a trickster, a deceiver, later meaning to *remove* a person, pull the wool over his eyes, perpetrate a stunt on him. The term *hocus-pocus* is a pun on the venerable Latin phrase *hoc est corpus* having to do with the transubstantiation (transmutation, transformation). *Conundrum*, by the way, has as its origin a collegiate joke, of which, God help us, there are a great many. This one is likely a parody (burlesque, mimicry) of some other Latin phrase (but no one seems to know what it is), directed at someone assumed to be a fool. But *hoax* is little more than an elaborate bit of deception designed to gull some halfwit into believing it. In other words, it is a pointless attempt, occasionally successful, to test some fool's potential for (or lack of) credulation, his readiness to believe any preposterous thing.

John Roach, in an article entitled "April Fools' Special: History's Hoaxes" for the *National Geographic News*, compiled a list of the more imaginative hoaxes, among them a shark's purported leap from an ocean to attack a low-flying helicopter, a mild winter's being responsible for a Swiss spaghetti bumper crop, a report of Taco Bell Corporation's having purchased the Liberty Bell from the U.S. Government (something altogether possible in 2014–2015), and another report that the State of Alabama had recalibrated the value of *pi*. In 1912 someone presented a half million year old skull that purported to be the long awaited Darwinian *missing link* between modern man and his beastly forerunners. The National Aeronautics and Space Administration, that for years has hoodwinked the American public and its moronic government in one way and another, was alleged to have staged its delivery of astronauts to the moon between 1969 and 1970 as part of the overly publicized *Apollo* missions; Roach says it was not, as suspected, a hoax aimed at befuddling the Soviet Union. Roach reminds us that the rumor attained its crescendo in 2001 when a television broadcaster revived the matter in a program entitled "Conspiracy Theory: Did We Land on the Moon?" Those who participated in that program argued that, at the time, the Apollo program lacked the technology to bring it off. "The main issue may have been put to rest," Roach noted, "when NASA pointed out that no one had examined 800 pounds of rocks encrusted from the Moon's surface."

Of course there are endless other such hoaxes targeted at fools who at times appear to have been entertained by them. Examples: Sweden's only television station in 1962 was still broadcasting in black and white until one of its tech people let it be known that viewers could receive color images if they so much as pulled a nylon stocking over their television screens. In 1998 Burger King revealed its having developed a hamburger for consumption by the nation's 32 million left-handed (if not left of center) citizens. A day later the company disclosed that thousands of customers had endorsed and requested the left-handed sandwich, while others expressed a preference for the older, road tested, right-handed version. In 1976, the British astronomer Patrick Moore spread a rumor over the BBC that when the planet Pluto vanished behind Jupiter, a temporary cosmic consequence would interrupt the Earth's gravitational system, and that his listeners might anticipate becoming airborne at the precise moment of this galactic event and discover themselves floating in space. Shortly after Moore's disclosure the BBC received hundreds of calls from fools attesting that, yes, they had experienced weightlessness. One perfectly normal woman claimed that she and 11 companions had risen blissfully from chairs and wafted, with the grace of larks and butterflies, across a room.

The list grows long and torturous, but the aforementioned Orson Welles Mercury Theater pre-Halloween "War of the Worlds" radio broadcast, suggested by an 1898 two-part novel composed by the prolific H.G. Wells under the same title, alarmed people nationwide who believed that yes, Martians had arrived, and yes they were eating everyone's lunch. On a somewhat more serious note, readers of the *Book of Mormon*, followed by members of the Church founded by Joseph Smith, discovered to their amazement that Smith had been summoned by an angel (no less) who ordered him to mount a hill where he was to discover two tablets containing the full manuscript of the book he was about to write, except that he had first to translate his miraculous discovery with the aid of two crystals that together formed some sort of reading spectacles. So, we are told, Smith completed the translation and then, per his understanding with the angel, was duly obligated to return the originals—meaning, among other things, that his book had supposedly preceded its author. Smith was later to make other such incredible claims, including his supposed translation of something called *The Book of Abraham*, that subsequent investigation revealed was a document that Egyptians burned with their dead. It later became known that the New York's Metropolitan Museum had a copy of its own.

On April 27, 2110, Fox News reported that "the remains of Noah's Ark [had] been discovered 13,000 feet up a Turkish mountain," according to information secured from a self-anointed troupe of *evangelical explorers* of Turkish and Chinese extraction who swore that the discovery of certain innocuous wooden beams that were indeed 4,800 years old. One dissenter, a chap named Yeung Wing-Chueng, cautioned that whereas it was not 100 percent confirmed to be Noah's ark, "We think it is 99.9 percent" likely the real McCoy. Moreover a spokesman from *Noah's Ark Ministries* was convinced that the wooden compartments were intended to quarter animals. One day later, *World Net Daily* claimed that "at least two seasoned archaeologists," some of whom arrived from the *Bible Archaeology Search and Exploration Institute*, had reviewed appropriate evidence, and redundantly concluded that it was a hoax and a fraud. An investigator proclaimed with supreme confidence that "the wood's in too good a shape to be that old," and another authority on such arcane matters ventured that "there's not enough H2O in the world to get an ark that high up a mountain," thus terminating the Bible Boat controversy.

There are other noteworthy occasions when people rather enjoy making satiric fools of themselves, and do so with astonishing *brio* and on an astonishingly grand scale. Consider for one outstanding example the 21st Annual New York April Fools Day Parade staged in 2006 with meticulous, not to say *exacting*, attention to the spirit of international foolery in this, allegedly the most cosmopolitan city in all America, therefore in all the world. According to a publication calling itself *Laughing Squid*, it involved an illustrious march down Fifth Avenue from 59th Street to Washington Square Park redundantly at 12 noon on April 1. It was a procession whose enlightened mission was "to remedy a glaring omission in the long list of New York's annual ethnic and holiday parades." Why on April first? It was, parade organizers felt, "the day designated to communicate the perennial folly of mankind." We might have presumed as much. It was organized also for the noble intention of delivering "people back in touch with their inherent foolishness" by celebrating "war, famine, pestilence, plagues, asteroids, earthquakes, volcanic eruptions, tornados, tsunamis, global warming and general impending doom." At parade's end there was to have been a public book burning and a *Take-Your-Chance Petting Zoo* with chickens, ducks and geese, sponsored by the makers of Tami Flu. Also on the program, a radio presentation called Best Racist Comments and a King and Queen of Fools selected by the volume of their public applause.

Meanwhile, the Berkshire Fools Festival purported to "bring together artists, organizations and businesses in a multi-media, multi-venue, always-surprising celebration with a dozen exciting events...with emphasis on the fake, absurd and mysterious." Why? Because some fools rather like to socialize with one another, since most socialization occurs between socially similar parties who have a better than average prospect of comprehending each other. Fools of a feather fly together and perch occasionally in lo, benevolently fraternal lodges of which multiple hundred have spawned across America over the years. Some are nothing if not rather imaginative in name and nature. The LuLu Temple (1913) situated itself in the "Oasis of Philadelphia, Desert of Pennsylvania" with its prolific camels and oases; the Machigoune Encampment (1872) served up in Portland, Maine, by the Independent Order of Odd Fellows who, being odd are more or less obliged to be independent; the Little Turtle Tribe (1921) stitched and cobbled together by a group calling itself the Improved Order of Red Men in Greenville, Ohio; the Moslem Temple (1907), the inspired work of the Ancient Arabic Order of the Nobles of the Mystic Shrine located in mystical Detroit; the Pontypridd Chapter No. 227 (1923) brought to life by the Sovereign Princes Rose Croix; the Sincerity Lodge (1895) composed of people whose outstanding feature was their impeccable veracity; the Sphinx Joy (1923) a *Mystic Shrine* that convened at the Foot Guard Armory in Hartford, Connecticut; The Tintic Lodge (1899) assembled under the mystic By-laws and Trial Code of Tintic Lodge in Juab County, Utah; the Walton Odd Fellowship in Walton, New York; We're Off For Middletowne (1930), another impressive *Mystic Shrine*, this one in mystic Erie, Pennsylvania.

It is even possible to join a mystic organization predicated upon one's indulgences, such as Alcoholics Anonymous, Debtors Anonymous, Gamblers Anonymous, Grey Sheeters Anonymous (for compulsive eaters), Narcotics Anonymous, Sex Addicts Anonymous, Online Gamblers Anonymous and so anonymously onward and forward. Those who enjoy murdering innocent people have the option of joining a jolly terrorist club where one can meet and learn from an appealing range of morons with similarly sadistic inclinations. If you happen to be living in the Philippines, fill out a membership application with Abu Sayyaf or possibly with Al-Qaeda if you live darned near anywhere. For other mystic terrorist organizations, consider Ansar a-Islam (Iraq), Arjned Islamic Group (Algeria), Hamas (Gaza Strip, West Bank/Israel), Hisballah (Lebanon), the Islamic Movement of Central Asia, the Islamic Movement of Uzbekistan and the Muslim Brotherhood (Hussein Obama's old favorite). For those committed to other forms of mystic delusion, one can always wade stealthily into magic. Yes. Magic is well represented, we are assured, by something called Wicca (that apparently refers to witches) circles, esoteric (meaning that they are understood only by a few privileged mystic personalities), arcane (secret) colleges and witches' covens (assemblies of 13 hags, ever at the ready).

Allow us to recommend a few of our own personal favorites, beginning with the Ancient Mystical Order of the Rose Cross, as good a place to discover comradeship as any; the Confraternity of the Rose Cross; the Order Militia Crucifera Evangelica; the Fraternitus Rosae Crucis; something calling itself FODOSI or perhaps Fudofsi; in a pinch, there's always the Servants of the Light; the old mystic standby Hermetic Order of the Golden Dawn that has a rather pleasant ring to it; the doggoned Ordo Templi Orientis that sounds damnably tempting. Any others? Well, yes. There's the old Sacred Fraternity of the Cross; the Ordre Martinisti; the Theosophical Society and (lest we forget) the A (with triangular dots after it) A (with three more mystic triangular dots that we've heard about but, to be quite honest about it, never felt motivated to investigate). Were there world enough and time, by Jove, we would join them all, and do so proudly. The A and A with the mystical three dots after them is a group of perfectly normal people who together pursue light and truth, not to say transcendent knowledge (with which, of course, we have no quarrel) and was organized, if you must know, by mystic Aleister Crowley (1875–1947) the noted British occultist, poet and (we like this) *sexual revolutionary*, of the sort whom you don't encounter every day.

We can't say with any authority whether or not the foregoing random lists of exclusive organizations pander to fools or not, although we've long been skeptical of those who flock to clubs and organizations and what they long to profit from their mystical allegiances. It may simply be the longing for mystic companionship. Or possibly they pander emotional support, encouragement, romance, an elevated sense of self esteem, instant prestige or a thousand other elusive things that may be, but probably are not, forthcoming. There are those who, in an effort to rise in the world, are convinced that it's best to cower in groups, while more independent minded people prefer to make their way alone, arguing that mobs of mystic people merely get in the way. On the whole, however, there's little gainsaying that it's far better to shun the company of blockheads (the Yiddis *golem*), for fear of becoming one of them. Sociologist John Macionis tells us that "the term socialization... refers to the life long experience by which individuals develop their human potential and learn culture," continuing that "social experience is also the foundation of personality, a person's fairly consistent patterns of acting, thinking and feeling." Among other considerations, one's social development therefore rests upon the care with which one painstakingly selects his companions, if any, meaning that he can exercise infinite options in the provocatively colorful company he chooses to frequent.

Foolery, as we plainly see around us, proliferates genetically, yes; but it also travels sociologically. Other sociologists generally define social interactions as "the process by which people act and react in relation to each other," that can obviously become beneficial, or quite the contrary. Growing up in a household of fools is going to leave its stamp, and trying to shed what one considers foolish behavior may be problematic, or conceivably ineffective. The dangers of embracing foolish ways of behavior can cripple a person's prospects in life because such ways are difficult to break and because one assumes that, as the cliché has it, *to get along one must go along*. One depends upon the consent and approval of his betters and his equals. To proceed otherwise is to risk being *different*, something received with profound disapproval indeed among those who function as best they can with the hearty endorsement of groups. To them, *different* is a code expression for *socially unacceptable, unpopular, distasteful*, and other unpleasantness that herds teenagers (for one good example) into disastrous conformity. Of course, fools are themselves different, and pejoratively so. This raises questions of how one elects to be a fool, and by whose assessment one is recognized as foolish. To refer to someone as a fool is to presume that the one who does the referring is not a fool, and is in a position to identify fools quite readily, even with the electricity out. Both of these assumptions may be outrageously presumptuous. To the contrary, it may be that he who calls others fools may be the biggest fool of them all. One may identify fools for any of several motives, among them as a deliberate act of effrontery, as a jest, as a way of concealing his own foolishness, as an affront to someone's presumed stupidity, as a way of making himself seem perfectly rational.

But suppose certain sane, rational and lucid thinking citizens, as determined by a studious jury of demonstrably wise and all-knowing persons, such as those who have resolved to read this book, have yet to encounter a fool; perhaps they may join and, with the greatest of pleasure become one. Let us divide this learned inquiry into two sections. First, let us assume that they had no control over their foolishness, and second (to the contrary), they have *deliberately* made fools of themselves. If it is the first option, those whose foolishness may have been hereditary, they have had no say in the matter because they possess limited mentality by reason of having selected the wrong parents, both of whom were idiots. If it's the second option, they are fools, be it in the form of fops, halfwits or (on a clear day) blockheads, because they wish with all their hearts to be crackpots. They believe that being a blockhead is quite funny, which it well may be, particularly if they devote their foppery to being professional entertainers of the comedic sort. In such an instance (to backtrack slightly) they may be counterfeit idiots. It sounds terrible, but it isn't quite so bad. After all: better a phony idiot than a real one. The world can gladly welcome another professional clown to bring merriment to the uplifting service of a fallen and corrupt society. If, on the other hand, he elects to be a fool of the sort we encounter in public places everywhere, that's anything but beneficial. Why? Because it contributes to the dissemination of fools over the earth's scarred surface, sowing the plentiful seeds of stupidity in the disservice of what intellectuals used to call the *human condition*, that, as we know, is well beyond the prospect of redemption. We all understand what *condition* suggests, viz: "belonging to, or characteristic of, mankind, distinguished from apes by superior mental development, capacity for articulate speech, humanistic development, and upright posture," as it's been articulated. Fools, we earnestly suggest, possess none of these elegant characteristics, and therefore ought not be encouraged to reproduce, consort with children, to approach civilized adults, or vote in elections—especially when those presenting themselves for public office are themselves fools of the worst, most despicable order.

> A cigarette that bears a lipstick's traces,
> An airline ticket to romantic places,
> And still my heart has wings.
> These foolish things remind me of you.

Jack Strachey and Harry Link composed the music, circa 1936, and Holt Marvell composed the libretto. A number of other, less romantic things, remind us of foolish people, and they involve language not quite so romantically wistful, as Marvell's fools have pernicious problems with words, and those problems involve the recognition of sentences and the wretched deployment of English and other language possibilities. In January of 1980 Martin Plessner published an article in the *Atlantic Monthly* entitled "1980: The Clichés are coming," that underscored the egregious miscarriages of language as it's been misapplied to politics, itself a disgusting and foolish *calling* better left uncalled since it belongs to those who enjoy destroying what was once taken to be civilized life in America and elsewhere. Politicians are hideous people with wretched judgment who concoct egregiously poor statutes intended mostly for their private advantage. By *egregious* we suggest towering, prominent, projecting, used here in the worst sense. The word *cliché* also cries loud for definition, since we are about to view a number of them along with other linguistic atrocities uttered by politicians and other roaches. *Cliché*, as one might expect, is a word of French origin that in its original sense meant the practice of deploying melted lead to obtain a casting that in turn might be used to mold a stereotyped plate, the purpose of which is to copy (say) printed material. In a lesser sense it meant (as the OED reminds us) to fix, to perpetuate an unchanging form that might also be used to reproduce images such as print and photographic representations. In language, cliché therefore means the repetition of a stereotyped expression that in the past has been over-worked and over-used and tortured until it no longer carries any vitality, freshness or novelty, if indeed it ever did. Clichés are commonly called *hackneyed* which (was, at least) a *Brettish* horse-drawn carriage for common use, which suggests something indiscriminate, commonplace, and vulgar. Hackneyed language assumes the form of clichés and other linguistic outrages popular with fools in their common discourse.

It was apparently with this in mind that Plessner wrote with ironic amusement and not a little horror about what passes for language among politicians and other imbeciles. There are few to no surprises here, in that one would expect nothing less than the hideous vulgarization of languages from such people who are neither politic nor sophisticated, subtle nor possessing the slightest sense of propriety. Plessner begins by referring to a certain revolting Indiana senator with a predictable "aptitude for the deadening cliché," that being an offensively, clumsy and moronic mode of expressing himself not much exceeded by *journalists* who follow such rubbish and (as the cliché goes) *hang on his every word*. The infinitely infertile variety of clichés overwhelms us. Suppose we begin by referring to some political sap as *dead in the water*, possibly because he had failed *to read his tea leaves*, ironic though that be, considering *his political smarts*, largely thanks to his being an *issues guy*, which makes him a *knockout artist* in the language of jackasses. Nevertheless, this scoundrel is *rapidly closing the gap* separating himself from other political punks, largely on the strength of his having *struck some responsive chords*, strangely enough, since he is (let us not forget) a *strict conservative* part of the time and a *knee-jerk member* of the *new* (or sometimes old) *left* on other occasions. All the same, he is universally celebrated by *party stalwarts* of undisclosed political persuasion who slouch *back to their drawing boards* so better to *clear the first hurdle* in *the presidential sweepstakes* by impressing other idiots with whom he passed words and kidney stones on the *campaign trail*, somewhere *off in the hustings* where he charmed the *party faithful* who adore having their *egos massaged* despite their being *battle scarred* from long having *kept their options open*. At the same time our candidate stays comfortably well within the *game plan* interlarding his speeches with meaty slogans (like "fired up, ready to go!") and reflecting what *opinion makers* want to hear, being, as they are, *seasoned professionals* who are *well oiled* if not always *finely tuned* when it comes to misleading ordinary fools out there in the *battleground states*, all of which are *pivotal* and invariably *barometers* and quite naturally *bellwethers* among the *fragmented Democrats* and Republicans perpetually *in disarray*. Mind you, it is no easy thing to *forecast the outcome* even if it's *comfortably predictable* given the *power of the incumbency*, leaving everyone's emotions *in shambles*, which is to say *coming unstuck* and *unraveling* despite a *flurry* of endless *secret meetings* with oodles of *street smart* jackasses and *wily old campaigners* who have (you may be certain) more than *tested the waters*, into which they have of course *taken the plunge*, if only to emerge *all wet*, yet dry enough to *catch fire* and stage a (yes) *late-inning rally*, thanks largely to an army of *party elders* who have benevolently *stepped in* so as to *unify the party* and to demonstrate that *the system worked.*

Fools, whether they come in the forms of blockheads, idiots and the rest of such rubbish, speak *in terms of* clichés. Were it not for clichés, they would be mute, speechless and dumb, thereby raising *issues* that might threaten their *windows of opportunity* that hitherto provided them a *leg up* and allowed them to *ramp up* instead of miring them in a *worst case scenario* at *this point in time.* For without the appearance of being articulate, quick-minded and sure of their positions that clichés enable them to e, they would be unable to *interface* with others to gather *feedback* or, to *make a long story short*, send them shopping for a *viable alternative* by *utilizing* (*timewise* and *spacewise*) a *meaningful relationship* with other cliché purveyors who, *claiming responsibility*, would resolve to *go for it*, once circumstances appeared *all clear on the horizon*, meaning that instead of *freaking out*, one might *last but not least* envision destiny as a *can of worms* from which one might *make the best of a bad situation*, not only *sooner rather than later* but in fact *like a bat out of hell*, *due to the fact that* their opponents were *bogged down* and all but *laid to rest*, we might well suggest in *the nick of time*, *albeit* they were *tickled pink* at this, the *eleventh hour*, when the *fires of passion* would customarily been *all the rage*, except that some of us were *dog tired* and became mere *bumps on a log.*

We'll get back to you to ask *what's the good word*, since we know that you've *worked your fingers to the bone* and *worked your butt off*, simply because *that's what it's all about*, considering that you're *between a rock and a hard place*, knowing, as you do, after a *rude awakening*, that you haven't a *snowball's chance in hell*; then you can *go by the book* or *throw caution to the winds*, and *do your own thing* the way *male chauvinists* invariably have since *time immemorial* even when it's *raining cats and dogs*. But *time flies*, something to which we'll all *swear on a stack of bibles*, especially when we're *spaced out*, or worse yet when we're *down in the dumps*, and *could care less*, even about bibles, be they *stacked against us* or *out of sight* (something that makes us *pleased as punch* but *you know how that is* because you're a *chip off the old block*). We ask that you refrain from *putting the cart before the horse*, or otherwise *counting your chickens before they hatch*, if we may beg to mix a metaphor. Let's merely say don't *bite off more than you can chew*, or you will be driven *up the wall*, if not *off the wall*, by *searching for a needle in a haystack* which, as clichés go is *beyond the shadow of a doubt* a *golden opportunity* where, *as far as we're concerned* it's *the more the merrier*, the better to *have your head together*, now that you've *wiped the slate clean*. You'll be left *shaking in your boots*, since you decided to *foot the bill*, *go to the mat* and *bite the bullet* even if it's *by the skin of your teeth*. However, we *have a bone to pick* and (if we may say so) an *ax to grind, but hey,* that's *water over the dam,* now that you've *found yourself, white as a sheet,* even if you're *black as the ace of spades,* and privately, at least as *queer as a three dollar bill. We'll let that pass, since we're drunk as a skunk, tough as nails, happy as a lark, crazy as a loon, cold as ice, sweet as honey, mad as a wet hen, nutty as a fruitcake, mean as a snake, stubborn as a mule, red as a beet* and *in the end dull as dishwater.*

That said, *keep your ducks in a row* and if need be, *drink like a fish* while you're having one of you goddamned *nice days* during which you squander your time stewing over *hidden agendas* and your moronic *lifestyle.* We have observed that you've taken a business school diploma and are now speaking pure, cliché-saturated commerce-*speak,* what with your insufferable *strategic alliances, your heads-up, cost-centered solutions to routine win-win situations,* your *game plans* that have *empowered* you to *capitalize* your every idiotic gesture and *conceptualize* every moronic effort *to position yourself to push the envelope* toward your *value-added* or should we say addled *passion* for *low-hanging fruit,* which we presume refers to your wife. We nonetheless admire your *resource constrained* and *smart sized synergies* that *touch base* with what you call your *intellectual capital.* Confound your insufferable *one-to-one innovativeness,* your damned *next generation methodologies,* your godforsaken *interfaces, holistic, cross-platform deliverables,* and *mission-critical cutting edges,* all of which are, with their *cross-media collaborative, brick and mortar shout-outs* with their 24/7 *bandwidths* and your foolish *web-ready relationships,* with their *back-end communities* and their infernal *architectures* of *one-time, intuitive supply chains,* since, however, *for all intents and purposes* or perhaps for *all intensive purposes* you at least *give credit where it's due* when you *prioritize* your *bottom line.* We feel genuinely moved to concede that your *line, bottom or not,* has done a *hell of a job,* having converted what used to be the English language into the *lingua franca* of a *buy-side, ankle-biting* and *cherry-picking double-dipping retrocession* in a *world class fox-trot economy* and *bring everybody on the bandwagon and on board.*

CHAPTER 4. FOOLS, ECCENTRICS & THE SONS OF MOMUS

Exists there a family without its blockheads and simpletons? Short of divorcing or otherwise partitioning oneself from vexatious relatives, one has little choice but to tolerate their presence, however reluctantly, until those family idiots are, thank heaven, a goodly horizon away. There are those who devise a way to deal with others by, say, relocating to Calcutta. Failing that, they have no choice but to remain under one roof and make the best of it, devising ways to coexist with a mindless passel of familial jackasses. Forbearance helps, providing that one exercises a more than ordinary talent for self-control, if that be sufficient to suffer blood relatives who have made a flourishing career out of inanity. Occasionally it may be necessary to accommodate a relative troubled by, shall we say, *cognitive impairment*, but this is not the sort of blathering fool we are addressing here.

A more creative solution to managing family fools, provided that one has the resources, is to shuffle them off to crime-captive Buffalo. Kyle McCarthy has written a surprisingly resourceful book called *The Complete Idiot's Guide to the Best Family Destinations*, although his use of the word *idiot* probably refers to the reader, not his family. Other idiotic guides address such timeless topics as *Finding Mr. Right*, *Family Reunions*, and *Successful Family Businesses*. Packing idiots off to distant points, however, may be as costly as it is temporary. We are put in mind of Gustave Flaubert's posthumous *Bouvard et Pécuchet*, an unfinished picaresque investigation of stupidity involving a foolish pair of Parisian office copyists and their failed attempt to discover a better, richer existence by hitting the road. The two undertake a Faustian quest to learn everything under the sun, only to become still more frustrated by

ambiguity, confusion and contradiction. In the end (so Flaubert's notes indi-
cate) they return to their mindless copying of mindless documents. Jean Paul
Sartre wrote a 3,000 page, unfinished five volume *true novel* about Flaubert
himself, calling it *The Family Idiot* (*L'idiot de la famille*). Even W. S. Gilbert,
of Gilbert and Sullivan, penned a few comical lines he appropriately called
"The Family Fool" that read, in part, "There are one or two rules that all Family Fools/ Must observe, if they love their profession. / There are one or two
rules/ Half a dozen, maybe, / that all family fools, / of whatever degree, / Must
observe, if they love their profession," that being to play the jester.

A source called *Jesters, Fools and Madmen: The World Turned Upside Down*
reminds us, if we had not long ago taken painstaking notice, that professional fools have substantially taken over popular entertainment, some by
way of such avenues as silent films. We refer, of course, to wise guys like
Joseph Francis "Buster" Keaton, Harold Lloyd, Joe E. Brown, followed by low
humor depictions of popular life as rendered by Laurel and Hardy, the zany
Marx Brothers, and even the low brow slapstick of Abbott and Costello.
Later, television viewers flocked to a popular and endless array of *situation
comedies*, many of them domestic in focus, such as *All in the Family* and *The
Golden Girls*. In recent years there was a television extravaganza called *The
Family Jackass* that presented a cavalcade of outrageous family nitwits for the
enrichment of adolescent audiences.

As if there weren't enough family fools to go around, time was when
those who had no jackasses in the household could hire a few, with a mind to
spicing up an otherwise merely elegant but dull domicile with professional
nitwits who were almost invariably not nearly as idiotic (except when they
lapsed into madcap posturing) as they might first appear. The acquisition
of household fools is one of the more bizarre practices one may encounter in
an investigation of evolving taste and creative entertainment. It is one thing
to ask an idiot to stop by and spit out a few salty one liners for the entertainment of a few tipsy dinner guests. It's quite another to take a professional blockhead as part of one's domestic entourage, as if to fortify it with
nitwits, of which there was never a shortage, then as now. And who were
the most celebrated of these hired jackasses? Some of them were, of course,
real people, some fictional. There are detailed accounts of the better, more
acclaimed court nitwits, usually beginning with a chap named Dag'onet, a
Scottish name sometimes rendered simply as *Dagonet* (it rhymes with *baronet*), remembered as King Arthur's jester and household fool. He is likely
to have been an invented, rather than real, person. There was once also a
fellow named Rayere, fool to Henry I. Today, Rayere signifies a variety of
Golden Retriever or an anabolic steroid. There was also a chap known only
as Scogan, jester to Edward VI. Scogan is remembered as a crafty sort of joker
who allegedly borrowed a goodly sum of money from the king that he could
not possibly repay. Resourceful knockabout that he was, he faked his own

death and was ensconced on a bier that was artfully presented in such a way as to attract Edward's undivided attention, whereupon the monarch in his mourning over the apparent passing of his merry mate, magnanimously forgave him his debt, only to see the knave return to life and express his profound, if obsequious, gratitude for the king's munificence.

A French clown named Triboulet, dressed in brilliant red, fooled around with Louis XII and François I. He eventually inspired Victor Hugo's *Le Roi S'amuse*, a play that eventually morphed into Giuseppe Verdi's *Rigoletto*. European courts found amusement in persons with mental and physical irregularities, which is one reason why Triboulet, a microcephalitic—a person having a head with a small braincase—seemed to be gladly received. There is an account, possibly apocryphal, that he informed his monarch that a certain nobleman had threatened to hang the jester, whereupon the monarch declared that if such a thing happened he would see the nobleman beheaded within 15 minutes. Triboulet then asked whether the beheading might be accomplished 15 minutes *beforehand*. On another occasion Triboulet swatted the king on his behind, after which the monarch threatened to kill him unless he could devise an apology that was yet more offensive. Triboulet replied that he had intended to smack the queen on *her* bums, instead. The role of jester seemed to imply that the professional fool might get away with impunity from nearly any outrage, but nonetheless he might still place his life and welfare in mortal jeopardy. Triboulet managed to survive a so-called *trick* in an early motion picture called *The King and His Jester* that depicts him as anything but funny. Triboulet's portrait, painted by an artist whose identity has been lost to history, carried the title "Portrait of a Dwarf," that amply depicts his unusual head.

Thomas Killigrew, known in his day as *King Charles's Jester*, was a dramatist and an actor who secured a warrant to open a London playhouse where he became a less than successful theatrical manager. He understood, at least, how to entertain, carry off a jest and evoke laughter—more than enough capability to tickle a king and curry royal political advantage for being an apparent halfwit. Speaking of Killigrew, we must not omit to mention a Scotsman named Archibald *Archie* Armstrong, jester extraordinaire in the illustrious court of James I. Archie was raised in an illustrious family of sheep thieves who had, nonetheless, a way with words and a way with illustrious people, hobnobbing as Archie did with James II and Prince Charlie. It was no laughing matter, by the way, that thanks to good connections, he acquired an alleged 1,000 acres of good Irish landscape. Back in London, meanwhile, he seems to have tried his hand at lending money. If we don't know when this prince charming was born, we at least know that he *passed away* in 1672 and is believed to be buried in an unmarked grave belonging to what is St. Michael and All Angels, also believed to be the place where King

Arthur's bones rest beneath the sod of what may once have been a Saxon battleground.

In his better days, Archie (according to reports) was both insolent and mischievous. That mischievousness may have prompted him to pit James I against Henry, Prince of Wales. History tells us that he was lavishly received in Spain, although he let fly with a few choice barbs aimed against the institution of Spanish marriage, a more than sensitive subject at that time. Archie had a glib and unbridled tongue, as a jester might well be assumed to have, and as a result he accumulated more than a few adversaries in his career as court jackass. Armstrong is known to have been twice married and to have fathered what court records call *a base son*. He died, of course, on April Fools Day. All in all, he did not do half badly and apparently passed his mature years in some degree of luxury, such as it then may have been construed. His biography aptly illustrates that (if it be yet unclear), there is money to be made thorough being a nitwit, real or feigned. He left behind a verse that he (or someone else) called *Archie's Dream* that contains a farewell to all that, saying, "And now no more words I in vain will scatter,/ But come unto the marrow of the matter."

This brings us to a certain Thomas Derrie (more familiarly *Tom Durie*) whose honor it was to play the idiot at the court of James I and whose professional resume included fooling around the court of Queen Anne of Denmark who later married both James VI and I. Time was when Derrie's portrait, painted by none other than Marcus Gheeraerts, was proudly exhibited at the Scottish National Portrait Gallery. A fellow known to us only as *Doctor Doran* or sometimes *Doctor John Doran*, recorded that Derrie freely participated in court revelry, as one might assume, and that "Derrie must have had to draw largely on his wits to amuse the Queen," who he says elsewhere "was the most amiable person possible when she was not put out." He also mentions in passing that any of the Queen's servants "could envy the condition of Derry the Merry Jester who is depicted wearing an ornate red jacket, a heavy gold chain, a high ruffed collar and hospitality cup presumably full of good red wine.

Noteworthy too is a woman named Jenny Colquhoun, granted, not a familiar face to most but still what we might call a *minor fool*, if fools be anything other than minor. Jenny is remembered by those who know as a predecessor to one James Geddes, in turn remembered as a damned fool to her nibs, Mary Queen of Scots. He is listed in his own day as a *prince of non-official jesters and coxcombs*, a dubious accolade if ever we heard one. Far better and more affectionately regarded is a cutup fondly known as *Patch*, a damned fool in loyal service to Henry VII's lovely wife Elizabeth. Some have theorized that *patch* was a code word for *fool*. The OED points out that the word was a nickname that none other than Cardinal Wolsey applied to his "domestic fool or jester," and that Patch's "real surname [was] Sexton." The term *patch*, it further points out, finds its origin in the Italian *pazzo*, meaning lunatic, fool, madman. It may also allude to Shakespeare's which is taken to mean one who does something idiotic. Be that as it may, Sexton's downfall arrived when he, like others of his calling, stepped over the edge when he pulled one spicy jest too many, thus ending his career as an idiot.

Of the jester Will Somers (aka *Sommers*) who ably played the fool in the court of Henry III, Robert Armin in his *Foole Upon Foole* penned the poor fellow's epitaph, saying, "Few men were more beloved than was this fool whose merry prate [chatter] kept with the king much rule. When he was sad the king with him would rhyme, thus Will exil'd sadness many a time." Somers indeed developed a reputation as *the poor man's friend* for his engaging ways that ingratiated himself with the king sometime between 1535 and 1537, and over time became a psychological necessity who, we are told, possessed the necessary tact and comedic skill to tow the monarch out of his emotional doldrums. Somers gradually became more of a counselor who engaged the king in comic gambits that involved rhyming jests. One may even think of him as a *psychiatric interventionist* by applying his wit and comedy as a form of therapy, thus illustrating the beneficial effects of jest in mood elevation. An engraving of Somers survives that depicts the canny jester as a diminutive man in an elaborate coat, the belt of which suspends the customary fool's cap. He died after spending much of his life in the king's service, jotting down his majesty's idiosyncrasies. Somers's career was celebrated in a biography called *A Pleasant Historie of the life and death of William Somers* that was reprinted in 1794.

Most of what we know about Queen Elizabeth' cutup William Frederick Wallet is captured in his autobiography entitled *The Public Life of W. F. Wallet, the Queen's Jester*, published in 1870, containing accounts of some ambitious forty years of playing the nitwit and his earlier, equally ambitious, itineraries through the United Kingdom and America, where he sailed the Mississippi and ventured to California with a mobile circus that billed him misleadingly as *The Queen's Jester*, in the company of the circus's entrepreneur Pablo Fanque who, oddly enough, later surfaced in a Beatles song that begins, "Being for the Benefit of Mr. Kite, There will be a show tonight on trampoline." The autobiography covers Wallet's raucous beginnings as poseur living on the ragged edge, written in an elegant but picaresque manner about his poverty-ridden fool's journey on the road. He subsequently performed at Windsor Castle before Queen Elizabeth, after which he had some legitimate claim to being her clown. Prior to that he was more a music hall dandy who played American cities such as Philadelphia where, once again, he persisted in billing himself as the queen's entertainer and idiot. His home town of Beeston, where he died, kept his name alive by christening an avenue in his memory.

Jean-Antoine Brisque, better known as Brusque (as in brusk) the jester was a phony medical practitioner and surgeon-turned-fool for his own profit and for the amusement of court hangers-on. His real name was Jean Antoine Lambert, which became over time *Brusquet*, rendered in French as *brusque*, meaning of course *abrupt*, as one who speaks sharply, snappishly, gruffly, bluntly and hastily—all of them not ordinarily identified with jesters, who traded in quick-witted retorts intended to pierce the armor of the unsuspecting. Legend has it that so many of his patients died that disgruntled survivors came perilously close to hanging him for what today we would call *malpractice*, but King Henry II rescued him and assigned him to be, strangely enough, a Parisian postmaster, where he might perpetrate less damage. The aforementioned John Doran in his history of fools reported that the bogus practitioner *with little knowledge of his profession* did at least have a comical side to him that King Henry seemed to appreciate, which led to Brisque's becoming a court buffoon who (history tells us) somehow superseded Triboulet although, as Doran cautions, "the wit of Brisque is oftener praised than cited." Doran also mentions that there was a time when *gros mots* were considered high hilarity, and the "grossest practical jokes were highly relished."

It came to pass that a certain cardinal who was ambitious to preach before the royal chapel was frustrated in that quest by court fools of Brisque's ilk, and departed from the pulpit immediately, occasioning a *matter of court and city*. What with Brisque's familiarity with Spanish and Italian, he ironically may have accompanied the cardinal on diplomatic junkets abroad. Brisque's perverse sense of humor evidenced itself when, following a royal banquet, he jumped upon a table, spread himself flat and as has been claimed, *rolled himself with plates, spoons, fruit, etc.* and so wrapped, rolled off the end of the table. A monarch thought this so extremely funny that he kept him on as royal jackass. "It is this," Doran comments, "that protects fools and infants." On a trip to Flanders, Brusque met with the former emperor Charles V who had a penchant for swapping inanities with nitwits. Having inquired about Brisque's health, he then asked, "Do you remember the day when Montmorency wanted to have you hanged?" Brisque said that yes, he did indeed, and that it was the same day "your majesty purchased those splendid rubies and carbuncles which now adorn your imperial hand," referring to "the gouty swellings which paralyzed the emperor's fingers."

The king was so enthralled with his court idiot that he dispatched him to France with a mind to making the old monarch wittier than he actually was. King Philip later rewarded Brisque with a gold chain which the fool immediately traded for a brass one, then informed Philip that he had done so, whereupon Philip threatened that he should be *flogged by the kitchen scullions* for being *such a wretched dullard*. A source known simply as *Brantome* opined that all of Brisque's stunts and foolishness would fill a bulky volume. Trickery, of course, cuts more than one way. Brisquet was himself, not surprisingly, the butt of nasty knavery when someone dispatched a messenger to his wife, claiming that her ostensibly provincial husband, believed to be in Paris, was instead beastly dead. Story has it that she subsequently married the messenger. Since Brisquet had masqueraded as a surgeon, he was no stranger to the inventive art of fakery. Some of his patients survived, but they may well have survived without his dubious services. His glib repartee and nimble posturing was such that he supposedly never fired the same wisecrack twice, and that he was up to his ears in not always good-natured trickery. He allegedly told his wife that the queen was eager to meet her, but that the queen was not only hard of hearing, but nearly deaf. He subsequently told the queen that his wife was deaf, as well. The result was that the two women screamed at each other. Like certain other fools and fakes, Brusquet could play many roles as befitted an occasion. He was appointed as a magistrate, somewhat, but not necessarily, inconsistent with having made a foolish reputation as a clown. Needless to say, a great many clowns have sullied the bench in purported courts of law, the primary difference being that a fool may don his familiar cap and bells, the magistrate his wig. In our time, when restriction upon free expression is a daily threat, the clown has on occasion emerged as the voice of liberty.

A personage identified only as *Chicot* became jester to Henri III between about 1553 and 1591. He figures in an 1846 novel by Alexandre Dumas *père*, titled *La Dame de Monsoreau*, known also as *Chicot the Jester*. It treats Chicot as friend and gentleman, but never as fool. Chicot liked to tell anyone with ears that he, not Henri, was King of France. His role in the court seems to have been a blend of idiot and protector, all the while a professional eccentric, about which we will have more to say in this chapter. Doran characterizes Chicot as long of limb, "all nerves, muscle and bone; active, addicted to raillery, ingenious in contrivances" and able to laugh *silently like an Indian*. We like the sound of that. As an accomplished mimic, he was adroitly able to switch identities. Henri apparently viewed him as (in Doran's words) a *sort of phantom-buffoon*, who died after the king ill-advisedly pummeled him over the head in a fit of rage. Elsewhere, Chicot left behind a reputation as one whose head was perfectly rational. There is a document called *The Parables of Chicot* claiming that his calculated mockery was a sure signal that he was of impeccably sound mind, if that be questioned. *C'est signe que Cicquot est bien tourne de teste*, a man of judgment, that can be claimed for many of his calling, since playing the fool was, and is, different from being one. Nor was it, to be sure, an occupation free of risk.

A person named L'Angli is today regarded as one of the last of the French court knaves, and by some accounts one of the temperamentally least foolish of them, associated with the court of Louis XIV. L'Angeli ironically came from a distinguished French family and ironically had served as a stable boy who in his time evidenced a talent for the jocund and the absurd that attracted the attention of the monarch. L'Angeli rose from being a mere jokester to what one might call a *fortunate fool*. Doran said that "if a courtier wanted a joke from him, he first had to damned well pay for it. If someone wanted to evade L'Angli's sarcasm, he had to pay for that, too. L'Angeli not only became wealthier, but more influential.

Others, such as Klaus (or *Claus*) Narr, became jesters to nut cases such as a certain Prussian fellow gratuitously named *Frederick the Wise* who apparently felt the need for a pseudo fool in his closet. Narr was a dwarf, and a funnyman who had in his youth abused the geese he was supposed to be attending. He was also, according to accounts, disgustingly foul-mouthed but (in his way) had wits enough to advise Freddy the Wise how much a certain valuable stone might be worth. Narr commented that it would require a wealthier jester to provide a yet more accurate answer. Narr's betters were intrigued with his foul mouth and his foul sense of humor that nonetheless kept him professionally afloat until about the age of 70. Erik Midelfort in his *History of Madness in Sixteenth Century Germany* credits Narr with being "no amoral merry prankster bent on inflicting his sadistic whims on the conventional and naïve," suggesting also that beneath Narr's lack of civility, he was paradoxically capable of forecasting just about anything and hence a purported example of a fool's uncanny gift of clairvoyance. Midelfort also advances the theory that "court fools seemed funny because they defied the increasingly delicate standards of courtesy, of restrained courtly behavior, of *Hoflichkeit*," meaning courtesy and politeness. He also reminds us that court rogues were known to be subjected to humiliation, pointing out too that "the prince bishop of Bamburg kept a fat, stammering fool at his table" and on one occasion ordered him to crack hazelnuts with his forehead until the poor wretch bled. On other occasions jesters were mercilessly teased and tormented on the inhumane assumption that "fools have to be driven and exercised, or else they go rotten and soft from lying around," being, as they are, *funny specimens of a distorted humanity*.

The real Yorick, jester in the Court of Denmark, of course puts us immediately in mind of Shakespeare's *Hamlet*, Act 5, Scene 1 where Prince Hamlet launches into his famous monologue on friendship, remembrance and death: "Alas, poor Yorick! I knew him, Horatio—a fellow of infinite jest, of most excellent fancy. He hath bore me on his back a thousand times, and how abhorred in my imagination it is! Here hung those lips I have kissed I know not how oft. Where be your gibes now, your gambols, your songs, your flashes of merriment that were wont to set the table on a roar? Not one now to mock your own grinning? Quite chap-fall'n? Now get you to my lady's chamber, and tell her, let her paint an inch thick, to this favor she must come. Make her laugh at that." The messages here are various. One of them addresses the vanity of living human wishes. Another addresses the transience of human life. Still another is a reiteration of *memento mori*: "remember death." Yorick's name also turns up, by the way, in Lawrence Stearne's novels *Tristram Shandy* and *A Sentimental Journey*. We find it too in Goldsmith's *The Vicar of Wakefield* where we are reminded of his Danish extraction, and of the real Yorick who served the Horwendillus court. He is sometimes referred to as *Horwendillus Rex*, whose time was eight centuries before Shakespeare. In any event, evidence of Yorick's deadly wit, when he was a court cut-up, has not, as people say, *come down to us*. The name *Yorick*, scholars have discovered, suggested a number of things, among them the jester minstrel as buffoon. Such jester minstrels were professional fools attached, at considerable risk, to royal courts.

John Heywood is customarily thought of as an Oxford educated Catholic playwright and poet whose sense of humor, judging from his *Witty and Witless, John-John the Husband* (a French farce), *The Play of Love, The Pardoner and the Friar*, were influenced by his having been a latter day court cutup, musician performer and purveyor of racy epigrams. He was better connected, however, than an ordinary court jackass, if only because he was a son-in-law of Thomas More and a grandson of John Donne. Nonetheless, Heywood became one of Henry III's favored jackasses. Henry himself was a good-time sort of chap who was not yet 18 when he ascended the throne. Heywood sounds less witty today than he apparently was in Henry's time, uttering such banal epigrammatic commonplaces as *Haste Maketh Waste, Look Ere You Leap, Better Late Than Never* and all of them impossibly mundane. He did, however, compose an epigram called "A Fooles Tounge" that reads, "Vpon a fooles provocation/ A wise man will not talke;/ But euery light instigacion/ May make a fooles tounge walke."

Dickie (sometimes *Dicky*) Pearce is identified with the Earl of Suffolk and immortalized, more or less, by an epitaph at the graveyard beside the Church of St. Mary, located in the village of Berkeley where he performed fool's service at the behest of the Berkeley family in Berkeley Castle in 1728 until (it has been supposed) he played one too many stunts upon one of the family guests. The legend on his tomb reads:

> Here Lies the Earl of Suffolks Fool
> Men Called him Dicky Pearce
> His Folly Served to Make Folks Laugh
> When Wit and Mirth Were Scarce
>
> ———
>
> Poor Dick Alas! Is Dead and Gone
> What Signifies to Cry!
> Dicks Enough Are Still Behind
> To Laugh At By-And-By
>
> ———
>
> My Lord That's Gone Himself Made Much of Him

Also nearly lost to time is Kunz (sometimes *Cunz*) von der Rosen, a so-called *private jester* in the service of Emperor Maximilian I. Kunz's likeness is preserved in all its belligerence with jutting chin and suitably misshapen head, as rendered by sculptor Daniel Hopfer, and once displayed in the Berlin Gallery. Today, Kunz's bust is to be found at the city of Innsbruck where Kunz has been designated (we can't imagine why) as the *mascot* of its museum where Kunz is presumed to accompany "children on their way back in history." Von der Rosen, like numerous other clowns, not only entertained but in more sober moments acted as an advisor to Maximilian, reminding us again that jesters were often, as Shakespeare recognized, more rational than their supposed masters. Shakespeare's *wise fools* is an irony, and yet all good, and great, writers are ironists. His not-so-foolish fools are to be found, for example, as Touchstone (*As You Like It*), Feste (*Twelfth Night*), an unnamed fool (*King Lear*), not to mention Trinculo (*The Tempest*), Costard (*Loves Labours Lost*), Gobbo (*Merchant of Venice*), Lavache (*All's Well That Ends Well*), another unnamed fool (*Timon of Athens*), Puck (*A Midsummer Night's Dream*), Thersites, a deformed and scurrilous Grecian (*Troilus and Cressida*), the clown (*Othello*), the two Dromios (*Comedy of Errors*), Speed and Launce (*Two Gentlemen of Verona*), the grave diggers (*Hamlet*), the citizen (*Julius Caesar*), Pompey (*Measure for Measure*), the Clown (*Winter's Tale*) Grumio (*Taming of the Shrew*), and the Porter (*Macbeth*) and Peter (*Romeo and Juliet*). His fools have served more than one dramatic purpose, such as relieving the heaviness of darker scenes so to balance lightness and comedy amid tragedy and horror. The fool is also capable of delivering a certain kind of corking good entertainment. Enid Welsford's book called *The Fool: His Social and Literary History* refers to the fool as "a man who falls below the average human standard, but whose defects have been transformed into a mainspring of comedy, which has always been one of the great recreations of mankind."

All the same, there remains an ambiguity of condescension toward the fool, since his message transcends foolery and tends to satirize his audience. Welsford reminds us that only in a culture "where the general level of sensitiveness is not very high" can one ferret out the fool's message. Elsewhere, such as in the Roman Empire, she says, some jesters were known merely as *moriones, stulte fatui* and were, as their titles imply, "mentally deficient" when such handicaps as imbecility and physical malformation were received with not so good-natured condescending laughter and derision, and when it was easy not to be threatened by their antics. Time was, and still may be, when some dunces find low humor in another's misery. All humor still contains some remnant of this passion for deriving satisfaction at the cost of other people's grief. Some household fools were expected to play the scapegoat and jack-a-napes, apparently to make their betters a little more satisfied with themselves. A lunatic, Welsford also notes, "is a victim who has lost touch with reality, on the theory that he is under the spell and damnation of an evil spirit," and therefore is to be treated as exactly that. Elsewhere, there have been those who interpret a fool's apparent signs of ironic sanity as a sure sign of his being under the influence of the devil. Whatever the presumed rationale for their deformity, dwarf-fools and hunchbacks, as Welsford also notes, were deployed to entertain dinner guests who preferred to view such wretches as nothing more than *silly slaves* and *subserving men* who were ordered to perform dangerous stunts that oftentimes led to injury and even death. There was a belief that such unfortunates might possibly become the household pets of their betters, through whose influence they might find their way into other comedic performances.

One of them was the *Feast of Fools*, a perverse reaction that took dead aim at the church, mostly (but not exclusively) in France during the later Middle Ages. It occurred at the first of the year during the Feast of the Circumcision, and may possibly have come about as a mutation originating with the pre-Christian Saturnian harvest festivals where conventions were turned inside out. Hence, social structures became inverted, revolution prevailed. Slaves became masters, civil laws ignored, chaos reigned, buffoonery was in flower. Revelers elected a Lord of Misrule, sometimes designated as a King of Fools, or *Preceptor Stulorium*. The idea was to appoint a mock pope and boy bishops as a deliberate satire belittling pious religiosity. The occasion was ideal for outrageous expressions of disorder. Licentious activities flourished. Paganism prevailed. Blasphemy was rampant. Cross-dressing was in style. Church alters became gaming tables. By 1431, however, the Feast of Fools was forbidden. Today, the church does its damndest to conceal the whole riotous uprising, even to the point of sweeping it under the pulpit. It was, withal, an excellent example of a foolocracy, the obverse of civilized behavior, emphasizing disorder over order, incivility over civility, madness over reason.

Fools might also find their way to another secular entertainment called the *Société Joyeuse* that was celebrated (so to speak) by the temporary suspension of what was presumed to be civilized behavior. The Sociétés Joyeuses were essentially ordinary citizens dressing as nitwits and behaving accordingly, selecting certain people of their number to assume the role of *Prince des Sots* and performing on a great stage of boneheads, acting out the *sub species, eternitatis*, reserving to right to say any damned fool thing they felt like saying without compromising themselves. Professional dunces elicit a certain elasticity of role that enables them to shrug insult and make fools of those who find amusement in their ridiculous dress and behavior. They possess a resilience that permits them to ignore slights and insults that others would receive with seriousness. Some have suggested that this principle plays out well in modern corporations and board rooms where, populated as they are by nitwits, some clever people have trained themselves to be oblivious to, and unaffected by, the commonplace stupidity that is present in the highest imaginable corporate circles.

"Qui non stultus?" Horace asked. Which of us is not a fool? In Erasmus's *In Praise of Folly* (*Encomun Morai*) the tables are indeed turned when a fool assumes command and belittles his arrogantly elevated and supposedly superior audience. Literary scholar Sandra Billington calls it "the most attractive point of departure for Fool Studies." In any case, such "clowns" on certain delicious occasions upset the prevailing imbalance that prevails between the lessers and their alleged betters. The celebrated theatrical fool Robert Armin in his *Nest of Ninnies: Simply Themselves Without Compound* concedes that "I think I am [mad], else I would not meddle with folly so deeply," acknowledging, all the same, that anyone being "wise enough...would wisely see into all men," except that "one foole cannot endure the sight of another." Langland in his *Piers Plowman* insists that the "artificial" (posing) Fool "is the Devil's agent," with a malicious capability for inciting chaos. The professional fool Tarleton learned the fool's trade (so to speak) by studying the ways of a *rustic simpleton*, insisting that "my attitude has always been that if I am a clown in the ring, I can and should be a clown out of it. Either you should be a thing, or not be it," although any actor knows, one can play a role on command and can, if he pleases, manipulate his audience, supporting Erasmus's claim that the fool comes equipped with a capability that can be used to undermine and satirize polite, civil behavior, especially in the foibles of courtly ill manners. Even so, the professional fool is a perpetual, and eternal, anomaly confusing his audience that is baffled by his ability, at will, to assume any bizarre identity. As one court fool confessed, his life would be less confusing if "...[he] were an innocent, a fool that...wear'd a pied coat, a cock's comb and a bell. And think it did become passive well," without alternating identities. Of the celebrated court fool Jack Oates, unaffected by his multiple identities, it has been wistfully and affectionately recorded:

> This fool was tall, his face small,
> His beard was big and blacke,
> His necke was short, inclined to sport,
> Was this our dapper Jack.

Unlike dapper Jack, other idiots have been likened to the somewhat contrarian somewhat passive, premonitional and foreboding role that the chorus plays in Greek tragedy. Speaking in one voice, the chorus reacts to, and warns of, what outrages are transpiring in the outer drama. Its role is somewhat similar to the narrative intrusion one finds in Henry Fielding, George Eliot and Leo Tolstoy, in whose novels the narrator cannot resist the urge to suspend the narrative and air a kind of off-the-record reaction to what's developing in the narration. Fools are by nature intrusive, interfering, gasbagging gadflies, persistently and outrageously irritating. They are rightly the sons of Momus, that irritating god of unceasing mockery, complaint, protest, and conspiratorial criticism, who was ejected from Heaven for bitching about the gods. Plato, in his *Republic*, discovered an object so impeccable that, he remarked, "Momus himself could not find fault with it." Nothing, however, is too sacred for the errant sons of Momus to obliterate. The classicist Edith Hamilton remarked, "to read Aristophanes is in some sort like reading an Athenian comic paper." True enough, although fools can scarcely be restrained from their irresistibly iconoclastic inclinations—particularly their urge to obliterate almost anything, usually by dismembering someone else's objects of veneration. The professional fool has claimed this as his occupational role, and has therefore felt quite free to blow anything he pleases to smithereens. His primary lethal weapon is vitriolic satire, which most of the time is comic, and therefore fair game for outrageous hilarity. Recall that Aristophanes, another son of Momus, had the audacity to take on none other than Socrates whom he depicts suspended in a basket from the roof of his sublimely philosophical *thinkery*, looking every inch the fool. This, incidentally, is the same Socrates about whom the noted classicist H. D. F. Kitto has written, "What society but Athens could have produced a figure like Socrates—a man who changed the current of human thought without writing a word, without preaching a doctrine, simply by taking to the streets of a city which he never left but twice—for the battlefield[?]"

Nevertheless, the professional fool claimed as his province satire and other means of derision as his occupational purview, and therefore felt quite at liberty to take aim at anyone or anything he wished, hoping all the while that others would not take aim at him in return. Freewheeling satire, Aristophanes well knew, could be, and often was, a dangerous and even deadly occupation. Welsford reminds us that "the fool's trade was too often a brutal one," insofar as the fool was liable to be judged either in light of his rational self or in light of his foolish persona. The so-called "natural fool" was a person bedeviled by some form of mental impairment, viewed as a *sub specie aeternitatis*, a subspecie viewed as an emissary of the devil. The *artificial fool* was, to the contrary, an actor, a professional comedian, a hired satirist occasionally regarded as a *stage fool*, expected to be rational and taken for that without retribution. Shakespeare evidently regarded many of his fools as truth tellers, owing to a fool's paradoxically inspired intuitive mind. If out of the mouth of babes come truths, so too the outspoken mouths of fools may reveal them as sooth-sayers. Strange though it is, we then have fools among the voices of reason, aiming their observations at those presuming themselves to be capable of higher judgment. Said another way, the fool transcends madcap nonsense and steps into the role of counselor to those taken to be in every respect his superior. To add insult to injury, the effect of a fool's remarks are all the more paradoxical because they issue from one presumed to be mentally defective and without any pretense of being intelligent.

A modern example is William Penn Adair "Will" Rogers (1879–1935) the Oolgah, Oklahoma-born, 'aw shucks' lasso-twirling wit who, in the august company of Texas Jack's Wild West Show, toured South Africa in the guise of the *Cherokee Kid*, later performed at two world fairs, turned vaudeville performer, joined the *Ziegfield Follies*, and eventually (while performing rope tricks) took to dispensing his view on life, love, politics, religion, culture, character, human events, and anything else that crossed his mind. Rogers subsequently appeared in Hollywood films (*Laughing Bill Hyde* in 1918, *Ropin' Fool* in 1928, *State Fair* in 1934) some 71 pictures in all, 48 of them silent. He was voted the most popular actor in Hollywood and allegedly authored 4,000 newspaper tidbits, became a radio political commentator, and had the gall to refer to congress as a *national joke factory*, jokingly campaigned for the presidency as the *Anti-Bunk Party* candidate in 1928, passed up an opportunity to become the governor of Oklahoma, hobnobbed with Coolidge and Roosevelt, traveled the world and died in an Alaskan plane crash near Point Barrow. There remains a memorial for him and his family in Claremore, Oklahoma.

Rodgers' persona was itself was a satire of some frontier nobody, drug-store philosopher and all-around damned fool, garrulously inclined, awkward-appearing prairie hotshot and know-nothing nitwit. "I am just an old country boy, trying to get along," he told audiences. "We don't need to worry about anything," Will said. "No nation in the history of the world was ever sitting as pretty. If we want anything, all we have to do is go and buy it on credit." As to his Americanism, he said, "My ancestors didn't come over on the Mayflower. They met the boat." Regarding his character judgment, he pronounced, "A man that don't love a horse has something the matter with him." On the subject of the sexes, he opined, "It should cost as much to get married as it does to get divorced." Politics? "A cannibal is a good deal like a Democrat. They are forced to live off each other." Elections? "I hope some of the men who get the most votes will be elected," since "no mathematician in this country has been able to figure out how many straw votes it takes to equal one legitimate one." All in all, he said of himself, "I could do a bum act with a rope that an ordinary man couldn't get away with."

A *New York Times* editorial claimed that "Will Rogers in the Follies was carrying on the tradition of Aristophanes, and not unworthily. His wry delivery is reminiscent of Mark Twain, in whose *Connecticut Yankee in King Arthur's Court* he appeared in its original talking version." His radio appearances were such that he rambled from one sentence to another, and was sometimes cut off in mid-sentence. Said Will over the airwaves, "What does a farmer need? A punch in the jaw if he believes that either of the major parties cares a damn about him after the election. Be careful that we're not getting all the government we're paying for. Everybody is ignorant, only on different subjects." In 1926 *The Saturday Evening Post* dispatched him on a

European tour where he met international figures and (of course) common people. Rogers was hardly a fool, although his pithy observations nonetheless originate bottom-up, from a persona who presumes, with more than a lick of irony, that he is proffering practical wisdom to some of those who fancy themselves infinitely more culturally advanced. It is more accurate to say that he was addressing his supposed homespun common sense that made its way culturally upward to an audience not nearly as astute as he ironically implies. His apparently unlettered, remotely anti-intellectual homespun messages puts us in mind of American 19th century Southwestern humor with its seriocomic, ever so earnest personae purveying a home brew of backwoods opinion, and does it in a uniquely American dialect bundled with backwoods foolishness. Southwestern humor was mostly a subliterary spin-off from what used to be known as *the old southwest*, especially Tennessee, Arkansas and Mississippi, with its use of the dressed-up tall tale and its gradually disappearing comic irregularities of spelling and articulation.

Not all practitioners of southwestern humor are remembered today. In their time, they were often newspaper men known by such colorful names as Thomas Bangs Thorp, Augustus Baldwin Longstreet, George Washington Harris, Johnson Jones Hooper and of course Joel Chandler Harris, author of the Uncle Remus yarns. Their subjects were an outgrowth of regional slave-holding culture centering upon such subjects as the frontier tall tale, back-acre trickery, comical foolery and local color situations involving the amusing cultural intrusion of the Eastern (New York, New England) tenderfoot upon the primitive west. Its narrators occasionally appear to be impossibly deficient in book learning and other civilities, but they were nevertheless read with interest and condescending amusement by literate audiences who presumed themselves quite above it all. Their literary influence eventually made its way into the work of Mark Twain and William Faulkner, both of whom drew heavily upon regional material.

Such comparatively unlettered narrations appeared to have been composed by and for fools, although the extent of their primitiveness is apt to be deceptive, their themes and messages ironically understated, originating as they did from barn and briar patch. Southwestern comedy survived more than 100 years and can be detected well into the 20th century in the work of Eudora Welty, Flannery O'Connor, Tennessee Williams, Truman Capote, Ellen Glasgow and Robert Penn Warren. It harks back to the professional fool of yore, what Barbara Swain in her study of fools and folly during the Middle Ages and Renaissance calls "the comedian's black face or the cockscomb and bells of the jester of literary history" who may be "distinguished by physical agility or awkwardness, by shrewdness or stupidity, malice, wisdom, garrulousness, or monosyllabic bluntness." Anti-aristocratic Southwestern foolery oftentimes was the work of writers mostly lost in literary history. Walter Hines Page (1855–1918) knew his gentleman's Greek, became a *literary adviser* at Houghton-Mifflin, rescued the *Atlantic Monthly* from extinction, became Woodrow Wilson's ambassador to England and was a lifelong observer and commentator on the American South, partly in the anonymously published, folksy pages of *The Southerner* (1909), a novel where we hear some choice testimony from a black slave identified only as Sam who opines, "dey say dat de niggers'll be free. I ain't gwine ter have non o'der freedom, I aint. May de good Lord carry me erway in er chariot o'fire." Hence, out of the minds and mouths of the humble and the downtrodden come scraps of backwoods philosophy that undermine what Southern literary specialist Gregory Paine called the *happy life of Negroes*, obliged to play the fool as one aspect of their survival. The fool is the one who chuckles derisively at such testimony. As Swain has observed, such a figure invites laughter "while it condemns him," for his apparent cultural innocence and for the ironic freedom that attends that innocence, mistaken for foolishness. Such a figure easily becomes an entertainer whose antics derive partly from his implied refusal to accede to prevailing codes of behavior among his betters. To carry this off, the fool needs to understand those codes. As a result, what has first seemed foolish is anything but that. When Erasmus assured us that "the greatest part of mankind are fools" he meant (among other things) that humor has as one of its principles that comedy arises out of exaggerated superior–inferior misalignment wherein the superior delights in the alleged stupidity of his inferiors, except that, as we have said repeatedly, the two roles are occasionally reversed. As Erasmus also tells us, through the voice of a woman, "friendship, you know, is seldom made among equals"; thereby evading the comedy of one party's finding comic absurdity in the other.

Comedy also reduces to questions of appearance and reality. Erasmus tells us that "what appears to be beautiful may chance to be deformed; what wealthy, a very beggar; what infamous, praiseworthy; what learned, a dunce; what lusty, feeble; what jocund, sad, what noble, base; what lucky, unfortunate; what friendly, an enemy; and what healthful, noisome. So it is between the fool and the philosopher." Erasmus also tells us that "all this life is but a kind of comedy, wherein men walk up and down in one another's disguises and act their respective parts." Furthermore, nothing is more foolish than preposterous wisdom, so nothing is more unadmired than an arrogant prudence. Hence, Erasmus's paradoxical title: *In Praise of Folly*, what elsewhere we might as well call a celebration of stupidity, or the appearance of it. To say it another way, the fool often represents our own defects. As Swain reminds us, during the 10th century the term fool was a synonym for *erring man*, one who makes mistakes. Nonetheless, Erasmus explores an entire culture of foolishness inside of which he has discovered grounds to defend, even recommend.

Such has always been the ambiguous role of the fool, although which of us would bother to quarrel over what appears to be the merits of a raving idiot? He may be what he appears, a rambling nitwit prepared to add a dollop of comedy to assuage our distresses and miseries. Of course, fools can be as annoying and as insufferable as a headache. A few of us actually live beneath the same roof with blathering jackasses and egregious morons, irascible nitwits, as if it is our cross to bear. Some people resign themselves to living within the same confines as blockheads, even encouraging their incessant foolishness, taking whatever they may from it. Author Jan Silvious has some thoughts to *share* about life among dunces and dipwits. Her book is encouragingly titled *Foolproofing Your Life*, by which she means how to survive among insufferable fools who intrude upon one's privacy. She suggests a number of coping strategies...many of which, by her own admission, don't work. One of her devoted readers responded that "I have plenty of fools in my life and I wanted to read more on the subject," which sounds encouraging, although she concedes that "we can't change our fools, anyway." Another testimonial admitted that "I was letting my 'fool' control me," which we find regrettable enough, although she was able to say in her own defense that "I was not going crazy," from which we derive comfort, but all the same the correspondent admits that "there's no way of dealing with the 'foolish' people in my life in a biblical manner," something that we find distressing. Regardless, Ms. Silvious's book does purport to show how one can approach idiots with strategies that enlist "a special kind of biblical wisdom," more specifically by searching the book of *Proverbs* with a mind to discovering "new insights" to assist in managing vexations with jackasses. We wish her well.

The assumption is that fools can be managed, which even from a distance sounds impossible. Not only is there little that can be done; it's hopeless. It is no more possible to cause a fool to be anything other than foolish than it is to cause a frog not to croak, even in those rare cases when household jackasses redeem themselves through an uncanny, if disarming, sense of perverse comedy. To add to our frustration we are not infrequently goaded into believing there may be some strategy that will restrain a fool from being foolish, an especially tantalizing prospect when one cannot isolate himself from nitwits. Deborah Katz and Angela Haupt collaborated on a brief article published in the *US News*, entitled "13 Fool-Proof Ways to Get Happier" (March 8, 2012) that reminds us of Wallace Stevens' "Thirteen Ways of Looking at a Blackbird," which manages not to say a damned thing about what the title purports to address. In like vein, Katz and Haupt propose to cite ways that we may all discover happiness *when life gets tough*. Their advice? "Spend $20 on an experience rather than an item," by which they mean blow it on theatre tickets and ski trips rather than on diamonds and cell phones. Point 2: "Pursue meaningful life goals" instead of getting all aroused about wealth and affluence. Point 3: "Be open to what's happening right now," in other words don't fret about your delinquent mortgage payment and your out-of-control credit card balance. Instead, be "moving on to other, more pleasant topics." Point 4: "Nurture meaningful relationships" on the dubious assumption that through them, "you only have that sense of belonging and acceptance." Point 5: "Reorganize your strength," as for example sucking in your breath and girding your loins after you've lost your job, your home, your insurance, your friends, your mind and your wits. Point 6: "Count your blessings" by saying things like 'at least I have my health' even though (back to Point 5) you've lost your health insurance. Another constructive thing you can do, the ladies suggest, is to associate "with others who are [even] less fortunate than you," having lost their homes, their jobs, their medical insurance and their food stamps. Point 7: "Keep an Optimism Journal," by Jove, a point well taken. What one needs to do is "every time something bad happens, think of the positive side to it." Point 8: Seek Advice From Your Neighbor," i.e., the fool next door. Example: "women makes more accurate forecasts about how they would enjoy a five minute speed date [whatever that may mean] when they read about another woman's experience with the man [what man?] rather than seeing his photo and reading his profile. Point Nine: "Get out and Sweat" on grounds that it fosters *feel good* brain chemicals like endomorphins and proteins that improve connections between cells in the brain. Point 10: "Do Unto Others," since 'Practicing acts of kindness has been shown to enhance well-being." Try giving blood or feeding a cat, since life is fundamentally a tit for tat equation; and consult a psychologist for whose services you pay by doing handyman or handy woman tasks around the house. Point Eleven: "Meditate" since, as everybody knows, deep breathing or meditating can do something, but we don't know what. Point 12: "Have In-Depth Conversations," if only because 46 percent of those who lost their homes, their jobs, their minds and their medical insurance strongly agree that their deep down conversations *were meaningful* (and also free) and Point 13: "Turn Up the Tunes," or as it were, *strike up the band*, because it's been duly reported that who listened to music "while undergoing a colostomy" (without insurance or life-support) "felt a whole lot better" about the occasion.

Hence we have 13 heart-felt, fool-proof paths to health, beauty and whatever else one may desire that should appeal to any fool willing to take them at all seriously. It is a couple of fools addressing a bountiful audience of abject fools, *abject* because the project is misleading and useless. Fools have always accorded other fools plenty of room and reason to make idiots of themselves. Someone (names omitted to avoid possible legal complications) commented that "fools only talk to other fools. They speak the same language," which is generally true. The language, however, is erroneous simplistic and misleading. There is, to be sure, nothing to be done about it and, as Benjamin Franklin himself told us, "it is ill manners to silence a fool," although on the other hand, "it is cruelty to let him go on," especially when one has no choice but to hear him out. There is a fellow out there named Kevin Lamb who authored a facile essay called *How to Avoid Becoming the Fool*, several pages into which he bravely addresses the dilemma he calls *Living With the Fool*, in which he warns that the fool in one's life is qualified through his example to advise others on how not to live theirs. This prompts Lamb to devise several paragraphs toward the matter of how to avoid developing into a flaming idiot, noting carefully that even a fish could avoid trouble if he kept his mouth shut. The poet John Donne composed a lyric called *The Triple Fool* that begins with the narrator's admitting that he is two fools, "For loving, and for saying so/ In whining poetry," and having done so, he concludes by declaring "and I, which was two fooles, do so grow three;/ Who are a little wise, the best fooles bee," which essentially says that were it not foolish enough to become enraptured, and admitting to it in verse, he exacerbated the dilemma by publishing it to the world, which is to say making a greater fool of himself.

It was Franklin (again) who memorably and unabashedly wrote that "a great talker may be no fool, but he is one who relies on him." All this is to say that he who keeps his own counsel and keeps his mouth closed at the same time will leave foolishness behind him. Ralph Waldo Emerson in his celebrated essay on self reliance tells us with his customary irony that "a foolish consistency is the hobgoblin of little minds," hobgoblin meaning a *bogy*, or *bogey*, a horrid apparition every bit capable of frightening children. Emerson also wrote quite unfoolishly that "to believe in our own thought, to believe that what is true for your private heart is true for all men—that is genius." Rather than playing the fool by aping the tastes and opinions of jackasses, it is self-reliance that delivers one from such abject folly. He furthermore argues that traveling is a fool's paradise, whereas "our minds travel when our bodies are forced to stay at home." Such matters as reliance upon property and governments signify "a want of self-reliance."

The word *eccentric* is to be understood as something not concentric, usually taken to mean something that shares a common center, a common axis, conveyed in the word *coaxial*, which means mounted on a concentric axis. To the contrary, an eccentric person is one who deviates from usual norms, and is not seldom taken to be rather odd, at variance from what is ordinarily thought, believed and done. He seems to be out of step with the great run of people, a fellow who seems to be capricious and whimsical, out of joint with ordinary folks. John Dryden in his *Conquest of Granada* applied the word to a chap "who moves eccentrique like a wand'ring Star" and is therefore abnormally aligned, hence at a distance from the center. Eccentrics, like some fools, can be a delight. Mark Twain, possibly in an attempt to rescue eccentrics from their detractors, remarked, "be virtuous and you will be eccentric." Robert Frost, an eccentric himself, defended eccentrics conditionally when he remarked that "a civilized society is one which tolerates eccentricity to the point of doubtful sanity."

Eccentrics are more fun that fools. They are also inner directed, rather than outer directed (like most fools). Inner directed people are just that: those who take direction from within. They are their own masters. Outer directed people look to others for direction. Their every preference and opinion originates from someone else. They apparently feel that they will be socially acceptable if they fall into line and profess what everyone else professes. The January 18, 1988, *Time* published a Pico Iyer essay called *Of Weirdos and Eccentrics,* that begins by citing an octogenarian named Charles Waterton whose wont it was to be seen clambering around the upper branches of an oak tree with what appeared to be the agility of an *adolescent guerilla.* Elsewhere, a source calling itself *Listverse* presented what it believed to be "10 Incredibly Eccentric People." Before we continue, be reminded that John Stuart Mill outspokenly defended eccentrics, observing that "the amount of eccentricity in a society has generally been proportional to the amount of genius, mental vigor and moral courage it contained ... [and that] so few people dare to be eccentric marks the chief danger of our time." That said, *Listverse* listed notable eccentrics from 10 to one in ranking, 10th among its allegedly arch eccentrics being a woman named Hetty Green, a miser known to those who knew her best as the *Witch of Wall Street,* supposedly one of the world's wealthiest women never to change her underwear nor her outerwear, for that matter. Her outerwear was her trademark black dress, comparable to the eccentric American poet Emily Dickinson's trademark white dress that she wore while leaving her home one dark night to view a church under construction. That white dress, now yellowed, hangs in her closet, 127 years after her death. Ranked 9th is the albino Dr. William Archibald Spooner (1844–1930) who made himself eternally, if unwittingly, famous as the fellow behind the Spoonerism which is a sometimes unwitting interchange of sounds, most likely first consonants or two or more words, such as "mardon me, padam, this pie is occupewed" (pardon me, madam, this pew is occupied), or "it is kisstomary to cuss the bride" (it is customary to kiss the bride), or "blushing crow" (crushing blow), or "can I sew you another sheet? (can I show you another seat?), or "well boiled icicle" (well oiled bicycle), or "let us glaze our asses to the queer old dean" (let us raise out glasses to the dear old queen). Spooner, all the while, was an Oxford don where, legend has it, people would attend his lectures on philosophy, Christianity and ancient history for the purpose of hearing him unwittingly turn his phrases inside out, creating a medley of howlers. To one of his lazy undergraduates he is believed to have said, "You've hissed all your mystery lectures and tasted two warm worms." Dr. Spooner was not amused, and to salvage his reputation he took to soliciting newspaper interviews.

The 8th nominee is a chap named Simeon Ellerton who, in the hearty name of physical fitness, became a foot messenger who eclipsed long distances in his English travels. On his return trips he is believed to have gathered ponderous stones that he balanced on his bean, the purpose being to intensify the exercise he was receiving, and also to gather enough rock to build himself a sturdy cottage for his dotage. He accomplished this, but it took him so fearfully long to do it that he continued to balance rock on his noodle for the balance (if you will forgive the pun) of his life that may have lasted 104 years.

The 7th selection is a fellow named John Christie, an opera fancier who, one memorable evening at the theatre, removed his glass eye, tidied it up and returned it to its rightful place. Next to him, incidentally, sat the queen, whom he asked whether his eye was properly restored to its socket. When the weather grew hot he was known to shear the arms off of the formal jacket that he would don along with a pair of ratty tennis shoes. His wardrobe was believed to contain 180 handkerchiefs and 110 shirts. Christie took to wearing lederhosen to the opera and expected his guests to do the same.

The 6th and the best known of all was Oscar Wilde, an eccentric name for an eccentrically irrepressible British poet and playwright given to extravagant, not to say flamboyant attire. During his Magdalen College, Oxford years he walked the streets with a lobster on a leash. A raving homosexual, he flaunted himself in such a way to represent what the proper English gentleman was not. "I have the kiss of Walt Whitman [the American bisexual poet] on my lips," he said after having met the fellow in 1882. Wilde was eventually imprisoned for sodomy, after which he took up residence for a time at the Hotel d'Alsace where, shortly before his death, he complained that "my wallpaper and I are fighting a duel to the death. One or the other of us has to go." Wilde was possibly outdone by the 5th eccentric on our list, he being Sir George Reresby Sitwell, 4th Baronet of Renishaw, an amateur gardener who, threatened by wasps, developed a pistol for the express purpose of shooting them. Sir George's estate housed seven libraries. The cows he kept were stenciled in blue and white to improve their appearance. He was the son, let it be remembered, of the redundant Sitwell Sitwell. Sir George was an accomplished hypochondriac who carried a huge pharmacopia on his travels. He is known to have invented a musical toothbrush and something called an *eggless egg*, consisting of a *yoke* of smoked meat, a *white* of rice and a *shell* of synthetic lime.

Our 4th screwball is Gerald Turwhitt-Wilson, aka Lord Berners, who harbored a variety of pigeons in his home, each of them dyed a different color. He also kept a pet giraffe that he regularly invited to high tea with him, and motored about in a Rolls Royce fitted with a harpsichord he could play while being chauffeured over the British countryside. Speaking of animals, the 3rd selection is William Backland, a naturalist uncommonly interested in animals, so much so that he opened his home to them and then ate them, one by one, in the company of his dinner guests whose tastes led them to mice, crocodiles, panthers and other sumptuous beasts. And speaking of dinner parties, our penultimate eccentric is Francis Egerton who threw a few noteworthy ones—for dogs, who were properly dressed for the occasion in the fanciest of finery, including shoes. Egerton himself wore a pair of shoes only once. He also kept partridges and pigeons in his household, but trimmed their wings so to make shooting them less difficult.

Our grand champion is eccentric Jemmy (James) Hirst. When King George I invited Jemmy to tea, he declined on grounds that he was training an otter to fish. He had engaged in other similar educational challenges before, when he supposedly taught a bull to assume the characteristics of a horse. Sportsman that he was, Hirst participated in fox hunts while mounted on his equestrian bull, and instead of relying upon dogs to flush the foxes, turned that ceremonial role over to pigs. Generous to a fault, Jemmy was given to blowing a horn to summon the poor to dinner, but when they arrived, he served them out of a burial casket. He instructed his many household maids to follow his casket (possibly the same one) during his funeral and enlist a bagpiper and a fiddler to play joyous music while he was lowered to his grave.

The object of our citing all such bizarre and outrageous eccentrics and their bizarre proclivities is to suggest that, all the same, such strange birds as these cannot very well be taken as fools, and that their questionable behavior is not to be viewed as remotely similar to stupidity. Nor can we suggest that eccentrics are in any sense to be seen as morons and dimwits. They are, to be sure, odd, something that certain of us may view with a certain forbearance and (yes) benevolent amusement, in the knowledge that all men are anything but equal, and that we have little choice but to accept eccentricity like the goofy fellows we are, secure in the knowledge that none of us is or has ever been the slightest bit off-center. Of course, we joyously encourage eccentricity so long as it does not threaten our safety and sanity. Our eccentric friends make the world a tad more colorful and rather oblige us to put our tolerance to the test. Fools, years ago, were eager to promote something they called *diversity*, which they believe themselves to have invented. It was simply the startling realization that there are some oddballs out there, and that they were to be tolerated and treated like *normal* people. It was to have been an act of consciousness elevation. Each of us, after all, might profit from having our horizons expanded the better to promote universal brotherhood and universally mutual understanding. Some of their number may have been reacting to a hideous slogan that read, "Join the army. Meet people from other cultures. Kill them."

To be sure, Will Rogers was something of an odd duck, but we are sufficiently liberal to tolerate such as he who blatantly prance about the world being exactly what they are: roving oddballs and other assorted misfits of varying shapes, colors and persuasions. A few of them may be found reading this page with smiling approval, but we decline to identify any. Mssrs David Weeks and Jamie James collaborated on a volume entitled *Eccentrics and Strangeness* that we earnestly commend to anyone who has ventured this far into our modest inquiry. They advance a number of astute observations, among them that *mad* scientists are fundamentally loners on average, and that loners could scarcely care less what the rest of the world thinks of them. They fear not much of anything. The authors cite Karl Popper's remark that such personalities "are creatures of [their] own minds" and are possessors of an almost poetic disposition. Even Newton, they remind us, passed his nights absorbed in the possibilities of alchemy and the prospect of turning base metals into gold. Newton also insisted that the mathematical theory set down in his *Principia* [*Philosophiae Naturalis Principia Mathematica*] arose from God's willingness to reveal them to a coterie of mystic philosophers *at the dawn of civilization.* They also cite the example of Robert Chambers, a 19th century Scotsman who relied upon (absurd as it now sounds) *phrenology,* a crackpot theory that the measure of one's intellect could be surmised by examining his skull. Weeks and James also record certain *eccentric scientists* such as Franz Anton Mesmer who theorized that the investigation of disease was more to be approached through physics than chemistry, and attempted to convert what he knew about astronomy and Newtonian gravitational theories into the science of medicine. "Good health," the authors assert, rested with Mesmer's belief that *inner magnetic fluid* is in synch with the *fluid that fills the universe.*

Be all that as it may, the authors have discovered that, according to the records of a large British hospital, "Only two out of 23,350 patients were deemed to be discharged with a primary diagnosis of eccentric personality," the conclusion being that the medical profession did not take eccentricity seriously, if at all. Such observations beg the question whether eccentricity is to be considered a personality disorder. Weeks and James also ask themselves whether eccentricity is the result of choice. If the answer is yes, they argue that the choice involves extraordinary bravery. Eccentrics, they also say, "revel in the feeling that they stand brazenly apart from most of the world, and experience ostracism because of it." They also estimate that something close to two thirds of eccentrics are aware by their eighth year that they stand apart from others. The urge to conform, the authors say, begins at home, and that parents want their children to be *normal.* Girls are more affiliative than boys and are more at the mercy of peer pressure, and thus are less likely to allow themselves to be recognized as eccentrics. Eccentrics are more likely to evidence a strong curiosity than the average bloke. Their sense of humor seems over the top, but by the same token they seem unable to comprehend other peoples' humor. Theirs is a pronounced self reliance, once a proud American characteristic, and *self-centeredness* that most would find unbecoming. But all the same, as the authors point out, eccentrics are happier than the rest of us. An eccentric knows what he wants, and how to find it, the rest of the world be hanged. Eccentrics, like other noteworthy people, evidence a necessary tunnel vision, something that extraordinary concentration demands. The penalty is that they're ordinarily anti social, singly directed, totally immersed. It's the cost of being accomplished. Eccentrics tend to stay by themselves because they candidly believe that most others are not worth their time, not worth knowing, being, as most of them are, fools and fatheads, blundering idiots who utter stupid remarks and bore the daylights out of any eccentric worth his salt. Notwithstanding, in 1882, there came into being a social club (of all things) called "The Eccentrics," a phrase supposedly lifted from the pages of Jules Verne's *Around the World in Eighty Days*. Theodore Roosevelt was supposedly one of its more visible members, if eccentric he was. It survived for 16 years in scenic Gloversville, NY, where it established a permanent residence in 1908, and where an estimated 600 alleged eccentrics celebrated together in a town without much of anything else to do except play billiards.

History, however, is punctuated by the presence of noteworthy individuals, who of course were at least in off-moments somewhat eccentric, as one might confidently expect. The arts, of course, have had their abundant share. Michelangelo lived in poverty and screamed at the statues he had created. So absorbed was he that he ate only when his body demanded it, and, like the Witch of Wall Street, refrained from changing his clothes, including his shoes that he wore to bed. He drew attention to himself by donning bright clothes and wearing an extraordinarily large, flowing beard. Similarly, Van Gogh lived in filth, whacked off the lobe of his left ear and rewarded it to a startled hooker. He irritated the pants off of his customers and was given to sudden outbursts of uncontrollable sobbing. Salvador Dali sported his strangely upturned mustache, confiscated the pens of those who solicited his autograph and habitually referred to himself in the third person. Picasso carved notches in his bedpost for reasons that one can only assume. Of course, culture rather demands that artisans display an eccentric exterior, even if they have to affect one. Should that happen, they're anything but eccentric. It is demeaning, of course for a person to impersonate someone else, but there are those who attempt it. To emulate eccentricity is patently foolish because it counterfeits a personality that is not one's own. It is also dishonest, a cosmetic alteration of one's personality. "The other day," wrote George Eldon Ladd, "I saw a man who fancies himself an eccentric. He sometimes wears strange clothes, a weird hat and often engages in quirky behavior," continuing, "I know another man who is a genuine eccentric. He is an expert in an obscure discipline, has unkempt hair [;] if you blindfolded him and asked him what he was wearing[,] he couldn't tell you...he is quintessentially quirky." He concludes, "genuine eccentrics are often very brilliant [whereas] pseudo eccentricity [is] sophomoric and annoying."

There is a bizarre 18th century account of an individual known as "Count Boruwlaski, the Polish Dwarf," no taller than a child of four who, oddly enough, chanced to encounter a certain Irish giant named O'Brien whose knee, we are informed, was nearly on a level with the dwarf's head. Boruwlaski, who believed himself appealing to women, made a fool of himself and succeeded only with women who treated him like the child he appeared to be. Be that as it was, Boruwlaski secured an audience with George IV, whereupon the king reportedly raised the little fellow up in his arms in a fond embrace, saying, "My dear old friend, how delighted I am to see you!" George picked the little fellow up, placed him on a sofa from which he jumped and was put back on, all the while addressing the monarch in French and otherwise commenced uttering a cascade of malaprops, revealing himself as pathetically confused about his eccentric identity.

A similar case of eccentric identity confusion turned up in a Bryan Miller essay entitled "Eccentrics on Ice," in the *New York Times* (December 30, 1991), having to do with the Rockefeller Center ice rink that, after 54 years of service, "has provided countless hours of slippery amusement for thousands of skaters from points near and far." There have always been, however, *regulars* who turn up daily, including a certain young woman known as the *Ice Princess*, who made her appearance at noon on Tuesdays and Thursdays in a "a pink tutu, a white fur stole and a glittering tiara" as well as her own music that she insisted be played before taking to the ice. The surprising thing was that the woman *could not skate*. More accomplished on the rink was a Bellevue Hospital nurse and sometime ballet student who, to the contrary, "put on a show that would give Ice Capades performers food for thought," what with her "twirling, stretching, crouching, splitting and arching into graceful swan-like movements" executed "with Olympian intensity" in, out and around "wooden-legged adults and elastic 6-year-olds" that terminated "with a flashy spin in the middle of the ice, a courteous smile to the imaginary crowds."

Hence the differences between a feigned athletic performance and a real one. Genuine eccentrics come by their eccentricities without trying. If, as Ladd claims, eccentrics may be more intelligent than most people (which wouldn't be difficult), it may be that their powers of concentration are such that they possess far more than ordinarily inquiring minds that demand a deeper, far more penetrating examination of what interests them. It requires what fools refer to as the aforementioned *tunnel vision* that has both assets and liabilities. On the plus side, it gives subjects their minute, sustained inquiry into something that occasionally results in their knowing more about less than anyone else. This can cause them to be celebrated and acclaimed as authorities over that certain thing, and on the strength of that, they are to be placed ahead, and possibly above, the rest of the human race. Such extraordinary concentration fosters eccentric behavior, if only because their uncommon attention to a single thing leaves them wanting in others. To a person whose mind is pointed in only one direction, little things don't much matter. He may wear socks that don't match or forget to carry rubbish out on Monday morning. The liabilities are far less significant. One can seem so absorbed in thought that he becomes what fools call *anti social*, having no patience with ordinary social interaction, with endless chatter and banality. Fools, as we have seen, tend to associate with other fools with whom they exchange blather. Some people, far from knowing an immense amount about one thing, are in direct opposition to people of tunneled vision and purport to know a tidbit about anything one can name. Such a person used to be called *well-rounded*, and therefore prepared to unload his shallowness at cocktail parties. An extraordinary talent at conversation qualifies him to be comfortably convivial.

Howard Robard Hughes, an American eccentric's eccentric entrepreneur was the errant son, born on Christmas Eve, of the first Howard Hughes who amassed a fortune by developing a drill capable of penetrating hard rock and leasing it to oil exploration companies. He was less good at drilling through to his son who, like many adolescents, had an adolescent will of his own that more or less precluded enrolling in schools. Like Steve Jobs in a much later era, Hughes was an endlessly curious, endlessly aggressive loner and tinkerer. His doting and rather psychotic mother died during surgery when he was 16, his father of an embolism two years later. At 18, Hughes had differences with his relatives who were then running the Hughes Tool Company, of which he inherited 75 percent of what was an estate of one million dollars, back when one million was a far larger number than it is today. Instead of waiting until the age of 21 when he could assume control of the business, he arranged legal emancipation into adulthood, bought the remaining quarter of the company and ironically married a Houston socialite named Ella Rice, two years after which they moved to Hollywood, the home of a screenwriting relative. Enchanted by the movie industry, Hughes began underwriting films, the third of which (*Two Arabian Nights*) he directed and won an Oscar; however, he lost his wife through divorce. Pursuant to his filmmaking he extravagantly invested in some 87 airplanes. Over time, Hughes underwrote 25 films, during which he acquired a passion for aviation that in turn led him to open the Hughes Aircraft Company in 1932 during the Depression when an estimated 16 million people (about a third of the work force) were unemployed. In 1935 he established an aircraft speed record of 352 mph, purchased aircraft along with engineers to look after them, and six years later with a crew of four circumnavigated the world, eclipsing a 1931 speed record then held by Wiley Post, another Texan who, with Harold Gatty, flew around the northernmost part of the earth in about eight and a half days. Post died in plane crash near Point Barrow, Alaska, that also claimed the life of Will Rogers. Hughes received a ticker tape reception in New York, a massive occasion at a time when he was verging noticeably toward antisocial behavior that eventually developed into his obsessive passion for privacy that some, at least, viewed as nothing more than an eccentricity. In 1936 he struck and killed a pedestrian, and amassed a net worth estimated at $60 million. Meanwhile, during his Hollywood period Hughes supposedly entered a protracted series of erotic adventures with both male and female motion picture performers such as Cary Grant, Errol Flynn, Rita Hayworth, Ava Gardner, Olivia deHavilland, Katherine Hepburn, Carole Lombard, Ginger Rogers, Faye Ray and Jean Tierney. During World War II, Hughes Aircraft contracted to develop a mammoth aircraft capable of transporting 700 people and airlifting a cargo of battlefield warfare including Sherman tanks. Its official name was the Hughes H-4 Heavy Lift Transport Flying Boat, popularly known as the *Spruce Goose*, a monster flying machine, much of it, because the scarcity of metals, constructed from birch. Hughes himself piloted it on its first test, but aside from that, it made only one flight. The brevity of its deployment is partly due to the lateness of its appearance. Loner or not, Hughes was obliged to appear in person before a body of Washington bureaucrats to defend the cost of his plane, for which he had received government boondoggle contracts that totaled $38 million that, according to newspaper columnist Westbrook Pegler, he obtained illegally.

Ever more eccentric and mentally troubled, Hughes continued to avoid public contact and become ever more reclusive, although he directed Jane Russell (for whom he designed a bra that she refused to wear) in a 1947 film called *The Outlaw*, and married actress Jean Peters, 21 years younger than he, in 1957. They divorced in 1970. Terry Moore, another actress, claimed to have married him in 1949, and the matter was settled out of court. He had earlier proposed to Jean Simmons and Susan Howard. Hughes continued to nurture an obsession for being alone, and in 1966 established residence in the Las Vegas Desert Inn Hotel. According to accounts, when the hotel attempted to be rid of him, he retaliated by purchasing it—at twice its assessed value. Moreover, he is said to have purchased three other hotels, maybe more, in addition to about 80 percent of Trans World Airlines, and during the Vietnam War he made another fortune marketing helicopters. Over time, his business acumen eroded, and he began to lose money and establish residences abroad. He died while en route from Acapulco (where he could easily obtain the codeine he craved) to Houston on a private plane, although the precise reason for his death has been contradicted. According to some reports, not even the FBI could establish that the corpse was Hughes's until they obtained fingerprints and discover broken hypodermic needles imbedded in his arms. Writer Scott Deitche has written that his body appeared more likely to belong to a homeless man than one of the wealthiest men in the world. "Emaciated with long hair and nails and covered with sores," Deitche reported, "he maintained his handlers [known as the "Mormon Mafia" because of Hughes's high opinion of Mormons] until he came to an ugly end." His private worth was pegged at $2 billion.

Hughes does not properly belong in any book of fools, except as an extraordinary example of an eccentric man who, while not foolish, in all probability suffered from madness by any other name we care to assign it. For all his faults and successes, he is the very antithesis of foolery. He had, at one time or another, been an aircraft manufacturer, owned regional airlines, owned a film studio, owned a medical research facility, and was lord over vast real estate properties. He had flunked out of a high school and allowed his mother to manage his life and forbade his from making childhood friends because she believed they carried communicable diseases. She also held him out of school for a year on some vague medical pretext. He did once injure himself badly when he crashed an aircraft in Beverly Hills while making a motion picture. He injured himself again when his fondness for morphine became an addiction. Psychological opinions of Hughes vary in emphasis. One theory proposes that he suffered from tertiary stage syphilis. Others have noted his obvious obsessive–compulsive disorder. There are those who suggested that he was the victim of pernicious dementia or maybe schizophrenia. Raymond Fowler, a psychologist at the University Alabama, allegedly studied Hughes for years and published the obvious in the May 1986 issue of *Psychology Today*, positing that he had become a "paranoid and eccentric recluse," the introverted son of a doting mother and a father who was mostly absent. Fowler also noticed an *avoidance disorder*, meaning among other things that although he sought friendships, his anxiety prevented his making them. He was apparently uncomfortable with himself and experienced what used to be called *nervous breakdowns* over a 13-year interval. When he was ensconced in Las Vegas hotels he would sit naked in a white chair that he presumed to be germ-free while he viewed old motion pictures. Later he began to repeat himself. He then engaged a pilot to fly him over the Southwest where he would hole up in darkened motel rooms. He insisted that those in his company wash their hands frequently and wear white gloves. They were forbidden to speak to him or view him directly. If he believed that he had been near a diseased person, he ordered that his clothing (which he often didn't wear) be incinerated. In his last days he continued his nudity, urinated on floors and remained perched on a toilet for an entire day. Fowler surmised that Hughes was psychotic and a disturbed man.

Any fool can assume that much, unassisted. Hughes, however, possessed an astonishingly creative mentality, and although he was patently destructive, he was inordinately, even absurdly creative and uncommonly successful at tasks that strike some people as unadulterated folly. His conceiving building and flying an airborne plywood aircraft of behemoth proportions, larger even than Jane Russell's breasts that for him presented an engineering challenge in the form of an underwire cantilever brassiere (he defined culture as the ability to describe her without using one's hands). Hughes undoubtedly applied his understanding of aeronautics to Ms. Russell, inasmuch as airplanes ordinarily possess cantilever wings. She tried the garment, deemed it uncomfortable and, on the sly, disposed of it. Hughes, for his part, left us with the impression of his being a rather deranged, uneducated individual who happened to demonstrate a genius for anything he felt moved to accomplish.

One could, of course, argue successfully that a man of Hughes's character was eccentric to the point of making preposterous, even stupid, lapses in practical judgment that qualify him for inclusion in any gallery of fools, and that his foolish side militated against him, whereas anyone with mere *common sense* (as we've commented earlier) ought damned well to navigate his life in a more rational manner. There has been a long held theory that madness is a necessary component of creativity. In her article titled "Creativity, the Arts and Madness," *Roper Review*, Vol. 21, pp. 47-50, 1998, Maureen Neihart, Psy.D. makes the case for one's *regression to more primitive mentality*, and writes that "to be creative requires a willingness to cross and recross the lines between rational and irrational thought." One ordinarily associates irrationality with madness and, more often than not, stupidity. Neihart defines creativity as "the production of something that is both new and valued," whereas madness is "a self-destructive deviation in behavior."

Opinions about creativity and madness have a long history. According to Seneca, Aristotle remarked one cocktail hour that "no great genius was without a mixture of insanity." Neihart claims that madness and genius have three features in common, namely what she calls "disturbance of mood, certain types of thinking processes and tolerance for irrationality." By *disturbance of mood*, she refers to such conditions as depression, dysthymia (a milder form of the same thing) and bipolar disorder. By *certain types of thinking processes*, she has in mind psychosis, a condition that bedevils a great many creative people. Her "tolerance for irrationality" speaks for itself. What she calls "translogical thinking" is essentially a "thinking process [that] transcend the common modes of ordinary logical thinking," not to be confused with ordinary garden variety stupidity and common foolishness. Most of Niehart's observations apply to artists of various kinds, although they also apply to gifted people in other odd corners of life. Her findings do not suggest that one must be mad to be creative, although such people tended to more than ordinarily at ease with irrationality around them.

Eccentricity has at times transcended the personal, and broadened to the cultural. Gregory James in an article called "Eccentric Biography and the Victorians," *Biography*, June 22, 2007, comments upon the Victorian "fascination with eccentric behavior" including *strange physiologies*, pointing out that between 1790 and 1901 "eccentric biography included almost sixty works, comprising periodicals, single works and multivolume books," all evidencing "an eccentric preoccupation with the marginal...aberrant [and] excessive," with attention to gender, but also with discussions "about British—

and especially English—culture and identity." Asked one bloke, "Breathed there a Victorian who was not eccentric?" Anyone who has read Dickens is aware that he traded heavily in impossibly eccentric characters and situations, apparently because his readers craved eccentrics and their oddball habits. James feels that such preoccupations reflect a long-held fascination for the "strange, violent and dreadful" that may have been influenced slightly by Sir Francis Bacon's taste for outlandish behavior. James cites an anthology collected by one John Timbs who characterized eccentrics as people *of wealth and fashion* who were obsessed by such engrossing things as "delusions, imposters and fanatic missions, hermits, fat people, giants, dwarfs and strong men, strong sights and sporting scenes, eccentric travelers, artists and theatrical people, men of letters and convivial eccentricities," which encompasses virtually a panorama of London life, consisting as it does of anything the slightest bit odd, peculiar, weird, outré, unusual, aberrant, disgusting, queer, strange, outlandish, ridiculous, outrageous, bizarre and (as one might suspect) indecent.

Such tastes as these presume that the world should rotate upon what is universally agreed to be quite safely and properly orthodox, unassailably moral, conventional, and universally acceptable. It recommends a culture predicated upon a tablet of assumed possibilities, all of them heartily endorsed by everybody, on the grounds that they are the way people and situations ought damned well to be, for the good of us all. It cuts no slack for anyone or anything perceived as culturally wide of the mark. We are put in mind of marching men in rank and file, each of them painstakingly attired in regulation military dress to the minutest detail. Furthermore, they are presumed to be of the same mind and mission, with no room for exception. There are and have always been conspiracies to stamp character from the same mold, and program it to the same ends, regardless of how mindless those tasks may have been. Such conspiratorial excesses are best suited to fools. Military culture demands that its members surrender their intellects and inclinations for what is allegedly the greater good, which renders them little more than automatons in the service of somebody else's motives. It means in other words submission to psychological indoctrination, and it is of course ideally fitted to obedient dunces. Religious indoctrination is one such example, with its catechization of the naïve and ignorant that ordinarily assumes the form of ritual questions and responses committed to memory. It has been suggested that children have been inappropriately subjected to ideologies better suited to intelligent adult evaluation, since it directly relates to such shopworn subjects for exhaustive speculation as God, man, religion, destiny, weather prediction and so forth. Now there are reports of quite the opposite, namely efforts to discredit religion by advancing partisan views at variance with those embraced by parents who on occasion have elected so-called *home schooling*. Of course there are other forms of social engineering, such as with athletic teams, choral groups and the secret societies already discussed at length.

Our outer directed marching men in uniform, though their services are forever in demand, are also in peril of combat catastrophes that may leave them disabled, if not decidedly dead. Certain kinds of personalities are obviously more suited to such horrendous possibilities. There are certain high-minded motives for protecting and defending one's country from external (but not internal, including governmental perpetrated threats) perils. It's what certain people do, and even like it, partly because it puts them safely in touch with others who seem to function well by taking orders and belonging to groups. The police protect, the firemen extinguish, the ambulance drivers ambulate the sick and injured and the morticians bury whatever they can find. These are no occupations for independently minded, inner directed eccentrics, however. Others see it as a fool's trap. A report issued by a group calling itself *The Project on Youth and Non-Military Opportunity* issues a warning to young people of independent inclination that military life entails abundant abuse and eternal humiliation. Those who volunteered for the privilege of donning a uniform and seeing the world found that the world they were destined to see, for what might come to seem like a very long time, was nothing like the one they had been longing to see. Nor were they truly prepared to surrender their privacy and submit to severe regimentation. Some will complain that the sales pitch they received from a recruiter with the straightest of faces was, to put it gently, misleading. Allegedly, a 1997 survey of enlisted personnel revealed that 50 percent were not at all pleased at having been fooled into uniform. Others complained that the job training they were promised was intended for military, not civilian purposes. Another 67 percent said that they were not accorded the kind of job training they had in mind. One can be punished without legal counsel and without a hearing. There are restrictions on what they are permitted to say. But this, after all, is military life, and if you don't like it, as they say, *tell it to the Marines*.

As Defense Secretary, Dick Cheney put it directly, :the military is not a social welfare agency; it's not a jobs program." Nor is it a convenient source of ready cash for university expenses. There are strings attached to everything, including this. Some 71 percent said that their pay was insufficient. Small wonder that about one quarter of military enlistees were accorded something less than honorable discharge. Another third find a way, despite obstacles, gracefully to duck out of the military earlier than they may have anticipated. Complaints about discrimination come from blacks, women and Hispanics. Many joined the military reserves, on the assumption that they would never be called to active duty, meaning that they would not, by some fluke, actually end up engaged in battle, with guns and bullets. Regardless of their reservations about the political nature of the conflict to which reservists have been sent, qualifying as a *conscientious objector* may not fly, and may instead land a soldier behind bars—not the ones at the officers' club. Those who attempt to leave the service are in peril of being punished. One must be prepared to participate in any military conflict anywhere and for any reason, even no reason at all. Offenders may find themselves among the colony of eccentrics incarcerated in the U.S Disciplinary Barracks at Fort Leavenworth, Kansas.

Such are the mixed rewards of regimentation where, if fools are to be suffered, eccentrics are decidedly not, nor do we suggest that they should. Eccentrics don't react well to being ordered around, although yes, there have been a few who took to the military life in their own peculiar ways, among them a cavalry officer whose idea of a good time was to inflate balloons that he attached to his body until he became weightless and capable of scaling tall buildings. There have been plenty of others, such as a certain John Malcolm Thorpe Fleming "Jack" Churchill, aka *Mad Jack*, who glamorously fought in World War II armed with a longbow, arrows and a *claymore*, which is a hefty double-edged sword identified with the Scottish Highlanders. Mad Jack asserted that any soldier who enters combat without a sword is *improperly dressed*. And speaking of being properly dressed, a certain Major-General Orde Wingate foolishly wore an alarm clock on his wrist and an onion around his neck. We have no problem with that, but Wingate greeted an Israeli ambassador while otherwise completely naked, and remained so until his guest departed hours later.

One must not, in his investigations of military eccentrics, overlook mention of dyslexic George Smith Patton, Jr., who at various times gave the impression of being irretrievably mad, even though he commanded the 3rd Army that led the way to the liberation of France and the defeat of Germany in World War II. He is remembered for a number of things, not all of them flattering. His habit was to arm himself with his prized ivory-handled pistols, should they come in handy, which they did when at the age of 26 in the 1932 Stockholm Olympics he won a pistol shooting competition from a distance of 25 meters, in addition to a fencing competition, a 300 meter free style swimming match, a horseback contest and a four kilometer cross country run. In times of battle he would remark, "You can't run an army without profanity, and it has to be elegant profanity. An army without profanity couldn't fight its way out of a piss-soaked paper bag." His men felt that whereas his was a treasury of salty language, none of it was anything close to elegant. His men didn't call him *Old Blood and Guts* for nothing; they amended it to read *Our Blood, His Guts*. One of his worst gestures was to slap two soldiers afflicted with shell shock and bedded down in an Army hospital. He was also responsible for killing more than one million Nazi soldiers. He designed and constructed a tank, but the Army wouldn't buy it, literally or figuratively. Dwight Eisenhower took him to task for willy nilly killing German prisoners. Quoth the old soldier, "I'd rather have a German division ahead of me than a French one behind me." Patton also saw to it that a certain German prison camp that held his son-in-law was liberated.

Patton, like Hughes, was no fool. He may have been insufferably mad, but he was more than ordinarily paradoxical. Inner directed eccentrics have been known to function surprisingly well within a highly structured organization. There are those who may be mistaken for fools when they're anything but that.

Those who pass their lives endorsing causes, including ones they don't begin to comprehend, may be perilously close to foolery, if not over the edge. The tenuous theory that to get along, one must go along, has misled a great many people who believed it was necessary to play ball with idiots.

Women, specialists advise us, may have greater affiliative tendencies than men, and they may also be at risk of endorsing other people's passions, one of the more corruptive of which are sororities that demean them into subjection. This can, and does, begin early in life. An organization known as WOG (Women of Grace) has directed attention to (of all things) Girl Scouts, that has been in existence since 1912 and is widely presumed to be a wholesome organization. Its founder was Juliette Gordon Low, a Savanna, Georgia, woman of good will and the best of intentions. Her idea was to model it partly on the Boy Scouts, by advancing such worthy ideals as responsible citizenship, benevolence, character and international friendship. The Girl Scouts currently claim more than three million members in at least 70 countries. What alarms the WOG women is the organization's affiliation with Planned Parenthood, and what they view as radical feminism. What's worse, they say, is its embracing something called *New Age*, an ambiguous innocent-sounding something-or-other that led to the Arizona Cactus-Pine Council of the Scouts which they insist was the insidious invention of something called *The Ashland Institute*. That in turn put together something called *Coming Into Your Own* that also looks reasonable at first glance, but which allegedly directs girls down the dubious road to politically correct causes, not the least of which is global warming. They also urge what they benignantly call *Journeys* that enlighten girls to *different archetypal dimensions* of themselves, the better *to work experimentally using dialogic and four quarter models* [whatever that may mean] together with story, imaginative and kinesthetic exercises to access [the] *whole self*. To make an even more complicated story short, one church warned that the Scouts' affiliation with Planned Parenthood led in the direction of contraception and abortion, inappropriate for girls of that age. We must say, parenthetically, that in our mad world of sheer foolishness, boys may now join the Girl Scouts, provided that they wear dresses. According to a Jan Vallorani article titled "Girl Scouts: Boot Camp for Feminists" and published in *Patriot Update* on March 21, 2012, it is "extreme liberals and fanatics [who] have hijacked this organization" and have linked it "to controversial issues such as radical feminism, gay, lesbian, bisexual and transgender issues [and] abortion rights." A cross-dressing fellow representing media relations allegedly "taught a workshop for the Girl Scouts based on a Planned Parenthood sex brochure called *Healthy, Happy and Hot*. The same character turned up at another "no adults allowed" workshop for the Girl Scouts, held at—where else—the United Nations, citing another passage from *Healthy, Happy and Hot*, this one claiming that "some people have sex when they have been drinking or using drugs. This is your choice."

Indeed. In saner times when you thought of Girl Scouts, chances are you thought of cookies. Writing for the same publication on February 22, 2012, David L. Goetsch noted that once upon a time "nice little girls in brown uniforms would peddle their sugary treats door to door, accompanied by their harried but smiling moms," but since the Scouts have become "an instrument of Planned Parenthood," he no longer eats their sweets. Children, like fools, are particularly choice targets for manipulation, including indoctrination under the guise of *education*. Responsible, disinterested (unbiased) teaching is one thing; indoctrination quite another. We take indoctrination to mean partisan, possibly sectarian opinion. One can present opinion for what it is. Children, if they remember anything (which they probably won't) are not equipped to evaluate the substance of what they've been fed. Nor can fools, who disseminate disinformation among themselves. Einstein said, "I never teach my pupils; I only attempt to provide the conditions in which they can work," which is to say an open environment, all of which politicians thirst to control, including educational systems, religious purveyors, the medical profession, the legal structure, the economy, the affairs of business and of every citizen living or dead.

Such is an ideal environment for the nurturing of fools who can be taken in by a blatant fraud. Edward Feulner, president of the National Heritage Foundation, in his article titled "Modern Academia: The Educational Equivalent of Fool's Gold?" in the October 27, 2008 *Capitalism Magazine*, warns that parents must exercise diligence over the courses into which their young and impressionable charges naively enroll. Rather than alerting them to the perils of frat parties and football games, they're warning them that they approach their academic affairs with prudence, particularly those that presume students to be aware of certain *talking points*, a euphemism meaning that they accept certain positions apt to be non-sequiturs, for example courses in *women's studies* that predictably begin on the assumption that marriage is "an instrument of oppression and a means of enslaving women," aimed at the same women who clamor after matrimony. For a course in *Black Marxism*, enrollees are to assume that "the growth of global racism suggests the symmetry of the expansion of capitalism and the globalization of racial hierarchy," or, to simplify: the non-sequitur that "capitalism equals racism." Feulner suggests that in times past students were introduced to traditional values accumulated from the best minds, and invited to evaluate them in open, academic, civilized discussion. If what we're told be true, then those days are behind us. Let's presume not.

Still and all, fools shall remain what they are. The world is brimming over with an inconceivably huge passel of stupid people whom we have little choice but to deal with as best we can, even if it's a hopeless quest. A more or less rational chap named Carlo M. Cipolla compiled a timely, if eccentric, treatise forthrightly titled *The Basic Laws of Human Stupidity* that offers some fresh thoughts on this endlessly perplexing problem. Chances are that your neighbors, pleasant though they are, are most of the time unimaginably stupid. Not even Cipolla himself can conceive of the stupidity that surrounds us. Nonetheless, the first of his so-called *laws on human stupidity* is simply that "always and inevitably everyone underestimates the number of stupid individuals. He also holds the opinion that moronic behavior is not parceled out in one gender over another. His so-called *golden* fundamental contention may be summarized by the principle that stupid people lose, while rational people win, assuming that people behave in a consistent manner. Stupid people, he holds, are *dangerous and damaging* because their behavior is both *erratic and irrational.* Intelligent people, he holds, consistently underestimate how dangerous fools are, and that attempting to deal with them is invariably a costly mistake. So it may be.

Andrew Romano had the gall to write a controversial piece called *How Dumb We Are*, for readers of *Newsweek* (March 20, 2011), in which he posing 1,000 American adults with the same questions that are put to citizenship applicants. The disheartening result was that 29 percent could not (or quite possibly preferred not to) identify the vice president, 73 percent could not explain why the Civil War was fought, 44 percent could not say what the Bill of Rights was, six percent could not find Independence Day on a calendar. In short, they are not only nitwits; they're worse. Such people are commonly identified as dunces and fools, but moreover as *philistines.*

The original Philistines, recall, appear in the *Old Testament* as savages inexorably inclined toward licentiousness seasoned with a healthy dollop of cruelty, idolatry and immorality. They're the ones who, we are told, were combative people of sinister origin who occupied parts of Palestine and preyed upon the Israelites. In modern parlance, *philistine* is taken to mean, or even denote, *outsider,* but the word today is more pejorative than ever, implying a base person, uncultured, unwashed and uneducated. Thomas Carlyle called them "bores, dullards, Children of Darkness." Besides being all that, they are jackasses whose existence threatens the intellectual fabric of the nations they poison.

Cicero said that a nation can (if it must) survive its fools, but anyone knows that their presence remains a cultural detriment, nay threat, especially if they are inclined toward philistinism with its perniciously bad taste and uncivil behavior. There are those who would have them deported to a distant island where they might languish in everything cheap and tawdry. They've even made their presence felt in the book trade. A site calling itself *Prospect* reported that "some of us persist in the belief that the book world has been over run by philistinism," whereas a few "can still rejoice in unprecedented levels of both quality and quantity." Would that it were so. Currently 85 percent of kids who turn up in juvenile courts are functionally illiterate. Over 60 percent of prison inmates, the same; 70 percent of those inmates cannot read above a fourth grade level. Illiteracy, like disease, passes from one generation to the next. Some 90 percent of welfare recipients can neither read nor write. An estimated 75 percent of food stamp people populate the lowest two literacy levels. *Education Portal* (June 13, 2011) reported that about 20 percent of adult Americans were assessed in the highest two levels that measure one's ability to comprehend documents, prose literature and ordinary mathematical computations.

Chapter 5. Idiotic Opportunities: Putting Fools to Work

Some of it's monkey business; some downright dangerous.

There is a place in the world, we prefer to believe, for darned near anyone. This does not exclude idiots, who at first glance strike us as being jolly well out of luck. And yet, as we've repeatedly said, fools do associate with other fools, and out of these crucially interpersonal colonies some productive exposure to opportunity may yet arise, but frankly, we don't see that happening. It's more likely to result in some explosively, unanticipatedly inflammatory outcomes. Still and all, when the full collective power of stupidity is properly harnessed, we're inclined to think that something laudable might yet inadvertently result. There have been days when sturdy individuals, by dint of their high purposes, their persistence and their conspicuous paucity of intelligence, caused startling things to occur. We can imagine that we personally might one fine day act in concert with substantial numbers of our blockheaded friends and nitwitted neighbors toward some more or less otiose common cause. We confess to imagining, we don't know quite why, being at the center of a huge, spontaneous outpouring of jackasses, converging on the streets, overturning flower pots and outhouses, urging nitwits onward to new and heretofore unimagined levels of inanity.

One means of making one's way is by functioning though an ingathering of halfwits, a flowering of fops, a march of morons, a bundling of blockheads marching to the cadence of quick stepping dumb clucks on parade. We imagine thriving in giggle-witted communities of imbeciles who, with one voice, make their message *resonate*, as nitwits say, through a festive commonality of morons. We further seize this opportunity to predict confidently that the outreach of foolery will rejigger the world into an international confederacy of foolocracy, embracing all nations in an unswerving commitment to world duncehood, their absorption in unbridled belching, wanton howls of gaiety and unbridled merrymaking, embracing all genders (shall we say) and all the world's spirited simpletons. Give stupidity a chance. Liberate monkeys and apes. Let communities commune. Raise garish temples to goofballs, dumbheads, fops and raving jackasses. Find a leader and follow him, wherever he wanders. Trust this nitwit with your life. Do precisely what you're told. Fool that you are, raise no questions. Look no further. Violate the rules. Ignite the firehouse. Let mayhem thrive.

* * *

Randolph County's Lynn, Indiana, is quietly situated near the intersection of highways 27 and 36, a few miles from the Ohio state line. Its population is about 1,100, and its police department is situated at Main Street and Church. The First Church of Christ offers a Ladies Bible Study on Saturdays at ten and sponsors a softball team. But that's not all the local news there was. In the 1930s the town dunce, who once bailed out of an airplane and into a haystack, confidently announced that he was about to leap off the Lynn water tower, then changed his mind — until two other town rowdies climbed the tower with him and pushed him over the side. Fortunately, he was wearing a parachute. The word *tornado* had not been invented, but in 1965 the town was struck by an enormous one, causing an estimated 875 injuries and 25 deaths.

Back in 1931 local townspeople named Thurmond and Lynetta Jones brought forth their only child and named him James Warren; years later he was believed to have greater than usual intelligence and a greater than usual ability at psychological manipulation. Those who knew him said that he appeared to be obsessed with religion and death. He was graduated from a high school in Richmond, Indiana, south of Lynn, in 1949, and married a girl named Marceline Mae Baldwin that same year when, strange to say, he was knocking on doors and attempting to sell monkeys. By 1953, he managed to become an *ordained* minister, meaning that he was, in the eyes of the Disciples of Christ church, somehow divinely accorded authority to dispense spiritual and other forms of privileged advice to the nitwits who were comparable to the fools who took him seriously when he was supposedly selling monkeys as one might sell Fuller Brushes. The couple moved to Columbus, Indiana, when he enrolled for a time at Indiana University, and then Indianapolis when he enrolled at Butler University from which he was graduated in 1961 with a dimwitted degree in elementary education. Jones saw fit to join the communist party, ingratiated himself with city politicians, got himself appointed to a Human Rights Commission by Mayor Charlie Boswell, affiliated himself with the Somerset Southside Methodist Church, and resumed selling what the gullible liked to contemplate: racial harmony, justice for everyone, socialist utopias and the promise of a red carpet welcome to a promised land. While in Indianapolis Jones took to the airways with his own radio program on WIBC, Indiana's flagship AM broadcasting station.

His supposed spiritual side by this time had eroded into rank socialism that he sold to mostly down-and-out fools who were eager to join his People's Temple and be taken in by what they believed was a religion suitably charismatic. Jones then eventually settled in San Francisco where he hobnobbed with some of the best, which is to say worst, of politicians. He assisted in seeing that one George Moscone be elected mayor in 1975, and was rewarded by Moscone's appointing the future mass murderer as his housing commissioner. Jones had the honor of buttering himself up with Walter Mondale, Rosalyn Carter, governor Jerry Brown and Harvey Milk, one of California's leading homosexuals who was murdered at the same time Moscone was. Time was when Moscone and Milk had some nice things to say about Jones in letters they sent to Jimmy Carter. But at the same time some not so complimentary stories were circulating about Jones. While this was happening he saw the possibility of transforming his makeshift church into a cult that soon gave rise to dark allegations of drug use, intimidation, beatings, rapes and other abuses of his parishioners who were mostly drawn from racial minorities, the poor, the uneducated and the stupid—all of whom he enlisted in the creation of an agricultural complex called the *Happy Haven Rest Home* for the use of his bogus *community*, to whom he advocated leftist politics.

By 1974 he and his wife had visited a site in the South American jungle in the Republic of Guyana, heretofore known as British Guiana, hemmed in by the Atlantic on the north, Surinam on the east, and Brazil to the south and west, Venezuela also to the west. Guyana's official language was English. Jones leased a spread of land and called it Jonestown, and by 1977 urged his following to join him there, partly, he said, to escape from American capitalism—not to mention the police and the corrupt IRS. In 1978 California's U.S. House representative Leo J. Ryan, a few newspaper people and a few more relatives of those by this time enslaved by the Jonestown cult, visited the site. Some of the cultists told visitors that they feared for their lives and welfare and wanted to leave. Upon hearing of this, Jones countered that his community was *being destroyed from within*. One of those eager to escape made his move barely in time to avoid the subsequent poisoning that murdered his wife and son. Jones then ordered that Ryan and his party be assassinated. He and four others died; the rest escaped.

Ryan, oddly enough, was posthumously awarded a Congressional Medal of Honor for being the first congressional bureaucrat to die (as they say) *in the line of duty*. Fearing that the murders would invite a more thorough investigation of the Jonestown catastrophe, Jim Jones ordered the faithful (as it were) to drink cyanide-laced, liturgically colored grape (of course) Flavor Aid. Being basically naïve and stupid, nearly all of them obeyed and nearly all of them died. When Guyana sent troops to find out what the hell was going on a day later, they discovered 913 corpses, 276 of them children, 210 unidentified and 16 survivors. Most of the bodies are buried in a mass grave at an Oakland, California, cemetery that, incidentally, offers a scenic view of San Francisco Bay. There has been a memorial service every November 18 when Jones, aware that his Marxist utopian dictatorship promised land was about to be exposed in all its horror to the world, ordered everyone murdered. Babies were the first to be poisoned; their mothers were next. It was the largest American civilian killing until September 11, 2001.

There are any number of ways to interpret this carnival of death, one of them being the inconceivable extent to which the weak minded can be gulled, subjugated, tortured, humiliated, subdued, and exterminated by a madman capable of capturing victims; in this case he told followers that he was a Christian prophet with the mystic ability to heal the sick and wounded, but then he massacred his weak minded captives through what he called a *revolutionary suicide*. Jones died of a gunshot to his head that was ruled a potential suicide—but the weapon turned up 200 feet away. American troops, including the Green Berets, punctured the bodies to free the noxious odor of decay.

Fools are where you find them. In Jonestown, hundreds came forward voluntarily like dumb animals and committed suicide after being ordered to do so. Reports claim that Jones had been more than able to hoodwink women, Hispanics and blacks who constituted a major proportion of his victims. After the Guyana affair, Congress did what it always does: appoint a committee to look into the matter and report back anytime it felt like it. Surprisingly, the committee did reveal some eye-opening details as to what preceded the mass murders and that shed some light on how easily the foolish can be goaded into astonishing actions. Jones's modus operandi bore a resemblance to that of certain totalitarian dictators whom the author read about as a Hoosier schoolboy, especially Stalin and Hitler.

He at first conspired to distance his followers from the past, including reducing all sources of communication and establishing himself as the only source of information. He then instituted a program of absolute obedience infused by threat and intimidation, even to the point of likening himself to Jesus and God. Jones punished certain people he deemed to be the slighted bit independent by depriving them of rest and nourishment and with more threats of severe beatings. Those threats were supplemented by mental and emotional pressure to recognize him as an omnipotent savior, all the while promoting guilt over such commonplace things as luxury, privilege, recognition and reward. He instituted public meetings where errant members of the cult were publicly interrogated, harassed, humiliated, reviled and disgraced. To accomplish this he relied upon a system of file cards he kept in the manner that governments use to spy on citizens, the better to control them. Nor was he above taking people to task for acts that they did not commit. His victims were made to believe, moreover, that Jones was aware of all things by virtue of his mystical transcendence. He also demanded that these fools inform on each other, including family and friends. As a result, people refrained from voicing anything that might be construed as subversive. His aides would reveal incriminating information to a person, and then wait to determine whether that person duly reported it. The intention was to contrive a culture where no one trusted anyone, except of course Jones's imperial self. It came to pass that family members, including spouses, children and siblings, turned each other in.

While this was happening, Jones extracted up to 25 percent of each person's income, and insisted that everyone sign over to the People's Temple (as it came to be called) all personal property. He even compelled unwilling partners to marry, and sometimes disallowed cohabitation between married couples. Fools were forced to sign blank sheets of paper, to which Jones and his criminal minions could attach any incriminating statements they wished. On other occasions the prisoners did not seem to balk at having their names linked with such things as theft and homosexuality. Jones freely attempted to ruin reputations, such as they may have been, by spreading lies like manure. At other time he posted operatives to spy on these fools and disseminate false information on them. At the time Congressman Ryan was murdered, Jones's gunnery squad open fired on what it believed to be other interlopers, namely Richard Dwyer from the U.S. Embassy in Georgetown along with the persons purportedly representing *Concerned Relatives*, and news reporters that included Ron Javers (*San Francisco Chronicle*), Tim Reiterman (*San Francisco Examiner*), Charles Krause (*Washington Post*), Steve Brown, Bob Brown and Bob Flick (NBC), all of whom were at first greeted cordially. Ironically, Ryan supposedly said upon his arrival that Jonestown "was the best thing that ever happened" to its prisoners that included about 150 children that Jones is believed to have adopted with the cooperation of California court orders.

Jones then took to his loud speaker system, exhorting his followers that their privacy had been invaded by outsiders, and that "well, it's all over, all over" and that they were to gather paper cups and consume poison out of a huge wash tub after having forced the liquid into the mouths of their children. Those who resisted were poisoned by way of hypodermic injections. Jones told them that were they to do it, otherwise they would be tortured by the *authorities*. He further said, "Don't be afraid to die. You'll see people land out here. They'll torture our own children here. They'll torture our people. They'll torture our seniors." As to the dead politician, he said, "I don't know who shot him...I tell you, get movin', get movin' get movin.'" According to the *Washington Post*, the fruit-flavored drink contained not only potassium cyanide (a toxic, rapidly fatal substance that deprives the body of oxygen) and potassium chloride (that can cause muscle weakness and irregular heartbeat), but Thorazine (used as a sedative), Demerol (a pain killer that also promotes sedation), Phaerengan (an antihistamine that also aids absorption of substances), Thallium (used in rat poisons), Haliopareo and Largatil (both sedatives). One of the victims was his wife.

Such are the catastrophes that befall those who are too easily led, easily persuaded, easily swindled, easily murdered, easily dumped into mass graves. Even those who had advance information about the atrocities refused to believe them. To compound the stupidity, there were circulated reports that Jonestown was the work of the CIA that had instigated the experiment in *mind control*, that Jones was himself a CIA operative who collected a huge colony of dimwitted *fanatics*, that the deaths were little more than a hoax, that the idiotic Guyannans were unable to count the deaths, that Jones was little more than a Bible-thumping fraud who displayed moist chicken livers as clinical evidence that his harangues miraculously cured his followers of cancer. Certain other allegations were true, among them that he was wealthy, that he swindled his captive fools (which he recruited out of mental hospitals) of their Social Security checks,, that despite the intense heat of Guyana his prisoners were forced to work as much as 11 hours a day.

Years later a rock and roll ensemble called *Jim Jones and the Suicides* appeared on the popular scene, as did Stephen Gandhi Jones, supposedly his only biological child, although there are others Jones is alleged to have fathered. Stephen played basketball on the concentration camp's team and was last seen in California where he claimed to be a businessman and confirmed that his father had been a drug addict. Duping large numbers of morons is not as difficult as it might sound. One would tend to believe that anyone with enough determination and fun-loving misanthropic inclination could (and has) accomplished it with surprising ease. Only recently an out-of-work improv actor, while not in the same murderous league as Jim Jones, pulled off an impressive stunt when he persuaded 4,000 idiots to remove their pants and participate in a movement he called the *No Pants Subway Ride*. His other claim to popular immortality was when he convinced 200 nitwits into freezing (so to speak) in one position inside New York's Grand Central Station. He has since written a book on the enlightening subject of removing one's pants, and of course has hit the university circuits, advising jackasses how *to stage pranks in public places*, which is probably more valuable in the end than the politically correct courses into which they have enrolled. In the meantime, the prankster has explained his silly preoccupation as *a sort of personal challenge to try something new.*

James Warren Jones staged more than a few pranks in public places, but took it to extremes when in the end he poisoned everyone. There's and old and unreliable saying that old maids are doomed eternally to lead apes through hell. We are reminded that Orpheus led Eurydice *out* of hell, although it eventually caused his death by suicide. The foolish and clichéd line *take me to your leader* is alleged to come not from history but from science fiction. Fools have attempted at times to lead themselves, which of course is not the best of ideas. Neither should they attempt to manage intelligent people. Under the heading of *My Time Pass Collection* comes a piece entitled *Working for Morons*, that divides into several *rules*, specifically that one ought not to use one's brain, since when working for fools, it's best to put one's intelligence aside and appear, at least, to comply with absurdity, for the time being, until a better employment opportunity comes one's way. Not to do so may cost one's job. It is of course best not to remind one's overseer that he's a flaming jackass, for the same reason. The next rule is to acknowledge that if something doesn't make sense, it's because it doesn't make sense. It's better not to ask for clarification, since the fool to whom one temporarily reports doesn't comprehend it, either.

When some horse's arse issues instructions, nod obediently and give the impression that you comprehend every syllable, and that it all makes perfect, rational sense, even to a jackass. Convey the serene impression that you're more than eager to carry out orders devised by some total moron, and that you wouldn't have it any other way. You live to obey directives, and to do so in a way that would flatter the pants off of any raving fool. At the first moment when this dunce is out of your sight, execute the job in your own fashion, partly because your way is far better and because this horse's fanny hasn't the intelligence to recognize it. Should you follow his instructions, no good will come of it. The result may be catastrophic and he may take you to task over it, even though it was his wretched idea. If this horse's ass says it's important, it means that some fool at a higher level believes that it is, which is why he is coming down on him, and why he's coming down on you.

Be mindful too that there is no rational need to extend yourself physically, emotionally or any other way. You need not forfeit sleep or go blind. He is not, after all, nearly intelligent enough to comprehend how difficult, or perhaps how absurdly simple, your assignment is, or appears to be. That said, make it appear impossibly difficult, then take your sweet time. Foster the impression that your tasks are breaking you down, compromising your sanity. Show evidence that you're working to the brink of exhaustion, and that it is for the sake of performing whatever inestimably lame-brained job has been given you. When this nut case peers at you over your isolation cubicle, promote the impression that you're laboring to distraction, even to the point of mental disintegration. It's all a charade, of course, but it has its rewards, namely that you will keep this nitwit off your case because he has the mistaken impression that you view your tasks as the highlight of your otherwise vacant life. Ask him questions that have no apparent answer. This will cause him to execute a quick and awkward retreat.

All such subterfuge carries with it a number of *hidden agendas*, as fools call them. Your hidden agenda is to protect your mindless job for as long as it requires to discover an acceptable one. Such strategies as we've cited are effective if only because there it's a fool's world out there; knowing this, one may just as well acknowledge and play it to advantage. It is not the slightest bit unusual for nitwits to become annoyed by circumstances that cause them to seem what they are, especially when overshadowed by a bewildering and highly visible authority. Positions of authority are parceled out by others of still greater authority who, heaven help us, do not want to be challenged in any way by the jackasses laboring beneath them.

Beverly West, who writes for a group called *Working with Fools*, cites an instance where a jackass hovers over a worker with a mind to witnessing his losing confidence in his ability to tackle whatever stupid task he's been assigned. The jackass observes his victim while he gradually becomes a little more than paranoid and begins to surrender his self-esteem, assuming that he ever possessed any. West's advice is directed at those who are biding time until they can shop their talents elsewhere, the better to accomplish feats without being supervised in the process. She further observes that people who meet the description of *boss* carry a label that demands some scrutiny. The *OED* reminds us that the word has an etymological history that suggests the term *botch*. It doesn't end there. It also carries implications of its being a *lump* or *protuberance*, which is to say a hump or a hunch as one might surreptitiously observe on someone's back. Boss also seems to denote a bulk, a bulky animal, also taken to mean *bose* or *boce* which is a large bundle, a butt, something stuck in a wine bottle.

Ms. West suggests that one may consider taking the horns by the bull, so to speak, and gently implies that one does not need to be supervised quite so closely, and that it is quite improper for an employee to take orders from a flaming idiot. Of course, one neutralizes this negativism by veiling his behavior. The objective is to work independently, which is to say without some damned fool bending over one's shoulder. Failing all that, West suggests certain effective recourses, to wit, that one turn his attention to other witless, bureaucratic and therefore impossibly foolish, not to say absurd, resources. Among them are *human relations* bureaucrats consisting of numerous nitwits certain to convene meetings that, several weeks hence, will do anything necessary not do anything to say much of anything bearing upon any problem, except that the committee will refer the employee to any of several other ineffective places. One of them may be *employee assistance* programs that will also evade problems partly because they don't comprehend them, and if they did, would do nothing anyway. West also refers us to a *career counselor*, another blockhead who will bury the employee in a sea of clichéd banalities. Result: no one vacates his job because, as Ms. West says, "it is too short for that," a limpid observation if ever we heard one.

A fool in the workplace is analogous to a house fool or court fool in days of yore. His task is to be foolish, something that idiots do naturally and, in their way, reasonably well. It may be that, contrary to good judgment, every office should have its fool to ease the hours of prevailing tension and long, insufferably monotonous silence. Our friends at *Mushable Business* offer some puerile yet suggestive ideas to lighten office dreariness short of tossing a lit firecracker into the privacy of one's assigned cubicle, or declaring a fire drill or a pat-down. One well-tested prank is to switch telephone plugs in such a way that one party is made to respond to a cascade of callers intended for someone else. Workers have been known to tape down the button that ought to rise when one responds to a call, the result being that the telephone persists in ringing, or whatever noise it makes. Another idea, petty though it is, is to tinker with someone's mouse. A better one is to lock someone in a lavatory stall. Honorable mention goes to tinkering with sound systems on computers in such a way that one is obliged to hear two minutes of a woman's orgasms. One creative prankster discovered a way to cause everyone's CD tray to pop open every 30 seconds. Not many fools would think of this one: swapping the five and the four so that when some dope punches one, he receives the other.

It's a cornucopia of foolishness intended to create temporary relief from the drudgery of mindlessly repetitive clerical work that continues for eight hours plus, and leaves some intelligent people mad with boredom. "The arrival of a good clown exercises more beneficial influence upon the health of a town than do asses laden with drugs," wrote the 17th century physician Thomas Sydenham. In our own time David Sobel, another physician, tells us that "laughter is an invigorating tonic that heightens and brightens mood, gently releasing us from tensions and social restraints." Probably so, but nonetheless there remain problems tolerating and managing jokesters on the job, mostly because one hasn't the option of unshackling himself from his desk and running for cover. Prolonged exposure to nitwits carries the veiled threat of becoming one, which is to say that prolonged exposure to dunces implies that one's in danger of becoming as big a jackass as everyone else. Elementary school teachers, not the most intelligent sector of society, over time begin to evidence childlike mannerisms that exacerbate their prevailing stupidity. It's altogether reasonable to be wary of influences that place one at risk of seduction. Consider, for example, being incarcerated among criminals for a prolonged time, and therefore picking up at least the veneer of, and then being lured into, criminal culture. Suppose too being charged with protecting mentally handicapped people, and being therefore influenced by their limitations.

We do know that stupidity is largely genetic, although there are those who come by their stupidity independently. Similarly, we presume that intelligence is also inherited, although it appears to be possible to enhance one's mental acumen. By intelligence, we simply mean comprehensive cognitive agility. Yes. It does more or less run in families, depending upon into which gene pool one happens to have tumbled. Some are gifted, others not. People are a rather unpredictable combination of the genetic mix, and then there is the question of what one does with his intelligence. We all know fools who come from what appear to be tolerably intelligent familial heritages. It follows that stupidity is also inherited, although there are environmental circumstances that foster, encourage and even reward it. There are even people who apparently feel that it is in some sense *shrewd* to appear foolish. This might be useful when dealing with morons, for example, since morons appear to relate best with other morons. In spite of that, there are nonetheless individuals whose social and psychological ploy is to appear cunningly stupid, and employ that ruse to gain the confidence of others who actually, obviously, plainly are stupid. We've heard the cliché *dumb as a fox*, which seems to say that what passes for stupidity is actually cunning, which in turn suggests being things like crafty, dexterous, resourceful, agile and clever. There are those who represent these enviable characteristics, all the while appearing to be stupid. The professional fools discussed in the previous chapter were generally of this disposition. It is they who are remembered for their ability to out-wit whomever they pleased.

Anyone who has ever been a teenager will attest that in the name of social acceptability he will gladly commit any stupid act, and commit it proudly. This kind of behavior has its analogues. Certain adults will perform like fools if it will carry them where they want to go. We had closer looks at certain idiotic groups earlier in these pages, namely social and secret organizations, clubs, cliques and all such rubbish expressly designed around, and for, fools. Were there no fools, there would be no such foolish flocking. Nonetheless some of them cluster toward any social abomination, even Jim Jones's fraudulent and murderous jungle cult where they were demeaned and humiliated in much the same manner those others will gladly tolerate so to be accepted into a college fraternity or volunteer with a military organization.

The naiveté of fools remains a perplexing problem for everyone. Debra Ronca has enumerated scams into which fools blunder while they're traveling abroad, if ever they do except in the military. One of those subterfuges involves encounters with counterfeit police whose counterfeit uniforms trick the unsuspecting who, of course, can't very well distinguish one uniform from another. Certain of these frauds inform their gulls that there's been a rash of bogus currency in circulation, and have the hapless tourist present everything in his pocket for expert scrutiny. Following a little *legerdemain*, the counterfeit cops return the cash, saying that appears to be the real McCoy, except that real or not, a goodly amount of it is missing. Other, similar ruses result in passports being lifted. Another technique is to direct a fool's attention one place while he's being swindled in another. When he redirects his attention, he finds that some of his property is gone. One of the distractive techniques is to spill something on the victim, and while he's wiping whatever it is away from his clothing, the thief has helped himself to whatever he can get away with. She also mentions the so-called *Good Samaritan* who assists the unwary at ATM machines where they not only steal money but steal cash cards. Another stunt, and this one is relatively easy to pull off, is to play games with currency, since most travelers are unacquainted with the value of foreign bills. Certain coins, for example, resemble other coins, except in value. Some frauds exchange counterfeit currency in exchange for legal tender. Ms. Ronca points our attention to taxi drivers who will deliberately drop a bill and then replace it with one of lesser value. There are those who, for a price of course, turn up at airports for the purpose of offering hotel discounts that, when the gull attempts to register, don't exist. Restaurants have been known to offer two menus, one for the locals, another for tourists. Some helpful souls offer to purchase fools tickets of some sort, accept a fool's money, and of course vanish. Out on the roadways, frauds point to tires that they claim are deflating, and while they are rummaging through the trunk of the car looking for a spare tire they steal whatever they can lift. At other times when a fool is busily fumbling with his camera, someone adroitly has his hand in the fool's pocket.

Not surprisingly, fools are particularly at risk for online swindlers. Bible frauds will be more than happy to sell gallons of Biblical holy water directly from the tap of Moses's motel room in Hackensack. Others in their number are apt to organize revival meetings with shills planted in the audiences who will be pleased to come forward and attest that their tumors have wondrously disappeared after a scam *preacher* placed his holy hand upon their afflictions. Others hand their money over to prophets on the prospect of its being an investment in a sure-fire scheme, only to discover that it disappeared, sure-fire, into the prophet's pocket of prosperity. Other Bible pounders extract money from their *congregations*, pledging to pass it on to certain holy causes such as treating themselves to a new Mercedes. Some profit from sob stories such as the need to cover some sad soul's burial expenses. At other times the sly preacher digs more from his captive fools to distribute at his holy discretion, which makes its holy way directly into his holy wallet. There is also the drop-off trick where some halfwit agrees to drop money on a church's steps, from whence it unaccountably disappears. Certain churches use their email accounts to send distress messages to nitwits who agree to send them whatever they believe they can spare. Other frauds move from door to door, collecting churchly donations.

A fool and his money, as the bromide goes, are soon separated. Some con artists dupe the crooked IRS into believing that they represent a tax-exempt religious organization, but few have been so diabolically successful as Jimmy Jones who eventually demanded and got his legions of fools, some of them not paupers, to relinquish their worldly goods, not excluding their entire property: cash, equities, bonds, other valuables—everything. There is always a fool waiting to be cheated and unraveled. Moreover, there are those who, Like James Hervey Johnson on behalf of the *Thinkers Club*, is convinced that all religious organizations are fraudulent. Johnson writes that whereas "intelligent men do not decide any subject until they have examined both or all sides," there remain "fools, cowards and those too lazy to think, accept blindly, without examination, dogmas and doctrines imposed upon them by their parents, priests and teachers when their minds were immature and they could not reason." *Thinkers Club* members apparently endorse the notion that "those who have a spark of intelligence will examine the facts" and thereby "stop paying tribute to the religious properties, and lose their fear of a mythological god and a mythical hell." What Johnson offers instead is his introduction to what he calls *Positive Atheism*. Various stupidities play mostly into the hands of dunces and others who are ideal targets as the insufferably gullible. There are other theological (if we may misuse the word) hoaxes out there including statues that weep tears, and it's of course possible to build statues that will not only *boo-hoo*, but sob until hell won't have it, or until its lachrymal tank runs dry. One may challenge the notion of raising the dead, or feeding thousands from one fish, or having virgins give birth or keeping our "seniors" alive for an amazing 800 years and Edenic gardens and all such, but one must at the same time be intellectually prepared to comprehend such things in any of several ways, not only theological, but possibly allegorical or as one may otherwise see fit.

Fools, in the meantime, are taken in by other manifestations of basic trickery. Even the IRS in all its impossibly-bloated shady bureaucratic magnificence has been taken in by thieves with invented identities and bogus impersonations of persons long deceased. Were someone to request a bogus refund, he might well receive it. Were one to ask a fool for his identity numbers, he might well surrender them. In the meantime, those who drone over their desks shuffling papers for behemoth bureaucracies are not conspicuous for their sophistication and intelligence. There is an entire *demimonde* of foolery, a subculture consisting of shadowy figures trading in scammery in the forms of ruses, deceptions, swindles, and frauds of all inventive descriptions that, as we have said, plays out best upon nitwits and dunces prepared to snap at any legitimate-seeming bait. Impersonations are an excellently inventive manifestation of deception, since they trade in representing themselves for what they are not. There are the purveyors of religions, those who purport to dispense advice on financial investments, home improvements, burial plots and encyclopedias. Others masquerade as detectives, imperson-ate the opposite sex, presume to practice law and medicine. A great many people pretend to have earned academic degrees and have even been hired by universities to profess things about which they know nothing. Some include counterfeit diplomas to support the bogus information they include on their resumes. Telephone marketers prey upon children, the elderly and the stu-pid. Others pass bad checks, and brandish phony documents attesting to everything under the sun. Fools themselves, living as they do existences of foolishness, silliness, stupidity and sham, inhabit a world separate from more rational, responsible notions of how life and society function best. The cleverest deploy their time and energy efficiently and effectively rather than dawdling their hours and days away, to the end that they direct their lives in a structured manner to ends other than folly, a word that suggests madness, a deficiency of comprehension and good sense, even wickedness, lewdness and wantonness.

In 1863 *The Saturday Review* attempted to differentiate between what it called *foolishness and wiseness*, somewhat pedantically commenting that "we are willing to believe that the folly that plays so great a part in the world is a taint in the blood. The fools we mean are not simply dull—on the con-trary, they are clever fellows," continuing, "folly is not folly until it proclaims itself," adding that when one declines to speak so as to keep his foolishness from showing, others may be listening. Fools are of course suited to ridicu-lous occupations that coincide with their world view of folly and nonsense, central to their constitutions and inclinations best described as light-hearted and *sans souci* in their approach to fun and frivolity. Certain kinds of employ-ment are adaptable to persons of little to no learning, since fools generally demonstrate a life-long aversion to it on grounds that it too time-consuming, too dull, possibly too likely to corrupt and distract, too theoretical, too open to common debate and deliberation, too damned much trouble, especially considering that one might of necessity have to arise by dawn's first light, pack off to a classroom, remain awake, even apply one's self to book learning with its dangers and discomforts. Better to be what others whimsically call a *child of nature*, free and unfettered as the breeze and guided by his natural instincts that tell him when to fill his tank and empty his bladder and when to write home (if write he can) for money.

Consequently, employment opportunities for jackasses, and fools of other descriptions, are rather compromised. Attracted as they are to expressing themselves through insufferable clichés such as "I'm no rocket scientist" and "I'm no brain surgeon," someone recently combined the two, declaring that *I'm no rocket surgeon*. Stupidity has its comic purposes, but in most cases does not advance a fool particularly far. To exacerbate the problem, the pernicious rise of technology can subsume almost all assignments, including those cur-rently occupied by government drones as well as those employed in bank tellering, envelope stuffing, stamp licking, automobile washing, telephone answering, ticket taking, snake oil selling, organ grinding, money laundering, window peeping, pipe smoking, pearl diving, egg rolling, salt shaking, floor sweeping, bribe taking, Bible pounding, wood chopping, bubble blowing, oil changing, beer guzzling, bear baiting, warrant serving, pocket picking and hand wringing—all of them career opportunities for nitwits. The problem, if we may call it that, is finding suitably useful opportunities to put dumb bells to work for the common good, paying for their lottery tickets and their moon pies. The US government, ever in an expansive mood and expansionist mode, may find a way to initiate a program to be called *Jobs for Jackasses*, modeled on the fabulously successful *cash for clunkers* program that was designed to block any self-righteous environmentalist dingdong from applying the admonition "reduce, re-use, recycle" to the engine components in cars that were still running but were no longer in good enough condition to be seen in our neighborhood.

Stupidity is not always cordially received. Montana governor Brian Schweitzer told the press that "49 percent of these jackasses," referring to those *serving* (themselves) in the United States Congress and who were complaining about the Keystone Pipeline, "one year ago wouldn't ever have known where the Keystone was," meaning that not even a jackass is fit to represent a constituency in that once august body, now transformed into a sewer of corruption. Another remark, this one included in *The New Social Worker* (Winter 1997), and authored by Judith Davenport, carried the disheartening news that the public perception of social workers is as "child snatchers, ineffective do-gooders, fuzzy-thinking liberals, parasites on the public purse, self-serving bureaucrats and fad-chasing jackasses." And while we're on that subject, consider an unsigned piece called *Jackasses, Blunders and Stupidity* that turned up in a site called *Suidoo* that attempts to clarify for us all what in general practice and by broad public opinion is meant when we utter the *j* word, so that we may attempt to form a consensus, however fragile it may be. Jackass, the writer begins, is "the ultimate anti-accolade, given to the individual or individuals who are so socially inept, so unaware of the consequences of their actions that there is almost no hope for their rehabilitation; extreme, almost pathological stupidity is the defining aspect of their character," to which we can all respond with a bravo and a hearty *heave-ho*.

Only recently, to our eternal regret, the less than esteemed national wastebasket stuffing and money burning General Services Administration that is *charged*, as nitwits say, with ferreting out, identifying and vilifying some of the reckless waste of taxpayer money, attempted to set new records of profligation by recklessly blowing a mere $823,000 on a Las Vegas orgy of conspicuous waste by bestowing a ludicrous honor upon one of its nitwit employees, appropriately calling it *The Jackass Award*, which was their idea of a good time that also included the "investment" of $7,000 in sushi,

$59,000 in *audio-video services*, and another $75,000 in what they claimed were *bicycle building* exercises for their fellow dolts. They're not by any means the only nitwits in Washington looking for new ways to piss public money down every toilet in town. Social Security bureaucrats are about to succeed in dumping all the money that subscribers, willing or not, were forced to pay into it and seem bent upon driving the whole blundering experiment over the precipice of bankruptcy. Recently they poured $770,000 of public money down the drain entertaining 675 of its politicians at the Phoenix Biltmore. *The Washington Examiner* (April 15, 2012) protested that such *boondoggles* will prompt taxpayers to see themselves as *jackasses* if they failed to see where their money was squandered, and for what.

Some jackasses actually hold jobs, although it's not always clear what sorts of employment they find. A source called *Gamespot* queried its readers about what they saw as the obvious places for them to find work. What ranked highest were opportunities, if any, in mail delivery and sanitation. One respondent suggested jobs as security guards because they require little to no learning or intelligence. But even that has it downside, since one is expected to purchase his own uniforms and then settle for about eight to ten dollars an hour. Said one respondent, "people who work at McDonalds are doing better." Points well taken, although there are other dismal possibilities out there, among them gatekeepers, by which we mean those dead souls who stand guard at gates including those created to prevent airline passengers from boarding their airplanes, and credential checkers who detain, interrogate and often frisk ordinary citizens, obstructing the normal flow of traffic and commerce.

These jobs require no intelligence, no learning, and judgment. It allows them to show the progress of damned near everything by imposing a mostly unnecessary delay. Dimwits love to obstruct because they imagine that it awards them the authority that they so crave. Toll collecting is another mindless activity better assigned to a robot. Aside from extracting money from motorists it has no prospect of doing anything significant for bureaucrats except to waste time, gas and money, and to erect more toll booths to extort more money from more motorists.

It's all quite hopeless, although jackasses have been honored, more or less, by having things named in their dubious honor. One sterling instance of that is Canberra, capital of Australia where, of course, the city is run mostly by bureaucrats, some of whom have risen to the level of jackasses who are damned fortunate to have discovered employment of any sort. It has come to light that, interestingly enough, the city's name has an Aboriginal source that nitwits called *Laughing Jackass*. It's popularly known and spelled a *Kookaburra*. Not everyone, even in Canberra, knows this. A recent prime minister proclaimed proudly that the city's arrestingly lovely name was a bloody shrewd choice. One apparent intellectual, whose identity will be protected for obvious reasons, published a learned piece in the equally learned pages of *The Queanbeyan Age*, claiming that as an authority on Aboriginal languages he had the authority to explain the curious implications of the city's hilarious name. According to reports, journalists then queried a fellow with the odd name of King O'Malley, minister of home affairs (what those might be, we'd prefer not to know), and that King O'Malley "dealt with this claim with aplomb," meaning with perpendicularity, self-assurance, exemplary poise. O'Malley too, we are assured, responded with a certain *philosophic calm*, resourcefully pointing out that "Even supposing it does mean the *laughing jackass*, that is infinitely superior to [someone's] sitting on a tree, croaking at progress." To the bloody contrary, King O'Malley abstrusely continued, "the jackass is a typical Australian bird [that is] merry and hopeful and buoyant and has a general attitude that conveys *faith in the future*," unlike a snake, the symbol of "groveling meanness." Well, it was game of him to try. However, one cannot summon much good to say in favor of jackasses and what they represent, except that, on the lighter side, there is a certain cocktail that bears its laughable name. In certain parts it's called *The Gent and the Jackass*, signifying the union of opposites within the confine of a coupe glass. Its recipe calls for one and one half ounces of Knob Creek bourbon, three quarters ounce of paprika simple syrup, four basil leaves, and two dashes of Fee Brothers Peach Bitters, to which one adds ice and shakes the glass instead of himself. It comes recommended that the portion be strained before consumption.

Regarding foolish employment, however, we would be remiss if we did not mention that Jack Ass Creek Land and Livestock in Ennis, Montana, was, the last we knew, in search of another employee for what appears to be a bank holding enterprise that in all probability would not entertain even the possibility of hiring an overt jackass. We may, of course, be assuming too much, or too little. After all, as Lyndon Johnson said (was he not an American president?), "Any jackass can kick down a barn, but it takes a good carpenter to build one." Points again well made. Speaking of jobs for jackasses, Harry Reid occupies one in the U.S. Senate where, upon hearing that *only* 36,000 voters lost theirs recently in a single day, responded, "That's really good," whereas a day when no jobs were lost was, in his opinion, *very bad*. Meanwhile, jackasses have the devil's own time finding work. Some may qualify for an assignment playing the piano in a sporting house, but that's presumably in Nevada where, according to unreliable government numbers, there are exceedingly few pianos, relatively few *houses of pleasure* and almost no jackasses who can read and interpret music. Nor is Washington any help. *UDBacklash.org.* reported on October 11, 2011 that "with all of the liberal pieces of crap in Obama's 'Jobs Council,' with No-Nothing, No Jobs Obama as their boss, there is little to no chance that they will create any jobs. These jackasses are too stupid to figure out how to create jobs, even when the people who know how to create jobs...have been telling them what needs to happen to turn things around."

As a rule, employers refrain from hiring halfwits, although certain avoidable errors have been inadvertently made. A *Palm Beach Post* reader in November of 1986 offered some suggestions for sorting the wheat from the chaff. "Go through the pile of applications," he said. "There are some really bright people in there, then sort out all the idiots, morons and tramps." Shall we then throw them out? "Heaven help us. Those are the people we want." And for what purpose? "Send them to Nicaragua to join the Contras." Brilliant idea. There is, we repeat, a place for everyone, otiose fools and all, if we knew what and where it is. In the 1974 film *Blazing Saddles* we discover an array of character types for whom some constructive opportunities may yet turn up. We refer, of course, to "rustlers, cut throats, murderers, bounty hunters, desperados, mugs, pugs, thugs, halfwits, dimwits, vipers, snipers, con men, Indian agents, Mexican bandits, muggers, buggerers, bushwackers, smugglers, horse thieves, bulldykes, train robbers, ass kickers, shit kickers and Methodists."

They all expect the *doors of opportunity* to open majestically before them, revealing what golden destinies glow luminously in the distance. But don't hold your breath. Kevin Mackenzie wrote an intriguing piece for *The Daily Mail* on October 9, 2011, called "Please Give Generously to Help a Halfwit" intended to raise money for the relief of "tens of thousands of rampaging stupid youngsters who have nothing to offer in either skills or manners, and may end up costing you and me a fortune in the years to come." Mackenzie warns, "they are without exception ill-educated, bad-mannered, foul-mouthed dimwits." Mackenzie's insidious plan is to "usher them onboard an airplane, fly over Eastern Europe, and push them out the door in such a way that they come to rest on the open areas of Poland and Lithuania which have been denuded of clever and ambitious youngsters" who have migrated toward the UK where they land some of the better opportunities.

Detroit, these days, is quite far down the list of attractive American cities, where jobs have disappeared and the population has declined by more than 25% in the last ten years alone; it has been paralyzed by crime, petty and on up, compounded with rampant stupidity that seems to flourish and flower from one ghetto generation to the next. We are now informed that an estimated 47 percent of those in the auto capital of the world can neither read nor write, nor have they any intention of doing so, since literacy is not much of an advantage to muggers, murderers and thieves, all of whom are far too stupid even to fill out forms for free money handed out by the optimistic folks at the Detroit Regional Workforce Fund, whose benevolent director wrings her hands over those Detroiters who have one hell of a time "reading prescriptions" to determine "what's in the bottle," how many to swallow, how often and for what purpose.

On the unlikely chance that a few of them manage to acquire minimal literacy, says the *Hallmark Employee Review*, odds are that prospective employers cannot detect it. Further, we are given to understand that to find work, "you must be polished," meaning that a company may hire "halfwits that look pretty but cannot distinguish what it is they're supposed to be doing for their pay," and moreover balk at having to show up "nights and weekends and holidays." Nonetheless, comments one interviewer, "any knuckle-dragging halfwit with the IQ of a rhesus monkey should know how to dress for an interview." While we're on that subject, Barry Ritholz's essay called *Here's to the Lazy Ones* refers expressly to "the halfwits, the bumblers, the square pegs in the round holes," all of whom "don't see things at all," and who have "no reputations to ruin," and whom some view as "lazy, or as merely lacking in intellectual curiosity." We agree that it's pretty depressing when fools cannot do much more than park cars, if that. Some can sweep floors or wash windows or empty the contents of dump trucks and rubbish baskets. One wonders what might have become of them and whether, had they taken stock of themselves, they might have done a little better for their own sakes. As it is, a few enroll in community colleges and university outreaches, but only the smallest fraction is ever graduated, or for that matter lasts for more than a few weeks in a classroom. In an effort to assist in the hiring of youths who could not or would not apply themselves to collegiate studies, British commentator Simon Swan reported that "in the three months to February, 2002, there were every bit 1.03 million 16- to 24-year-olds" who might well apply themselves to what he calls a *National Service*, once mandatory, but which ended in 1960 and which at least provided them with *something to do* while at the same time possibly steering them away from what he also calls *bad influence and lethargy* such that when they return to normal civilized life they may be "capable of opening a tin of beans and making their own beds," rather than surrendering themselves to their "customary drinking and mugging." In the USA, meanwhile, census figures show us that 48.5 percent of the population dwells in a household that receives some sort of handout in the form of subsidized housing, cash welfare, Medicaid (medical assistance to the poor) or food stamps. Reliance upon government has played a part in the lack of commitment to higher learning (or any learning) and other forms of self-reliance.

Opportunity surrounds and engulfs us, but it's not for everyone. There is an outfit called *Boneheads* that is in the business of selling seafood restaurant franchises. The folks there refer to it as a "complete turnkey Restaurant Development Support System waiting to set the ambitious and the industrious up in the food business," therefore no place for an idiot. There is a similar outfit called *Expect Success*, also in the business of business that offers quite a bit of advice on the bonehead problems that enterprises routinely encounter. "Let's be clear," they warn. "There will always be boneheads" who "do things to embarrass the company." We assumed as much, but what to do? The answer: "shackle and tackle them," which strikes us as far easier said than done. Anything else? Yes. Boneheadedness is occasionally open to question, subject to interpretation. We use the term *bonehead* advisedly, since it denotes a person endowed with a more than ordinarily thick skull that all but prohibits clear, rational cognition. We cannot well deny that some fools may, especially the more patient of them, demand that they be accorded a chance to prove themselves.

Not so long ago did a Texas woman win a prize while attending a Grand Prairie Air Hogs baseball game. All we know is that Irving's Chapel of Roses Funeral home collaborated with Oak Grove Memorials Gardens to donate a $10,000 funeral. Said the neck-braced recipient, "I almost croaked several times," which we interpret to mean that this windfall was a cosmic signal that her life had been extended long enough to win the free funeral. Others who were vying for the grand prize dressed for the occasion and participated in a pallbearers' foot race. Another arrived dressed as a mummy. In the meantime, however, the lucky Texas woman pledged to select a casket and plot at the earliest opportunity. "I'm going pick a spot under a tree, out of the Texas heat," she informed the *Dallas Morning News*, "and let's hope it's a pet-free cemetery. I don't want to get watered on." One bystander suggested that since this was, after all, a baseball promotion, the Texas woman might more appropriately be buried beneath home plate. The whole incident remains subject to closer interpretation. If it is not boneheaded, it is at the very least a bizarre business burial.

Australia's *Daily Telegraph* published an account of a German travel company that offered to arrange an all nude flight of East Germans bound for an obscure, not to say obscene, Baltic Sea island, but thought better than to follow through. It was an idea whose time had come, even when the nudes didn't. The flight was at first completely subscribed, with 50 passengers whose intention was to take it off following takeoff, then enjoy a thoroughly naked holiday journey without the encumbrance of clothing. There was talk of staffing the plane with an all nude crew, but nothing came of it. Suffice it to say that the whole scheme came unraveled. The idea strikes us as more absurd than boneheaded, if we may advance that fine distinction. Consider that if some people are pleased to embark on a naked flight to a remote destination, it bespeaks an astonishing confidence that they would ever recover their covering. It is such nagging uncertainty that may dull the ardor for a kind of naked voyage. We do not, let us be clear, regard this regrettable misadventure to be necessarily foolish. Eccentric, yes. But even so. We are ever on the prowl for fresh, new adventure, wherever it may take us. That includes Rio de Janeiro, where another open-minded travel company conceived of organizing a tour of that great city's not so great slums, and while on that curious quest, throw in as a bonus a photo opportunity with some of the biggest names in the Brazilian drug trade. What might the folks back in River City say? As with the German nude flight plan, others had, shall we say, *concerns* about such a bizarre opportunity. Some of the cooler heads in that steamy Brazilian city thought better of the idea, and came down with bureaucratic authority on the very idea of tourists posing it up with drug lords. One of that city's newspapers dispatched a reporter, armed with a camera and a Hawaiian sport shirt, to a slum fest and a generously long visit to a district known to locals as the *bocas de fumo* to have his photo taken with a few of the better known slum bums and heroin heros. The journalist reached the conclusion that this sort of outing wasn't one of the best of moronic ideas, although it offered a different perspective from what one might otherwise enjoy on that that city's golden beaches.

So-called bone headedness is abundantly evident in American universities which admit the strongest freshman classes they can attract, then find that those same supposed students, despite their purported high school academic records, cannot demonstrate even minimal competency in mathematics and rhetoric. The result is that universities roll out remedial courses intended to bring youngsters *up to speed* academically before enrolling them in collegiate studies, if indeed that ever happens. This is not altogether a new phenomenon. One California remedial woman said that "when you ask a UC student to take a percentage of a number and he whips out a calculator, you know you have computations issues." Another person close to the problem asks how kids can write a coherent composition when "their go-to language is computerese and texting." A university professor reported reading a student essay that had one sort of grammatical problem or another in each of its sentences. Public education bureaucrats are developing something they call *Common Core Standards* that they expect to unveil in 2014, on the assumption that presenting a correct answer *only gets you so far*. The object of remedial courses is for the student to understand *why the answer is the answer*. But learning how to write and compute requires a great deal of time and desire—which most would-be students haven't got. To the contrary, their objective is *to get by—for now*, never realizing that to make certain kinds of errors in the real world can be fatal.

The best employment for fools remains with the United States Government, one of the largest, most abominably inefficient, ineffective and inane monstrosities on the face of the globe, enabling and enacting directives and stern regulations that only professional paper shufflers and career bureaucrats can endorse. So impossible is it that in April of 2012 a bill was entered in the Missouri legislature prohibiting the "Missouri state government from recognizing, enforcing or acting upon interference of certain actions of the federal government," which is a cloudy way of saying, we gather, that the Feds keep their hands off such state matters as the right to bear arms, legalize and/or fund abortions, destroy embryos, applaud homosexual marriage, interfere with the relations between church and state, even require trading in carbon credits (whatever that may mean), or impose a tax on carbon emissions.

No wonder. Gary North has written an essay he calls *Government Drones* arguing that it's an exaggeration to say that the government is run by fools, since the real fools are the voters. There is a site that calls itself *Washington Fools*, meaning ambiguously that Washington is in the business of fooling everyone, and that Washington is awash in jackasses. If what Washington says is any index to its abject foolishness, then we rest our case. Barrack Osama claimed that "all the choices we've made have been the right ones," which comes as a surprise to intelligent Americans everywhere. His none too intelligent vice president proclaimed, "Look. The Taliban *per se* is not our enemy. That's critical. There is not a single statement that the president has ever made in any of our policy assertions that the Taliban is our enemy because it threatens US interests," which is another ambiguity, saying on one hand that the Taliban is not our enemy because it threatens us; it's our enemy for some other (undisclosed) reason. Harry Reid, also conspicuously unintelligent, told the world that *seniors* somehow adore receiving junk mail. "It's sometimes their only way of communicating, or feeling like they're part of the real world," yet another ambiguity, suggesting that they actually communicate by receiving post office trash, and that they're not somehow part of the *real world*, but can be coaxed into believing that they are. Said the inscrutable Nancy Pelosi, "We're trying to save life on this planet as we know it today," a puzzling remark if we've ever heard one. She's the same fool who said it was necessary to pass bills through Washington bureaucracy before understanding what's in them...

All such stupidity calls to mind socialist George Bernard Shaw who opined that democracy is a form of government *of the fools, for the fools, by the fools.* To that point, Ron Ewart in his *Fools Rule America* argued that the danger is not so much in the man who claims to be president, but in that "vast confederacy of fools who made him their prince," and that yes, "fools rule America...because these fools can vote." And once the fools have elevated other fools to fool around in Washington, foolish things predictably happen often, for example, $2.1 million spent for the encouragement of grape genetics research in New York; another $1.7 for barnyard odor in Iowa, $1 million for Mormon cricket control in Utah; $650,000 for beaver management in North Carolina and Mississippi; $1,951,500 for "sustainable Las Vegas," whatever that may mean; $2 million "for the promotion of astronomy" in Hawaii; $167,000 for the Autry National Center for the American West in Los Angeles; $238,000 for the Polynesian Voyageur in Hawaii; $200,000 to assist gang members in having their tattoos erased; $209,000 to pick up blueberry production in Georgia. Such is supportive evidence that America has turned itself over to fools, as is in tacit acknowledgement that the world has gone so mad that it confuses up with down, left with right, cold with hot, and therefore may just as well turn itself over to nitwits and jackasses who will exacerbate problems and drive the nation ever deeper into the realm of the absurd, out of which there is apparently no escape, no turning back.

Absurdity, indeed. One symbol of that absurdity is a governmentally mandated light bulb, the product of an absurd congress and an equally absurd EPA. The absurd light bulb contains an absurd amount of mercury that, if unleashed in an aircraft, would constitute an absurd terrorist attack. One wag absurdly suggested that "You'll need to hire a federally *licensed* light bulb fool to assist in bulb replacements." In the meantime, we understand that Los Angeles will soon outlaw both paper and plastic bags, even though having once contained perishables that may contain dangerous bacteria. Another congressional fool, if he has his way, will require the purchase of dog insurance, "mandatory [of course] for all owners of male, [non] neutered dogs weighing 20 or more pounds." The wisdom behind this is that such policies will "cover any damage to you, your dog or to another person while off its leash." That sounds like a damned fine idea to us. The jackass who wrote the bill adds, however, that "this does not in any way penalize dogs, or prevent people from enjoying the benefits of dog ownership," whatever those benefits may be. Heather Macdonald, writing for the *Manhattan Institute,* complains that "it's bad enough that the Education Department...spews out a constant flood of misguided regulations, which usually embody the view that schools and universities are bastions of petty-minded bigotry that only federal bureaucrats can check with their superior, enlightened wisdom. But alongside the regulations," she continues, "comes a more wasteful flood of grant programs," concluding that "every federal agency, of course, is engaged in the same shell game. Federal grant money recipients appear to believe that they've received a windfall—that federal money is free money."

Plainly enough, government work is the closest thing to appropriate employment for halfwits and duds. Fools, in the meantime, haven't even a chance to land a job supervising intelligent people and thereby screwing virtually everything up. Suppose we posited, stupidly enough, that there are but two sorts of people in the world, i.e., those who create and those who destroy? Common fools decidedly belong in the latter category. We've all known people who, presented with a damned fine idea conceived by some intelligently constructive person, set about systematically ruining it. You destroy an automobile battery by leaving your lights on overnight. You destroy its engine by allowing its oil level to diminish. We are told that you ruin a *relationship* (whatever that may be) by attempting to alter someone else's personality, or by completing his incomplete sentences, or by presenting him with a summary of his glaring deficiencies. You ruin damned near anything by attempting to *improve* it. Improved websites, especially those pertaining to hard and software, are invariably worse than they originally were, until they become virtually useless. Robert Maynard Hutchins, who actually improved the University of Chicago, astutely argued that "football, fraternities and fun have no place in the university. They were introduced only to entertain those who shouldn't be in the university," speaking of which, Henry Mencken interestingly commented that "college football would be much more interesting if the faculty played instead of the students, and even more interesting if the trustees played. There would be a great increase in broken arms, legs and necks, and simultaneously an appreciable diminution in the loss to humanity." Someone else, we forgot who, said that football players and prostitutes ruin their bodies for the entertainment of others.

When fools find employment, they devote themselves to fouling everything possible. Bill Clinton's dalliance with Monica Lewinsky is a minor, even irrelevant example of this, except that it disgraced the purported *president* and got Lewinsky into hot water: after having sold herself inside the Ovarian Office, she then tried to sell her lurid narrative to various publishers, one of whom remarked, "I'm as big a whore as anyone, but I'd rather die first" than publish her misadventures. Another publisher advanced a reported $2.75 million up front for Georgie Stephanopoulos's golden days in that same oral orifice, only to develop cold feet because of "the famous debacles and triumphs of an administration that constantly went over the top," that we assume to mean went to impossible excess. On a grander scale, the US government practically specializes in debacles that defy comprehension, except that they're the work of high salaried, prancing jackasses. The more public money they squander, the more they command in wages. Moreover, these predators rarely lose their jobs, and are rarely made to defend their morbid stupidity to the public that is paying for them. In Illinois, at least, the last two fools who presumed to hold the governor's office are behind bars, also at public expense. In Washington, the economic recovery has all but disappeared. Fossil fuel restrictions set in place by an army of idiots has resulted in higher fuel prices and more foreign oil dependence. Foolish subsidies for corn ethanol caused shortages in food grain and ruined engines. So-called *air quality standards* have taken their toll upon the economy. The simpletons' stimulus failed to stimulate. Shovel-ready projects scooped only animal waste. Now the federal government has granted itself permission to confiscate various foods, supplies and even water for its own profligate use, effectively placing America under martial law at the hands of fools, although one would expect nothing less from a foolocracy, a government of fools, for the benefit of other fools. It is, in short, a universe of foolery that is in turn fundamentally a reaction to reason and rationality. Sydney Smith first used the term foolocracy in a letter he composed in 1855, and it has become a more or less regrettably common word in our time. So too, a *foolosopher* is nothing but a perversion of the philosophic, which is to say who pretends to have learning and the wisdom it can bring, and a nod in the direction of those whose intellectual acumen is fatally compromised. It further suggests surrender to stupidity, a triumph of moronic practices among those who cannot comprehend anything nobler.

Reason is its opposite, denoting as it does a declaration of fact, real or occasionally alleged, presented as support for some assertion, belief or notion. It has been used as a major premise, an explanation, possibly a fact, maybe an incident, sometimes a rationale, often a governing principle, conceivably a foundation of logic. Even lower animals rely upon it, associating some event to some action. It is sometime presumed to be *apriori*, "from the former," meaning in turn self-evident, having been presupposed by experience, which is to say *presumptive*. Reason, unlike mere foolery, has a distinguished history, celebrated in aphoristic citations, often when Reason assumes the allegorical form of a woman, as in "Hear Reason, for she'll make you feel her," otherwise "hearken to Reason or she will not be heard." Elsewhere we are warned, "better to die than turn your back on Reason," and "Reason is the life of the law," and "Reason succeeds where Force fails," and particularly "without good Reason for doing a thing, we have a fine Reason for leaving it alone," and "neither great Poverty not great Riches will hear Reason." There was once, and perhaps still is, something called reality therapy, a mode of psychoanalysis aimed expressly at those who had a hell of a time, and we can see why, confronting Reason in the early 1970s.

To the contrary, anthropologist and anatomist Ashley Montague observed that "human beings are the only creatures...able to behave irrationally in the name of reason," a statement which we cannot challenge rationally. Another such remark comes from the voice of prophetic Ayn Rand when she averred that "ever since Kant divorced reason from reality, his intellectual descendants have been diligently widening the breach," but hell; that may not be so awful. After all, free thinking Samuel Butler, possibly best remembered for his autobiographical and evolutionary novel *The Way of All Flesh*, was wont to say that "to live is like to love—all reason is against it, and all healthy instinct for it." Shaw, whose contrarian opinions are ingeniously paradoxical, said that "The man who listens to Reason is lost; reason enslaves all whose minds are not strong enough to master her," which is especially true of fools. Even the nearly forgotten William Jerome, whose popular songs include *Chinatown, My Chinatown*, and *The Green Grass Grew All Around*, whipped up a little ditty that further belittles the boundless efficacy of mighty Reason. It goes,

> You needn't try to reason,
> Your excuse is out of season,
> Just kiss yourself goodbye.

Blithe though he was, Jerome was not the only not-so-foolish thinker to treat this serious matter with levity, seeming to say something profound without believing it. No one we know wants to sound like a raving fool. One means of possibly covering one's stupidity is to expound on certain *eternal truths* that appear to rest upon the fortress of Reason. Allow us to present some examples of pomposity in action. None other than James Madison orated that "to the press alone, checkered as it is with aliases, the world is indebted for all the triumphs which have been gained by reason and humanity over error and oppression." Hence, anyone not armed with Reason will sound like a fool, and in all probability qualify as one. To orate without Reason is pure nonsense, something that our neighbors and acquaintances spew at random. Nonsense means what it says: something that carries no sense and is patently absurd, which is to say unsubstantial, totally worthless (unless perhaps intended for comedic purposes). One way that fools purvey nonsense is through the *non sequitur*, meaning "it does not follow," a logical fallacy, a proposition that alleges a conclusion that does not follow from the evidence. Suppose one should say that "you wife is Italian, and is therefore an excellent cook" or the old favorite, "since dogs are animals and cats are animals, then dogs are cats"? There is a comic strip called *Non Sequitur*, the creation of Wiley Miller, one of whose sequences shows a little girl waiting at a bus stop, saying to a little boy, "Jeffrey? The bus stop is over here." He acknowledges that, prompting the little girl to say, "So why don't you stand here next to me?" to which he responds, "Because I can read," a *non sequitur* that leaves the incident up in the air, possibly suggesting that he's read something that precludes his standing next to her. One never knows.

Logic, however, is the study of reasoning. There are plenty of pitfalls besides non sequiturs, and fools bite on them all. There is something called an *appeal to authority*, when one cites alleged authority who may, but probably does not, settle a dispute. One may say that since Christ drank wine, there's no reason why we can't do the same. Another is to rely on precedent, for instance, "there is nothing wrong with dropping bombs on people; it's been going on for decades." Another is to make one's point by threat of force, as in "you'll do it my way, or I'll break your arm." Many are familiar with the use of *ad hominem*, literally "against the man," which means attacking one's person instead of his argument, as opposed to *ad rem*, "to the thing," which is to say "to the matter at hand," or staying on the subject. Another is the fallacy of presuming that because someone is silent, he must be guilty. A favorite of ours is the *fallacy*, that presumes something is either *this* or *that*, when in all probability is it something else entirely. A *reductio ad absurdum* (reduction to absurdity) is the practice of deflating a proposition by demonstrating that it leads to nothing. Another common error is what some call a *slippery slope*, arguing that one situation inexorably leads to a number of others: If, like Jesus, one drinks wine, it leads to drunkenness and poverty, panhandling, peeing in alleys, and eventually ending one's days in a flophouse. There are any number of slippery, fallacious non-arguments that lean on such insubstantial factors as fear, pity, spite, wealth, flattery, religion, received opinion and so on. But if it does not rely upon reason, it won't fly either in a court of law (usually) or a barroom brawl. It's the chatter of fools and nitwits who lack the ability to enlist reason to their discourse, for lack of education and lack of intelligence, causing them to forfeit every gambit.

All of this begs the question of what, if anything, can a fool do instead of or besides passing his life as a moron, halfwit, idiot, jackass, dunce and dimwit. If one is a fool as a consequence of heredity, the problem would appear at first glance to be altogether hopeless, since one cannot exchange his genes with the ease that he might exchange his jeans. But it's worth a try. Some unfairly believe themselves stupid because they've been made to, whereas their dilemma is more a question of low self esteem, a problem that can, with or without help, be addressed. One can at least attempt to mask his foolishness through a cosmetic effort to disguise his moronic personality. Many of us do that routinely and without much thought, if any. One can at least, as they say, *hold his tongue*, so not to embarrass himself and others. Chaucer, of all people, refers to this practice in his *Tale of Melibus* when he counsels, "Thee is better hold thy tongue still, than for to speak," an admonition that one hears in wedding ceremonies when one is solemnly advised to speak now, or forever hold his peace rather than raise some thorny point of conjecture.

One can, of course, remove fools from his *circle*, should it come to that. Whereas it's occasionally necessary to clear one's garage, it also may be necessary to clear one's friends and companions, as well. Fools after all are by their nature useless, if not altogether destructive. This does not *rule out* (as idiots are fond of saying) discretely pruning out a few of one's relatives, as was mentioned at the beginning of Chapter 4. *Out with them*, we say. No rational person wants the absurd company of fools when he could rid himself of them as he might rid himself of fruit flies, namely by swatting them (metaphorically, of course). Getting rid of people is one of the easiest tasks to which one can apply himself, although relatives remain a nuisance that is more vexing to control. Of the rest, we merely say *be gone!* It's every bit as simple as that. This elementary procedure eradicates fools from one's life, while it assists one in not being a bigger fool than he presently is. So does refusing to dress like a fool, which is to say by donning unusual clothing such as a conical dunce's cap better suited (if you will forgive the pun) to clowns and nitwits. People assume that if you look like a dope, chances are that you are one. Looking like a fool is not ordinarily a good idea. One may also choose to cease viewing television, since easily 99 percent of its programming is directed at fools, and discontinue as well harkening to the banter of jackasses, particularly those who have devoted themselves to the foolish calling of politics, an activity best suited to rogues, liars, chatterboxes, criminals, self-serving horse's asses and baying hounds.

Were it so that fools were readers, it of course would be appropriate to read what rational people of learning, sophistication and civility have written. Odds are that the longer ago they wrote, the more valuable their discourse. Of course, one needs to read with discretion, and read the best. The most mentally active readers consider reading a matter of give and take, who feel free to comment, supplement, delete and sometimes quarrel with the author, rather than accept *carte blanche* any damned fool thing he felt moved to write. Life is brief, and one might just as well select the best. Should a person read carefully enough, books become his better, more intelligent, enduring and dependable of friends. And he is far less of a fool for having done it. One must periodically overhaul his rhetoric, as well, so not to sound like a jackass. One means of accomplishing this is to aspire to grammatical *correctness*, which relatively few of us possess. Grammar and usage ultimately find their often arbitrary standards set by the better educated among us. If those supposed standards sound ridiculous, nonetheless they're the only guidelines we have. Indeed, as E.B. White tells us in the preface to his and William Strunk's influential grammar and style manual fittingly entitled *The Elements of Style*, the advice it proffers is of course "somewhat a matter of individual preference." Accordingly, even the pages of Strunk and White contain problematic language, even outright errors, as do the pages of this book. But at the very least, even a fool, trying as he may to shed his foolishness, must assume control of his language by attempting to write and speak properly, and with the authority which the best of preferential writers attempt to present and maintain. The probability is that anyone who speaks and writes discerningly will not be taken for a fool. Finally, the best means of not appearing like a fool is to observe the fools that surround us and learn by their wretched examples. This is quite simple, inasmuch as society is thick with morons, nitwits, dunces and dolts. They're everywhere one looks; they're climbing in the windows and hiding under the sink. Even if fools were *teachable*, which most of them are not, their wretched habits would still threaten the rest of us.

There are distinct advantages to being even relatively intelligent, informed, literate, amusing and educated, well *put together* and reasonable. Most people are not. Those who enjoy most of life's advantages are at the same time the targets of jealousy. If one does not attract jealousy, it says that he has nothing upon which to attract it. If, on the other hand, one is the object of even virulent jealousy, it confirms that he's doing something well enough to merit it. The more jealousy, the better. And what is jealousy? It's an unattractive, out of control emotion fixated on the achievements of other people. It's a compulsive feeling of ill-will aimed at the conspicuously successful. If one is on the receiving end of jealousy, he cannot but count himself fortunate. Fools are no exception. There comes a time to capitalize on their foolishness, ever cutting up in theatres, royal and otherwise wealthy households. Fooling in cunning ways that entertained, amused and in not a few instances even informed, they discovered rewarding, profitable ways to repackage their foolishness before larger, more grateful, even envious audiences. They performed before their alleged intellectual superiors, who enjoyed the antics of low-born, uneducated know-nothings whose knockabout comedic levity provided temporary relief from life's ugly realities.

We must be reminded too that the terms *folly* (variously spelled *foli, fole, folik, foly, follie, follyche* and the Middle English *follich* and *follies* all denote foolery, and in their time came to suggest such related things as evil, wickedness, sexual looseness, licentiousness, criminality and so forth. Folly therefore has a semantic track record that reaches as much toward the salacious (lustful, lecherous) as toward the merely funny and entertaining. We have all heard of people who regret the folly of their youth. It originally suggested a form of low brow amusement adjusted to the unsophisticated. As entertainment, follies became Parisian entertainment associated with the cabaret tradition, meaning a tavern turned racy nightclub. All the same, the tendency to associate follies with elaborate theatrical entertainment ideally identified with Les Folies Bergères, the *iconic* Parisian cabaret. *Bergère* variously suggests a shepherdess, a lover, a young woman. Les Folies became celebrated as a *theatre of the people* for its glorified risqué middle class rowdy boldness and glorification of the Paris that once was, with is bawdy badness and libertine lust. Inside the Le Folies customers were accorded dimly lit tables whose lamps were suggestive of a bordello's inner sanctums. Folies customers were abundantly entertained with array of vaudeville jugglers, tight rope walkers, chorus lines, sleight-of-hand acts, tumblers and acrobats combined with playlets, salacious nudity, occasional richly colored lights, brassy music, and other deafening racket. Its erotic side of course appealed to American GIs seeking glitter and glamour, the illusion of sex and promiscuity that accompanied the liberation of France in 1944. Charlie Chaplin. W.C. Fields and Stan Laurel shared the spotlights at Les Folies, assisted in carrying off its charm, lurid sensationalism, puff and pretense, all of it good nonsense and splendid erotic entertainment, out of which came a few memorable performers, among them a woman called Josephine Baker.

Her birth name was Freda McDonald, and she came not from Montmartre but from St. Louis. Baker was an irresistible slinky, slender, light-complected woman who during the war had assisted with undercover work for the French Resistance. She became a spotlight performer who wowed audiences at Les Folies where she performed her eye-popping *banana dance*; adopted a dozen children whom she called her *Rainbow Tribe*; and she became a civil rights activist who refused to perform before segregated audiences. Her name was a holdover from one of her husbands who happened to be a Pullman porter. She had appeared with the *Chocolate Dandies* at Harlem's *Cotton Club* in the 1920s, when she also showed her stuff in Paris at

La Revue Negre and became a French citizen. So popular was Baker that her admirers rewarded her with expensive automobiles, jewelry and what were liberally reported to have been as many as 1,500 marriage proposals. Besides loving her children, she loved animals and owned a leopard, a chimpanzee that wore a diamond studded collar and joined her act at Les Folies, a pig, a snake, a goat, some parakeets, a few fish, three cats and seven dogs. Her *Banana Dance* was a blend of the ludicrous and the lewd, during which she was attired a skirt of what appeared to be large, somewhat obscene Freudian bananas. Baker captured the full attention of her audience when a theatrical voice called out, "Mesdames et Messieurs, Les Folies Bergères present mademoiselle Josephine Baker!" It was more than anything a tease that she executed, for some reason, with her eyes crossed. Baker later danced the Charleston to the accompaniment of largely self-taught Sidney Bechet, the American saxophonist. *The Los Angeles Times* commented that, provided one can find the banana dance on surviving film clips, one will "be treated to an explosion of pure playfulness" that "allowed her to combine the Charleston, the Folies Bergères and the hokey pokey into a free for all in which her hips swing with the precision of a Machine Age engine." An admirer of Baker's wrote wistfully, "Well, it's Paris again, but this time it's fall/ Misty and cool, but alive. / I've been to the sites from the Louvre to Pigalle, just waiting for night to arrive, / For all the papers and posters I've seen/ They talk of nothing else but Josephine/ Down at the Folies Bergères./ Down at the Folies Bergères that lustrous haven." Having in the end fallen on hard times, she was rescued from poverty by Princess Grace, and she is buried in Monaco.

Josephine Baker was in no sense a fool but an inventive up-from-nowhere entertainer perfectly fitted to an audience of limited sophistication and less than ordinary culture. This much cannot be challenged. Hers was a genre intended for an audience that comprehended and identified with it. Baker, in the end, discovered a side of entertainment especially suited to popular notions of gaiety, cabaret nights, suggestive theatrics. Married four times, the first at 15, she knew firsthand the East St. Louis riots of 1917 and ran off by herself at 13 (some reports say 15). Her mother had fantasized about becoming a chorus girl but settled instead for marrying a vaudeville drummer. Baker first worked as a laundress and at the age of eight became a white woman's maid, was relegated to sleeping with a dog in a coal cellar, and was punished for adding too much soap to the laundry by having her hands scalded. She sailed with other black performers to France at time when black performers were especially in vogue. Picasso, e.e cummings, Jean Cocteau and Hemingway numbered among her admirers, while at the same time they too were in the throes of artistic ascendancy. She married the French industrialist Jean Lion (the marriage helped her become a French citizen, but ended by 1940), took up with the Resistance, became a Red Cross nurse, and in time overcame the humiliation of minority life, performed in *The Forest of*

Paris and became known as *La Bakaire*, whom the *New York Times* passed off as a mere *Negro wench*.

Josephine Baker was born in 1906, a year before the Ziegfeld Follies opened with a bang in New York with a platoon of buxom beauties strutting through theatre aisles banging drums and exposing their charms to what we presume to have been an appreciative, primarily male, audience in search of saucy, high-pitched low-brow titillation tailored for decidedly bottom end tastes. What taste there was came from Florenz Ziegfeld, Jr., born in Chicago in 1867 and, according to his biographer John Kenrick, as a kid sold tickets to other kids for the privilege of taking a long look at *invisible fish* swimming gracefully in a bowl of water. Ziegfeld was destined to sell more tickets to more people to view more invisible fish for the balance of his life. What he marketed was, like Les Folies Bergères, pedestrian erotica for the birds that flocked to his box office for a peek at his saucy entertainments. Ziegfeld, who looked much very like comedian Eddie Cantor, wasn't paying all the bills for this noisy commotion. It was his financial backers who shelled out for the extravaganzas and rewarded Ziegfeld $200 a week for creating and supervising erotic mayhem. Flo claimed (he wasn't above inventing apocryphal stories about himself) as a youth to have hit the road with Buffalo Bill's Wild West Show. His father too had certain promotional inclinations aimed at mostly idiots, when he spread wide the doors of the *Trocadero* nightclub coincident with the 1893 New York World's Fair. All went well at first, then faltered, then suddenly prospered when his son adjusted the entertainment by hiring a strong man named *Sandrow* to amaze his dimwitted viewers with miraculous feats of strength. Flo later took Sandrow on a vaudeville tour where he daringly wrestled with a drugged lion.

Yokels loved anything Flo dished out. James Traub, in his book called *The Devil's Playground: A Century of Pleasure and Profit* (2004) wrote, "what Broadway lacked, at the turn of the century, was a figure who could fuse the naughty sexuality of the streets and the burlesque show with the savoir faire of lobster palace society—someone who could make sex delightful and amusing, What it lacked was Florenz Ziegfeld," who at considerable expense imported a Polish-Jewish beauty named Anna Held who became a draw at the Ziegfeld Follies and, according to Flo, indulged and immersed herself in milk baths and later formed a sprightly chorus line called *The Anna Held Girls*. In the meantime, Held obtained a divorce and let it be known to stage door johnnies that she was now married to Flo Ziegfeld, which was an apparent fabrication. In any event, Flo had a demanding personality and was addicted to gambling. He began chasing another matinee cutie named Lillian Lorraine, a termagant woman given to emotional outbursts. He gradually moved toward organizing his opulent follies into a series of annual cornball theatricals. In 1908 Flo brought out a new edition of his entertainments using as his unlikely theme *the history of civilization* that featured popular songs like *Shine on Harvest Moon* as a representative nightclub ditty to illus-trate the march of civilization, with the Ziegfeld Girls dressed as robust New Jersey mosquitoes, wings and all. In 1909 the girls were dressed as battle-ships while they belted out a song called *The Greatest Navy in the World*, after which a few honeys flew over the audience in a simulated Wright brother's airplane. Audiences of dimwits were flabbergasted. In 1911 he introduced the sensational Dolly Sisters dressed as Siamese twins, while his chorus girls gave *The Texas Tommy Swing* their all. A year thence Flo planted his perform-ers in the audience where they commenced audibly to quarrel about what kind of entertainment explosion should open the night's follies. The whole charade ended with a *Society Circus Parade* with ponies and scantily clad girls leading the procession. It was too damned much.

In 1913 the Follies opened its gala 7th edition at the New Amsterdam where, we are told, "Ann Pennington's high kicks and dimpled knees" kept the boys in a constant state of uproar. In a gesture of low humor, comedian Leon Errol's pants fell down, and the house went crazy while the Ziegfeld girls executed their dance routine calculated somehow to suggest the open-ing of the Panama Canal, locks and all. The simpletons were on the edge of their seats. A year later, Flo's director Julian Mitchell stalked out in a huff, leaving Errol to take over, opening as *Joe King the Joke King*, a lowbrow play on words the Follies audiences could comprehend and even find remotely amusing. Errol worked for Ziegfeld from 1911 until the 1929 stock market catastrophe, during which Flo set his sights, and sometimes his hands, on the admirable task of *Glorifying the American Girl*. Errol was no dumb bell. Born Leonce Errol Simms in Sydney, Australia, he studied medicine at Syd-ney University before he surrendered to the performer in him that got him-self genuinely excited about appearing as everything from a circus clown to a Shakespearian character, before yielding to the raucous lure of Ameri-can burlesque, which is where Ziegfeld discovered him in the role of what Flo called *a rubber-legged society inebriate*. Errol eventually appeared in both silent films and talkies, and made a number of 20-minute reels in which he was the top banana. He died of heart failure at the age of 70.

Historians credit Ziegfeld with revolutionizing the Broadway musical, geared primarily for consumption by the less refined market for big noise, banal humor and catchy dance routines, all of which were readily available as relatively inexpensive glitzy big city adult entertainment that dealt in eye-popping theatrical stunts and everlasting comment in the press, especially in the gossip columns. The mainstay was of course the showgirls, a few of whom used their Ziegfeld days to launch themselves into lifelong theatri-cal careers. Josephine Baker was one of those, although when she returned stateside in 1936 to work for Flo, the show tanked and she returned to Paris. From its beginnings the follies catered to lower and middle class ticket buy-ers who had the opportunity to witness an array of ultimately famous personalities. As early as 1909 Flo had engaged the services of Sophie Tucker (née Sonya Kalish), the racy Russian-born music hall and burlesque queen, whose career stretched to 62 years while she traded her brassy, sassy, semi-lewd banter that secured her reputation as *The Last of the Red Hot Mamas*. By 1910, Fanny Brice, whose stage career gave rise to the Broadway musical *Funny Girl*, had come to Ziegfeld after an apprenticeship in burlesque and vaudeville. Her family was hardly poor, having accumulated a fleet of New Jersey saloons. It was at the Follies that Brice developed her *Baby Snooks* routine with which she charmed middle class radio audiences. By 1915, W.C. Fields and Ed Wynn joined up. Fields had but a 4th grade education, if it can be called that, and an abusive father. Nonetheless, he nurtured his theatrical talents and found a place at the Folies Bergères, then remained with Flo Ziegfeld until 1921. Zany Wynn, who carved a place for himself portraying nitwitted fools, turned down the title role in the *Wizard of Oz* because he believed the part to be *way too small*, and later armed himself with an 11 foot pole to contend with fools he wouldn't touch with a ten footer.

Also on parade in 1915 was Ina Claire who, unlike most of Flo's hired help, became a celebrated Broadway and Hollywood actress whose demeanor suited her best for parts in cerebral dramas created by S.N. Behrman, Somerset Maugham and even T.S. Eliot, none of whose dramatic presentations were for the likes of fools. In 1916, down home Will Rogers joined the fun. His time there is the subject of a book by Arthur Frank Wertham, appropriately called *Will Rogers: At the Ziegfeld Follies*, where he not only performed his customary rope tricks but was an active performer in other vaudeville skits. Eddie Cantor, who performed with the Follies in 1917, was raised by a grandmother on New York's Lower East Side. He later teamed with song writer Earl Carroll in his review called *Canary Cottage*, and his performance recommended him to Flo Ziegfeld and in turn positioned him to make the acquaintance of Fields, Brice and Rogers. By 1922, Barbara Stanwyck and the Olsen–Johnson comedy team were making theatrical reputations. Stanwyck (known on the street as Ruby Catherine Stevens) became a 1922–23 *dancer* at the Follies at a time when she, a high school dropout, was trying to make ends meet after her mother died beneath a streetcar where she had been pushed by a drunken passenger. John Sigvard "Ole" Olsen and Harold Ogden "Chick" Johnson dished up what was then called *Hellzapoppin*, an impossibly cornball comedy of Hoosier slick one-liners that played well enough on the vaudeville circuits to find them a place with the Follies. By 1923 popular bandleader Paul Whiteman brought his *symphonic jazz* to follies audiences. Between 1924 and 1925 Flo signed his Blonde Beauty, later his wife, Mary William Ethelbert Appleton "Billie" Burke. She, the daughter of a singer and sometime circus clown, became far more notable after her rocky marriage to Florenz Ziegfeld, but even gossip columns averred that she would not have done half so well had she not opted for the right husband. Nonetheless, Burke had an appealing voice and an engaging personality combined with some of her father's knack for foolishness. After Flo died in 1932, she was so engulfed in the debt he left behind that she returned to Hollywood where she had little choice but to accept less than enviable roles such as those availed to her in Hal Roach's inane *Topper* series, and another playing alongside Oliver Hardy in a film called *Zenobia* in 1939, although she is identified today mostly in her role as Glinda the Good Witch in *The Wizard of Oz*, also released in 1939. She was herself the subject of two films portraying her late husband's rakishly eventful life. Myrna Loy played Billie's role in *The Great Ziegfeld* in 1936.

The primary reason for Ziegfeld's decline and fall was the financial crash that began on October of 1929 and cost him his entire estate, estimated at nearly $3 million. He more than once attempted to render the Follies as a motion picture, continuing to bill it, somewhat misleadingly, as *Glorifying the American Girl*, only to have it ill received by critics. Flo attempted to resuscitate the Follies in 1931, when it failed esthetically and financially. Contemporary accounts had it that Flo was reduced to leaving the theatre under cover of secrecy to evade creditors. While Billie was in Hollywood, trying to rescue the two of them from financial ruin, Flo had transformed their Westchester home into a private bordello, using what appeared to be an unending parade of chorus girls, one of them being Marilyn Miller who had not long to live, dying at the age of 37. Miller was the daughter of an Evansville, Indiana, telephone repairman; her stepfather was a vaudeville acrobat. After performing in London she joined the Follies, where she acted and sang in 1918 and 1919, but not without Flo's exacting an erotic price that eventually ended their professional relations. Miller thereafter acquitted herself well on Broadway stages, commanding $3,000, which at that time was reportedly the highest payout to any actress. Her role in *Look for the Silver Lining* lasted for 570 performances. Her first husband perished in an automobile accident; her second (Jack Pickford, brother of Mary Pickford), ended in divorce, as did her third.

Gypsy Rose Lee, the world's most celebrated ecdysiast, made her way to the Follies after having appeared with her sister in vaudeville, later earning her keep by removing her clothes at Billy Minsky's Broadway Theatre in 1931, then joining the Follies in 1936. She too was later portrayed in a Broadway musical called appropriately *Gypsy* that emphasized her as the child of an uncommonly pushy stage mother, although she passed much of her career in tawdry burlesque houses catering to drunks and assorted riffraff. Gypsy, née Rose Louise Horvik, was born in Seattle. Following a divorce, her mother moved herself and her daughters to Hollywood where the girls became the delightful darlings who appeared in their mother *Madame Rose's Dancing Daughters*, that Lee parlayed into motion pictures, including one called *You Can't Have Everything* and another titled *Ali Baba Goes to Town*. Gypsy later remarked that "I could be a star with no talent at all," which at the Follies in 1936 would not have much mattered, since it featured Gypsy doing a comparatively tame scene with Bob Hope while he belted out *I Can't Get Started* to Eve Arden, who had been ordered to junk her real name, which was Eunice Quedens.

Milton Berle (born Milton Berlinger) began his theatrical career at the age of five when he dressed like and mimicked Charlie Chaplin. He was a latecomer to the Follies which he joined in 1942 during World War II when he was accorded higher billing than Follies itself, and lasted for 553 performances at the Winter Garden, wearing a silly hat and a fool's costume. Berle was the product of New York's tenement district, out of which he made himself into a hot property in movies, radio, theatre and eventually television. In vaudeville he made a contentious reputation for unabashedly stealing material from other comedians, who never let him forget it. Nor did he mind being called *the thief of bad gags*. When he played at the Follies, he used material concocted by Doug Whitney, who said, "You know what would happen if I left you?" Berle confessed that he didn't. "You'd go back to making $7,500 a week." Berle was endlessly amused by his writers. "Listen," one of them said, "I don't have to sit here and let you tolerate me." Milton told audiences that he met a panhandler on the street. "I recognized him as an old actor friend. I asked him if I could buy him some lunch. He said, "But I haven't had breakfast yet." About Hollywood, Berle remarked, "Things are slow out there, Abbott and Costello haven't made a picture all day."

This is all good street humor. No pretense, No challenge. No way not to laugh. The personalities who played the Follies were some of the great names in American theatre. Even Tallulah Bankhead was another latecomer, so late that the Follies had left New York and opened at Boston's Schubert in 1956. "Tallulah," an anonymous writer recorded, "wanted to star in a review, and quickly signed on for the Ziegfeld Follies, although it bore no resemblance to the original production. She appeared in a variety of skits and recited Dorothy Parker's poem, *The Waltz*." The show closed after a four week trial. It had been a grand effort but without the bordello rowdiness of the 1930s. Even Bea Arthur had a go at the Follies, same place, same time as Bankhead did. The original members of the cast were, as someone rightly commented, "former waitresses, farmers' daughters and office workers who dreamt of becoming part of Ziegfeld's own grand dream of glorifying the American girl, preferably with measurements of 36-26-38. Some went on to further careers on the stage and screen...some disappeared into obscurity." Arthur never began at the Follies, and most certainly never ended there. Popular entertainment is, after all, expressly calculated to amuse popular, and not select, audiences. There are those who elect to be entertained there for motives of their own and to be regaled by the loud, the lavish and the preposterously absurd, allowing entertainment to drive out reality for a time. Existence is always more arduous for fools, if only because they are culturally maligned, passed over, left wanting and waiting. Their prospects are circumscribed and delimited, their destinies perilous and problematic. If, as Shakespeare declared, all the world is a stage, the stages we've examined constitute a fool's microcosm, a little world, a world made small, but still a telling cultural representation of how it really is.

BIBLIOGRAPHY

Aichmayr, Michael. *Der Symbolgehalt der Eulenspigel-Figur im Kontext der eratureuropaischen Narren und Schelmenil.* Goppingen: Kummerle, 1991.

Anderson, Sherwood. "I'm a Fool," in *Horses and Men.* New York: Huebsch, 1917.

Arden, Heather, *Fools' Plays.* Cambridge, N.Y.: Cambridge University Press, 1980.

Armin, Robert. *Fools and Jesters.* London: Shakespeare Society, 1842.

Augarde, Tony (ed). *The Oxford Dictionary of Modern Quotations.* (New York: Oxford University Press, 1991.

Barnes, Margaret. *The King's Fool.* Chicago: Sourcebooks, 1959.

Beaumont, Cyril W. *The History of the Harlequin.* New York: Arno Press, 1976.

Berne, Marie. *Eloge de l'idiotie.* Amsterdam: Rodopi, 2009.

Berry, Edward. *Shakespeare's Comic Rites.* New York: Cambridge University Press, 1984.

Billington, Sandra. *A Social History of the Fool.* Brighton, Sussex: Harvester Press, 1984.

Boskin. Joseph. *Sambo.* New York: Oxford University Press, 1988.

Boucquey, Thierry. *Mirages de la farce, fete des fous.* Amsterdam: J. Benjamins Publishing, 1991.

Bowman, W. Dodson and Douglas Fairbanks. *Charlie Chaplin.* New York: Kessinger, 2007.

Bradbrook, Muriel C. *Shakespeare's Clown.* New York: Macmillan, 1972.

Brant, Sebastian, *Narrenschiff.* London: Cambridge University Press, 1911.

Braun, Johannes. *Das Narrische bei Nestroy.* Bielefeld: Asthesis, 1998.

Brooke, Henry. *The Fool of Quality.* London: John Lane Company, 1909.

Burton, Robert. *The Anatomy of Melancholy* (ed Floyd Dell and Paul Jordan-Smith). New York: Tudor Publishing, 1941.

Busby, Olive M. *Studies in the Development of the Fool in Elizabethan Drama*. Oxford: Oxford University Press, 1923.

Cavendish, George. *The Life and Death of Cardinal Wolsey*. London: Early English Text Society, 1959.

Chambers, E. K. *The Mediaeval Stage*. London: Clarendon Press, 1923.

Cline, Paul. *Fools, Clowns and Jesters*. La Jolla, Calif,: Green Tiger Press, 1983.

Cliver, Sean. *Jackass*. New York: Pocket Books, 2002.

Clouston, William. *The Book of Noodles*. London: Elliot Stock, 1988.

Collins, Cecil. *The Vision of the Fool*. Chipping Norton, Oxfordshire: Kendos, 1981.

Cox, Harvey. *The Feast of Fools: A Theological Essay on Festivity and Fantasy*. New York: St. Martins, 1995.

Crowley, Bridget. *Feast of Fools*. New York, McElderry, 2003.

Davidson, Clifford. *Fools and Folly*. Kalamazoo: Medieval Institute Publications: Western Michigan University, 1966.

deVries, Manford. *Lenders, Fools and Impostors: Essays on the Psychology of Leadership*. San Francisco: Jossey-Bass, 1993.

diBartolomeo, Albert. *Fools' Gold*, New York: Viking Press, 1986.

Disher, Maurice, *Clowns and Pantomimes*. London: Constable, 1923.

Doran, John. *The History of Court Fools*. New York: Haskell House, 1966.

Dull, Anna. *Folie et rhetorique dans la sottie*. Geneve: Droz, 1994.

Earman, J. *A Primer on Determinism*. Dordrecht: Reidel, 1986.

Eichenwald, Kurt. *Conspiracy of Fools: A True Story*. New York: Morrow, 2005.

Erasmus, Desiderius. *In Praise of Folly*. Mineola: Dover, 2003.

Esslin, Martin. *The Theatre of the Absurd*. London: Methuen, 2001.

Farmer, John S. "A Knack to Know a Knave," in *The Tudor Facsimile Texts*. New York: AMS Press, 1970.

Firth, David, and Alan Leigh. *The Corporate Fool*. Oxford: Capstone, 1998.

Foucault, Michel. *Folie e deraison*. Paris: Libraire Plon, 1961.

Fowler, Erlene. *Fool's Puzzle*. New York: Berkley Prime Crime, 1994.

Fradon, Dana. *The King's Fool*. New York: Dutton, 1993.

Frazer, James G. *The Golden Bough*. New York: Oxford University Press, 1994.

Gaffney, Ed. *Suffering Fools*, New York: Bantam Dell, 2006.

Galdone, Paul. *The Wise Fool*. Toronto: Pantheon Books, 1968.

Garner, Harvey. *The Guizer*. New York: Greenwillow, 1976.

Gierach, John. *Fool's Paradise*. New York: Simon and Schuster, 2008.

Gobin, Pierre. *Le fou et ses doubles*. Montreal: Presses de l'Université de Montréal, 1978.

Goldsmith, Robert. *Wise Fools in Shakespeare*. East Lansing: Michigan State University Press, 1955.

Gordon, Alan. *An Antic Disposition*. New York: St. Martins Minotaur, 2004.

Harris, Joanne, *Holy Fools*. New York: Morrow, 2004.

Heers, Jacques. *Fetes des fous et carnivals*. Paris: Fayard: 1983.

Highet, Gilbert. *The Anatomy of Satire*. Princeton: Princeton University Press, 1962.

Hinchliffe, Arnold P. *The Absurd*. New York: Barnes & Noble, 1969.

Holcomb, Chris. *Mirth Making*. Columbia: University of South Carolina Press, 2001.

Hornback, Robert. *The English Clown Tradition from the Middle Ages to Shakespeare*. London: D. S. Brewer, 2009.

Hornby, John. *Clowns Through the Ages*. New York: H. Z. Walck, 1965.

Hotson, Leslie. *Shakespeare's Motley*. New York: Haskell House, 1971.

Hudson, Paul. *Mystical Origins of the Tarot From Ancient Roots to Modern Usage*. Rochester, Vt: Bear & Company, 1972.

Ivanov, Sergei. *Holy Fools in Byzantium and Beyond*. New York: Oxford University Press, 2006.

Hyman, Robin (ed). *The Quotation Dictionary*. New York: Macmillan, 1962.

Janik, Vicki K. *Fools and Jesters in Literature, Art and History*. Westport, Conn: Greenwood Press, 1998.

Kaiser, Walter. "Praisers of Folly." *Harvard Studies in Comparative Literature*. Cambridge: Harvard University Press, 1963.

Karr, Kathleen. *Fortune's Fool*. New York: Knopf, 2008.

Keene, Carolyn. *April Fool's Day*. New York: Aladdin, 2009.

Klein, Robert. "Le thème du fou et l'ironie humaniste." *La Forme et l'intelligible: Ecrits sur la Renaissance e l'art moderne*. Paris: Editions Gallimard, 1970.

Killinger, John. *The World in Collapse*. New York, 1971.

Krueger, Derek. *Symeon the Holy Fool*. Berkeley: University of California Press, 1996.

Laing, Ronald David. *The Divided Self*. New York: Pantheon Books, 1969.

Lerner, Ralph. *Playing the Fool*. Chicago: University of Chicago Press, 2009.

Loewer, B. "Determinism and Chance." *Studies in History and Philosophy of Modern Physics*, 32:609-620.

Macionis, John J. *Sociology*. Upper Saddle River, NJ: Prentice-Hall, 2003.

Magill, Frank (ed). *Magill's Quotations in Context*. New York: Harper and Rowe, 1965.

Maguire, Gregory. *A Couple of April Fools*. New York: Clarion Books, 2004.

Marshall, Roderick, *Falstaff*. Longmead, Shaftsbury, Dorset: Element Books, 1989.

Meeks, Wayne A. (ed). *The Writings of St. Paul*. New York: W.W. Norton, 1972.

Mencken, H. L. *The American Language*. New York: Knopf, 1963.

Midelfort, Erik. *The History of Madness in Sixteenth Century Germany*. Stanford University Press, 2000.

Mieder, Wolfgang ,et al (eds). *Dictionary of American Proverbs*. New York: Oxford University Press, 1992.

Moore, Christopher. *Fool*. New York: Morrow, 2009.

Moore, Leslie. *The Jester*. New York, Putnams, 1915.

Morley, John D. *The Feast of Fools*. New York: St. Martins, 1995.

Murav, Harriet. *Holy Foolishness*. Stanford: Stanford University Press, 1992.

Nashe, Thomas. *A Pleasant Comedie Called Summers Last Will and Testament*. London, 1600.

Nicole, Allardyce. *Masks, Mimes and Miracles*. London: Harrap, 1931.

Novakovich, Josip. *April Fool's Day*. New York: Harper Collins. 2004

Otto, Beatrice. *Fools Are Everywhere*. Chicago: University of Chicago Press, 2001.

Paine, Gregory. *Southern Prose Writers*. New York, American Book Company, 1947.

Patterson, James and Andrew Gross. *The Jester*. New York: Warner Books, 2004.

Phillips, Tori, *Fool's Paradise*, Toronto: Harlequin Books, 1996.

Pyle, Sandra J. *Mirth and Morality of Shakespeare's Holy Fools*. Lewiston, N.Y. 1998.

Ran. Faye. *The Tragicomic Passion*. New York: P. Lang, 1994.

Robb, David (ed.). *Clowns, Fools and Picaros*. Amsterdam: Rodolpi, 2007.

Robey, Edward. *The Jester and the Court*. London: W. Kimber, 1976.

Rowley, Samuel. *When You See Me You Know Me*. Oxford: Malone Society, 1952.

Ruelle, Karen, *April Fool*. New York: Holiday House, 2002.

Sandmel, Samuel. *The New English Bible*. New York: Oxford University Press, 1976.

Saward, John. *Perfect Fools*. Oxford, N.Y.: Oxford University Press.

Simpson, James B. *Simpson's Contemporary Quotations*. Boston: Houghton-Mifflin, 1988.

Skeat, Walter W. *The Concise Dictionary of English Etymology*. Ware, Hartfordshire, Wordsworth Editions, Ltd., 1993.

Smith, Lacy Baldwin. *Fools, Martyrs, Traitors: The Story of Martyrdom in the Western World*. New York: Knopf, 1997.

Smith, William G. (ed). *The Oxford Dictionary of English Proverbs*. Oxford, Clarendon Press, 1963.

Southworth, John. *Fools and Jesters at the English Court*. Stroud, Gloucestershire: Sutton, 1998.

Stewart, Elizabeth-Anne. *Jesus the Holy Fool*. Franklin, Wis.: Sheed & Ward, 1999.

Swain, Barbara. *Fools and Folly During the Middle Ages and the Renaissance*. New York: Columbia University, 1932.

Tett, Gilliam. *Fool's Gold*. New York: Free Press, 2009.

Toole, John Kennedy. *A Confederacy of Dunces*. New York: Grove Weidenfeld, 1980.

Treffert, Darold, M.D. "Savant Syndrome: An Extraordinary Condition." *Philosophical Transactions of the Royal Society*, May 27, 2009.

Videbaek, Bente A. *The Stage Clown in Shakespeare's Theatre*. Westport, Conn: Greenwood Press, 1996.

Von Grimmelshausen, Hans. *Adventures of a Simpleton*. New York: Continuum, 2002.

Warde, Frederick. *The Fools of Shakespeare*. Los Angeles: Times-Mirror Press, 1923.

Weeks, David and Jamie James, *Eccentrics: A Study of Sanity and Strangeness*. Kodansha International, Tokyo, 1995.

Welch, James, *Fools Crow*. New York: Viking, 1986.

Welsford, Enid. *The Fool*. London: Faber and Faber, 1935.

Williams, Andrew P. *The Restoration Fop*. Lewiston, N.Y. 1995.

Williams, Paul. *The Dunces of Doomsday*. Nashville, Tenn.: WND Books, 2006.

——— (ed.). *The Fool and the Trickster*, Totowa, N.J.: Rowman & Littlefield, 1979.

Wiles, David. *Shakespeare's Clown*. Cambridge: Cambridge University Press, 1987.

Willeford, William. *The Fool and His Scepter*. Evanston: Northwestern University, 1969..

Yolen, Janes. *Queen's Own Fool*. New York: Philomel Books, 2000.

INDEX